The Distribution of Income between Persons

The Distribution of Income between Persons

D. G. CHAMPERNOWNE

Professor of Economics and Statistics,
University of Cambridge

CAMBRIDGE
at the University Press
1973

Published by the Syndics of the Cambridge University Press
Bentley House, 200 Euston Road, London NW1 2DB
American Branch: 32 East 57th Street, New York, N.Y.10022

© Cambridge University Press 1973

Library of Congress Catalogue Card Number: 73–75859

ISBN: 0 521 08546 2

Printed in Great Britain
at the University Printing House, Cambridge
(Brooke Crutchley, University Printer)

Table of Contents

Table of contents

      * Items marked with an asterisk did not appear in the
original dissertation.

List of Charts

List of Charts

List of Charts

1. Introduction

1. This book was originally submitted in November 1936 as a dissertation for a prize fellowship at King's College, Cambridge. The choice of the subject 'The Distribution of Income between Persons' had arisen from a suggestion to the author, as an undergraduate, by one of his supervisors, Mr J. M. Keynes, that he should search for an explanation of the remarkable degree of conformity with Pareto's law displayed by many statistics of income-distributions published by the taxation authorities of various countries. Having discovered a possible explanation, the author decided that the theoretical model involved was worth generalisation in order to provide the framework for discussing a much wider class of questions concerning income distribution. The dissertation was concerned with this generalized model.

Traces of the influence of Keynes crop up at intervals in the dissertation. For example, the obscure section on p. 62 of Chapter 5 on the prices of land and money was evidently based on a slightly imperfect understanding of remarks dropped by Keynes about the properties of money and land as means of storing wealth: another distorted echo of Keynes is heard in Chapter 7, p. 76, where we are told that 'in order to discover the forces determining the nature of the distribution of income...we shall accordingly have to study carefully those links between past and present distribution that are provided by this tendency of the aggregate value of qualifications to preserve the continuity ...We have seen that there are likely to be many links between the income of a man in one year and his income in the next year, and many links between the income of a father and his son and between the income of a man and his heir, whereas there will be fewer links between a man's portion of any one particular qualification at different dates, since he may exchange one qualification for another.' These sentences plainly echo the many passages in Keynes' *General Theory* where he refers to capital as the link between the present and the future: these are but echoes, since the links pointed out in this book are of a very different kind from those discussed by Keynes. But although the book is much concerned with the effects of particular fiscal policies on the ability of individuals to save and thereby increase their incomes, it contains virtually no attempt to adapt any parts of Keynes' *General Theory* to throw light on the determination of personal income distribution.

2. The reader may enquire why this short book should be offered for publication thirty-six years after it was submitted as a prize-fellowship dissertation. It has lain during this interval in the library of King's College, Cambridge, and has been consulted by a number of persons interested in income distribution. The number of these has increased in recent years and the author has been asked on a number of occasions to make the ideas expressed in the dissertation more generally accessible by publishing them.

He had the choice of publishing the dissertation almost exactly in its original form, or of writing a new book bringing his ideas up to date in the light of later experience and recent theoretical developments. After carefully reading through the dissertation, he decided that it included a number of ideas expressed with a freshness and directness which he could not hope to recapture if he rewrote the whole book. It contained also a number of naïve and flippant passages, which it was hoped that readers would find inoffensive in a dissertation submitted by a youth twenty-four years old for a competition judged on 'promise' as much as on solid achievement.

Naturally, a prize-fellowship dissertation submitted in 1936 contains very many faults, which are rather clearer to the author today than at the time of writing. As will be explained in the new supplement to Chapter 2, there are several serious objections to any attempt to construct a stochastic model of income distribution between persons: many of these objections indeed were anticipated in the later chapters of the dissertation and some attempt was there made to deal with them, but such attempts were only partially successful.

This very fact that the theory as then presented was still so imperfect provides another reason for making the dissertation more readily available. For the questions with which the dissertation is concerned are of lasting importance and interest in them is probably considerably greater today than it was thirty-five years ago. The methods of approach in the dissertation to these questions seem capable of much further development, and the opportunities for such development are now much greater owing to the availability of far more statistical data and of the high-speed computer which then simply did not exist. Perhaps more important still, the supply of otherwise idle young persons with mathematical training, paper qualifications in economics and financial support sufficient to enable them to play with and competently develop such theories and models has, at a guess, increased a hundredfold since the dissertation was written. Since many of these young persons may be at a loss for respectable subjects by whose study to justify the enjoyment of research grants, it may be hoped that the revelation of so many imperfectly followed trails may tempt a certain number to carry through to a finish some of the tasks which are left uncompleted in this dissertation.

3. It has therefore been decided to offer for publication the original dissertation with a minimum of alterations: these were confined to the correction of a few minor slips, provision of improved versions of some of the charts and the substitution in Chapter 3 of the statistics of the 1938–9 income distribution for the United Kingdom, for the very imperfect statistics of the 1919 distribution, which was the best available at the time when the dissertation was written. The following new material also has been added:

i this introduction to the book.

ii an appendix to Chapter 2 in which further comments

on the plan of the dissertation are given in the light of the author's further thoughts during thirty-five years.

iii an appendix to Chapter 3, which brings up to date where possible the tables and charts of income distributions in various countries and the analysis of them in that chapter.

iv an appendix to Chapter 8, which brings up to date the charts of the changing distribution of income among surtax payers in the United Kingdom and comments on the changes during each of the 12-year periods, 1927–39, 1939–51 and 1951–63.

v Chapter 24 (plus an appendix) indicating various directions in which the contents of the dissertation need further development. Particular attention is paid in this chapter to the study of approach towards equilibrium and to the complications arising from feedback from changes in income distribution on the forces of change of income.

vi a further general appendix 5, giving some numerical illustrations of some of the theorems established in appendix 3.

vii a further general appendix 6, consisting of the reprinting of an article by the author on 'a model of income distribution' from *The Economic Journal* for June 1953, by kind permission of the editors of that journal.

The publication of this article in 1953 had certain undesirable effects. In order to compress it sufficiently for it to be published in a journal and in order that the conclusions might be both intelligible and established with sufficient rigour, it was found necessary to concentrate on the mathematical skeleton of the theory and to dispense with most of the 'flesh' concerning conjectures about the effects of particular measures and of relaxing the extreme simplifying assumptions associated with static equilibrium. Also, in order to make the article more quickly intelligible, the theory was introduced first in terms of the particularly simple example of forces of change such as would lead to the observance of 'Pareto's law' in equilibrium. As a result the article probably gave a false impression of what had been the main

Introduction

purpose of the original theory, namely to provide a theoretical apparatus for determining the effects of particular economic influences upon the distribution of incomes between persons.

4. It will be noted that the object of the book is not primarily to *explain* the observed forms of income-distribution: nor is it to provide a *theory* or model of how income-distributions are determined: the object is to provide a conceptual framework within which one may discuss the probable effects on income-distribution of particular measures and policies.

However, in order to construct such a framework, some theory or model has to be provided. Most of the book, Chapters 9 to 23, is concerned with a fairly general pseudo-stochastic* model, which although of a type which will be familiar to many readers today, was rather novel at the time of writing (1936). It will be seen to be considerably more general than Gibrat's model (1931), which is discussed rather unsympathetically† in Chapter 9. But the author also was very much on his guard against advancing this stochastic model as a *complete* theory of income-distribution. One obvious shortcoming is that it treats a man's income as homogeneous and the causes of change in that income likewise as homogeneous: whereas, in real life a man's income may stem from a variety of sources, each with different causes of change. Aware of this, the author only introduced his stochastic model after a digression of three chapters discussing various aspects of the heterogeneity of the sources or 'qualifications' for obtaining income. These chapters are concerned with the distribution of income between regions, between factors of production, and with inequality arising from monopoly. There is in fact a very real difficulty in

---

* *Pseudo*-stochastic in the sense that it incorporates a transition matrix determining the proportions of the occupants of one income-class which move to specified other classes and not merely the probabilities of such movements.

† R. Gibrat, *Les Inégalités Economiques* (Paris 1931). The author had, as a matter of fact, completed the first draft of the dissertation before getting hold of a copy of Gibrat's book and was somewhat disturbed then to find that a stochastic theory of income-distribution had been in circulation for four or five years.

reconciling any stochastic theory of personal income-distribution with the orthodox theories, based on competition, supply and demand and so forth, which attempt to account for the relative rates of reward of the various kinds of labour, capital, land and enterprise. The author's solution was to appeal to the notion that to some extent 'qualifications' for obtaining income can be bought and sold and thereby exchanged for one another. A man's income is determined by his total 'hand' of qualifications, and so are his prospects of change in income. This was taken as justification, as a first approximation, for regarding a man's total income as a single parameter summarising his prospects of change of income in the future. But the author did admit that this approximation was only a good one for people who were fairly well off, since it was these people who most frequently sold and bought qualifications (such as a well-situated house or good education) for themselves or their families. Many of the later chapters are concerned with the determination of 'equilibrium distributions' by 'forces of change', and the degree of inequality is regarded as the outcome of a battle between equalising and dispersive forces. But the object of the enquiry is not to study equilibrium so much as to consider how these equilibria will be shifted by particular measures.

The author could then be forgiven for confining his examples to an entirely artificial set with invented numerical values, and for his airy deferment for later consideration, of any idea of getting down to work on any useful application of the theory, with the explanation: 'although we shall generally assume such information to be given, and thus avoid the temptation* of an interesting field of research, whose too hasty cultivation would lend a spurious impression of precision to our results, yet we may suggest briefly the orders of magnitude for the forces of change for particular influences, which research might possibly reveal'.

---

* At the reflection that he is still avoiding the temptation, the author occasionally feels slightly uneasy.

2. Plan of the book

1. We shall construct a theoretical apparatus for determining the effects of particular economic influences upon the distribution of income between persons.

2. The phenomenon is obvious enough: a large proportion of income for buying the good things that there are to buy, goes to a small proportion of people. There exists statistics – imperfect ones – which give us a vague mental picture of the throbbing shape of these complex structures, the distributions of income between persons in the various communities of the modern world: we can guess at the proportions of the income which go to the richest half, quarter, tenth or thousandth of the people, and at how these proportions change from decade to decade in war and peace. depression or prosperity.

3. The phenomenon is obvious enough and so are the explanations of it. Each man's income is obtained in virtue of his possession of various qualifications: the possession of ability, property, bargaining power and good luck enable a man to obtain income, and the difference between the incomes of the different individuals in a community reflects the difference in their qualifications.

The distribution of incomes depends on the distribution of qualifications for obtaining them and on the relative values of different types of qualification: these in turn depend upon the social structure of the community under study, and upon the economic conditions of the times. Economic influences affect the distribution of incomes by altering the distribution of qualifications for obtaining them, and by altering their relative values. We know what are the important influences today which shape the distribution of incomes, and we can guess their particular effects. Death-duties and progressive taxation cause a transference of property and other qualifications for obtaining incomes from the rich to the poor and thereby decrease inequality of distribution. The fact that it is the rich predominantly, who save, causes the qualifications to accumulate into their hands; this causes incomes to be the more unequally distributed. In similar manner we can roughly reason about the kind of effect which any economic influence is likely to have upon the distribution of incomes.

4. Yet the whole system of ideas remains chaotic and incomplete; we know that this effect is likely to increase, and that effect, to decrease, inequality, and yet we have no ordered picture of how these processes will work out together, and no complete framework in which to arrange our theories of these causes and their effects. We have no systematic form of exposition which will relate all minor phenomena of change and economic influence, to the resulting developments in the central organism, the distribution of incomes among the community.

5. This book aims at supplying such a system of ideas: the plan of the book is this:

In Chapter 3, we shall learn to describe and chart the distributions of income and to measure their properties by numerical co-efficients; later in Chapter 3, we shall practice these arts to describe the actual distributions revealed by available statistics.

Chapters 4, 5, 6 and 7 form a very necessary digression into the question of what are the important qualifications which must be possessed in order to obtain income, and to what extent they can be regarded in order to obtain income, and to what extent they can be regarded as homogeneous, or divided into types which cannot easily be substituted for each other.

In Chapter 4 we consider how the income of a country may be divided up into streams flowing:

a   From different geographical areas.

b   From the possession of different qualifications, e.g., the ability to work, property (capital and land), monopoly advantages and good luck.

We find that it is difficult to keep these streams separate, and after discussing this system of classifying qualifications in Chapter 5, we reject it in favour of another classification. In Chapter 6, we remind ourselves very briefly of the principles determining the size of each stream relative to others and in Chapter 7, we turn to the problem of what determines how the income in any one homogeneous stream will be divided between individuals.

6. This brings us back to our main theme. We have found that in a modern community, where transport facilities are well developed and different types of qualifications for obtaining income can be bought, sold and thus exchanged, it may introduce more error to consider different types of income (from different qualifications) separately, as if in isolation from other types, than to consider distribution of all income as if it were homogeneous.

We find that the distribution this year depends largely on what it was last year: but that influences increasing some incomes and decreasing others often increase inequality: others, by enriching the poor and impoverishing the rich check inequality. It is the measurement of such effects that will be our chief concern.

Two types of influence are distinguished: those which are acting every year, or every generation, to change the incomes of individuals, and those which act just once for a short time only. The former category, we shall call 'forces of change', and the latter, 'impulses of change'.

In Chapter 7 we develop our main theme. The properties of the income-distribution are being moulded all the time by the forces of change. Under their action, the properties of the distribution move towards equilibrium, but never reach it, because they are shaken away by impulses of change, and also because the forces of change are themselves smoothly altering. This thesis is illustrated by the changes in the distribution among English super-tax payers since 1910.

In Chapter 8 we give a brief account of attempts to account for the distribution of income as an example of the law of normal error, which rests on the assumption that the causes of change act alike (proportionally) on the incomes of rich and poor, and are many and independent.

In Chapters 9, 10, and 11, we develop a theory based on the idea that at different income levels the influences affecting incomes will be different, but that for neighbouring income-levels the proportionate effect of influences upon incomes are likely to be similar both in:

i Their average effect.

ii The degree of, or lack of, uniformity of effect.

Having learnt to measure the strength and nature of individual economic influences (upon the basis of sufficient information), we develop the idea in Chapter 12, that corresponding to any given set of forces of change, there is an equilibrium set of properties of the income-distribution towards which the properties of the actual distribution would settle if the forces of change remained constant. The concept of equilibrium enables us to picture far more clearly the gradual development of the properties of the actual distribution under changing economic influences. It is as though, in seeking to account for the movements of a dog, we suddenly proceeded to a study of the (relevant) movements of his master.

In Chapter 13, we discuss the form that the equilibrium distribution is likely to assume, under given circumstances.

In Chapter 14 we discuss the effect on the equilibrium distribution of various measures, such as taxation and medical care of poor children. In Chapter 15 we discuss the effects of various systems of inheritance and death duties.

In Chapter 16 we discuss the limitations imposed by our

supposition that the forces of change are constant and abandon the supposition.

In Chapters 17 and 18 we modify our analysis to allow for increasing income per head and increasing population, and discuss the effects of high birth rates and high mortality among the poor.

In Chapter 19 we discuss modifications in our results which must be allowed when the forces of change are smoothly altering. In Chapter 20 we investigate the result of sudden disturbances (impulses of change), like capital levies, wars and slumps.

In Chapter 21 we investigate the reactions of changes in distribution upon the influences causing the changes: we find that their presence may make the distribution either less or more sensitive to given measures designed to influence distribution: in extreme cases they may cause instability in distribution.

In Chapter 22 we shall learn to square our theory with the facts of distribution in the world today. This is difficult because of the inadequacy of information about the actual distribution in modern communities, and about the changes of individual incomes from year to year. Nevertheless, we are able to show that the measure of the actual influences at work is not unlike that of those which according to our theory, would produce the distribution of income actually found. We are also enabled to explain certain properties of actual distributions, such as their approximate conformity to Pareto's law, which, without our theory, cannot so simply be accounted for.

In Chapter 23, we shall summarise the conclusions which emerge from our analysis, and the impatient reader is invited to pass over the intervening pages.

Finally, for those who may suspect the assertions made in the text, with no further justification than remarks, 'common-sense suggests', 'it would seem natural that', or even 'it can be proved by mathematics that', there are provided appendices containing mathematical proofs of these assertions: to the pure mathematician, all things are suspect.

In addition, the appendices provide digressions on interesting points, whose inclusion in full in the text of the book, would have distorted the emphasis.

In Chapter 3, we turn to our first task; the description and charting of income-distributions.

APPENDIX*

There are certain points in the above introductory chapter to which the reader's attention may be drawn. At the start, the object of the book is set out as being 'the construction of a theoretical apparatus for determining the effects of particular economic influences upon the distribution of income between persons'. The reader is asked to keep *this* purpose in mind when reading the book and to remember that to construct a general theory of income-distribution is *not* the main purpose. Underlying the discussion of the effects of *particular* economic influences on personal income-distribution, there has, of course, to be a skeleton in the form of a simplified mathematical model of the process of formation of the personal income-distribution, and in its basic form this model is a stochastic model which tends in the long run to bring the income-distribution to an equilibrium, whose nature will depend on all the particular economic influences: the method suggested for studying the effect of any particular economic influence is that of partial equilibrium analysis, namely that of finding the effect of the addition or subtraction of the particular influence on the long-run-equilibrium distribution of income.

An earlier version of the dissertation had been submitted a year earlier in November 1935 to the prize-fellowship electors of Kings College, Cambridge, and had very properly been severely criticised for the indecent display given to the mathematical skeleton and the scant attention paid to purely economic considerations. Accordingly in this later (November 1936) version, the mathematical skeleton is tucked away in the cupboard of the appendices and only allowed to emerge fitfully into the main text: indeed the first glimpse of the theoretical model is only permitted in Chapter 12, where in an aside the general formula $b = 2I_1/I_2$ is released; upon this one formula most of the remaining chapters of the dissertation depend. It gives the slope at each point of the equilibrium income-ratio-curve in terms of the 'forces of

* Written in 1972.

change' acting on income of the size which corresponds to that point. The whole of the remaining chapters of the dissertation may be thought of as (i) working out the implications of that formula, in particular contexts, and generalising the formula in various respects, such as allowing equilibrium to incorporate steady growth of various kinds; and (ii) trying to answer some of the large number of objections to and difficulties in developing such a stochastic-equilibrium-model for discussing the determinants of the equilibrium distribution of personal incomes.

The purpose of the next chapter on the description of personal income-distributions is twofold: first, there is the superficial purpose of portraying the statistics and bridging the gap between the theory and the real world, but second, there is the deeper purpose of accustoming the reader to accepting its logarithm as the measure of a person's income; more particularly, it is to accustom him to the people-ratio-curve or the income-ratio-curve as providing a summary of any income-distribution, since it is the slope of the latter curve which will be so simply given, in equilibrium, in terms of the forces of change by the general formula, $b = 2I_1/I_2$ and the slope of the former curve at each point will then be given as $b - 1$.

The next four chapters (4 to 7) were as a matter of fact among the last to be written and they are amongst those whose main purpose is to meet some of the objections to developing a stochastic-equilibrium-distribution model. They resulted from a mild question by Mr David Bensusan-Butt as to how I squared my theory with certain other theories which purported to account in various ways for the distribution of income between the 'factors of production'. Mild, the question might be, but it was characteristically devastating: it was also very stimulating and led to second thoughts which greatly assisted my understanding of the nature of the process which I was attempting to analyse.

It was in these chapters, in attempting to meet the implied objection that if these quite different theories were right, then mine must be wrong, that the idea was developed that a man's income depended on his qualifications for obtaining it, and that its growth or decline would depend on his trading in qualifications and on changes in the effectiveness of individual qualifications for obtaining income – as, for example, in the particular case of a man who obtains his income in the form of dividends on a portfolio of shares which he modifies by purchases and sales. I would now give much more importance to a point which then only got a bare mention in the introduction, namely that the values of these various qualifications are not primarily determined by marginal productivity and the price-mechanism, but 'depend upon the social structure of the community under study, and upon the economic conditions of the times'.* The answer to the question how to reconcile theories of the distribution of income between factors of production with the present theory of personal distribution of income is suggested in Chapter 7, in the form 'the other theories are useful for discussing the distribution of income from owning particular qualifications such as land, capital, monopoly advantage or skill to work, but more is needed for the study of the distribution of aggregate income from all such qualifications'. Here, the influence of yesterday on today is stressed – the effects of inheritance, heredity and continuity: it 'will depend on how good are the qualifications each individual possesses for obtaining income: this will depend on how much he had a year ago and on how much he has lost or gained since then. His aggregate income will largely depend on his start in life and on the use he has made of that start. Any person who has been 'dealt' a set of qualifications by nature and his parents may be considered as spending his life trading with these qualifications, in order to increase their aggregate value and his income. By exchanging qualifications, he will increase his stock of some qualifications, and will reduce his stock of others, but the aggregate value of his qualifications will remain less affected by these exchanges than will the values of the stocks of particular qualifications. When a man dies he will hand over to his

* Chapter 2, §3.

15

sons stocks of other qualifications for obtaining income besides inborn ability. These stocks may be mainly in the form of capital, land, monopoly advantages or expensive education, but the aggregate value of them is likely to depend largely upon the aggregate value of the father's own stock of qualifications. Hence some sort of continuity can be traced between the aggregate values of the father's stocks of qualifications and the aggregate values of the son's stock of qualifications, although little continuity can be traced between the father's stock of and the son's stock of each single qualification for obtaining income.'*

In Chapter 8 the idea of an equilibrium distribution of income is at last introduced. But no sooner has it been mentioned than objections to the use of the concept are anticipated. Of what use is equilibrium analysis since in the real world all is in a state of flux so that equilibrium is never reached? That is the basic objection and the attempts to answer it are scattered through the remaining 15 chapters of the book. Already in Chapter 8, three types of equilibrium (apart from the trivial case of 'dead' equilibrium) are distinguished; static, quasi-static and moving equilibria. In Chapter 9 yet another tiresome 'rival' theory, that of Gibrat, is unsympathetically discussed and thrown aside. In Chapter 12, at long last, the basic theory of the static equilibrium personal distribution of incomes resulting from fixed 'forces of change' is provided. The two previous chapters (10 and 11) have been used for introducing the 'forces of change' in the form of parameters summarising the properties of the transition matrix, that is of the set of frequency distributions of proportional change of income from various income levels.

Apart from the working out of illustrative examples, the remainder of the book (Chapters 13–23) consists of successive generalizations of the theory to allow the concept of equilibrium to embrace various forms of smooth growth and change, and to anticipate and meet various objections to the crude form of the theory presented in Chapter 12.

* Chapter 7, §4.

These are very real objections and some of them have been met only very imperfectly, so that a great deal of further work remains, which might be well worth doing. It may be useful at this point to outline some of these objections.

In static equilibrium, although individual incomes change, the frequency distribution of all personal incomes does not change at all. It may be well objected that this model of static equilibrium is particularly unrealistic since, apart from anything else, actual personal distributions of income usually display gradually increasing income per head, even in real terms, and even more so in terms of money: moreover, the total number of incomes, which remains fixed in the model of static equilibrium, increases in many countries of the actual world. To meet these objections the concept of quasi-static equilibrium is introduced: this allows a constant percentage increase of income-per-head and also a constant percentage increase in the total number of incomes in each year, but no change in the proportionate frequency distribution of incomes expressed as a proportion of their own average. The extension of the static equilibrium of Chapter 12 to this more general case is pretty simple. The necessary modifications to the formulae for the slope of the income-ratio-curve are given in the text and illustrated by examples: the proofs are tucked away in the appendices.

The next generalisation of the concept of equilibrium allows the percentage rate of increase of average income and the percentage growth-rate of the total number of incomes to vary from year to year, provided the proportionate frequency distribution of income expressed as a proportion of the average income still remains fixed: again no essential complication of the theory results. In this form of the model, it is not assumed that fertility or mortality are independent of income level and the model can be used to investigate the effect of contrasts in mortality and in fertility between rich and poor.

In all the models so far considered the 'forces of change' at any income fixed as a percentage of the (equilibrium) average income have themselves been assumed fixed. In an attempt to break free from this assumption, the concept of 'moving equilibrium' is introduced, which is a path of steady change which is supposed to be approached in the long run from any initial income distribution, provided the 'forces of change' alter in a given slow smooth manner. But it is found that the simple basic theory does not extend to this case: the author has to admit that the initial distribution may now affect the final outcome, and in place of references to proofs in the appendices, he now has to fall back on a rather unconvincing process of making conjectures. The picture conveyed is one of an actual distribution being smoothly modified, and following with a time-lag in the path of a smoothly moving equilibrium distribution, like an elderly dog following an elderly master.

The next objection considered was originally pointed out to me by my supervisor, Mr (now Professor Lord) R. F. Kahn, the deviser of the 'multiplier'. Why should one regard the 'forces of change' as exogenous? Suppose that they are endogenous, being determined partly by the form of the income distribution itself. This objection is far more fundamental than I realised when writing the dissertation and I shall have some more to say about it in Chapter 24. The purely formal answer to it provided in Chapter 21 was however fairly simple: it is that if the 'feedback' effect of income distribution on the 'forces of change' is of a certain particularly simple kind and is known, then the 'multiplier' that must be applied to the effect of a particular measure on the slope of the income-ratio-curve at various income-levels can be calculated by means of a simple formula: it will exceed unity for positive feedback and will be non-negative and less than unity for negative feedback.

The final objection considered is the vital one that in the long run we are all dead. One should be more concerned with measuring the fairly short-run effects of economic measures on income-distribution than with what they would be after a hundred or more years, under a set of unrealistic assumptions about other circumstances remaining unchanged all that time. Very little attention was given in the dissertation to this extremely important question, but it was not entirely overlooked. The study of the path of adjustment from disequilibrium towards the equilibrium distribution of income is perfunctorily discussed in Chapter 20 pp. 169–70 and in rather more detail in Appendix 4. There, a mathematical treatment leads to a rough description of the manner in which a curve plotting the slope b of the income-ratio-curve will approach its equilibrium position. This question also will be taken up and further discussed in Chapter 24.

3. Description and charting of income-distributions

1. In England (1936), some twenty million income-receivers share a total income of between three and four thousand million pounds. One seventh of these people share one half of the income; one fiftieth share a quarter; one five-hundredth share a tenth, and one forty-thousandth (500 people) share over one hundredth of the total income. Curiosity is tickled by such facts as these, and it is interesting to devise a theory to explain them.

2. The best information available concerning the distribution of income in modern communities is contained in publications relating to the collection of income-tax: as the most convenient definition of 'income' in any community, we may accordingly adopt whatever definition the taxing authority prescribes.* In cases where this definition does not normally cover incomes below the exemption limit we must extend it by analogy to include these incomes.

   For some, the study of distribution of income derives particular interest from its relevance to the human problem of the waste involved in unequal distribution of the opportunities for enjoying life. To that problem, other definitions of income would be more relevant; but for the purpose of building a theory which can be measured against actual information the definition of the taxing authority is preferred.

3. A convenient method, in common use, for describing the distribution of income amongst a group of people, is to set out in a table

---

* The reader's attention is drawn to the fact that 'income' always refers to income *before* payment of income tax [1972].

Description and charting of income distributions

i   the number,

ii   the aggregate income

of the people whose incomes fall between each of a series of pairs of limits. The people in the group are thus classified into a series of income-classes, and we are told the number of people and their aggregate incomes, in each class.

Table 1 is taken straight from the *Statistisk Årsbok 1936* for Sweden, being curtailed in order to save space.

TABLE 1. *Sweden: incomes of private individuals declared in 1931, classed according to their size*

classes of income in kroner	number of persons	aggregate income (hundreds of kroner)
Under 1,000	1,072,953	5,873,849
1,000–2,000	785,616	10,732,244
2,000–3,000	385,930	9,264,270
3,000–4,000	184,273	6,218,446
4,000–5,000	74,366	3,260,427
5,000–6,000	37,470	2,022,225
6,000–8,000	35,837	2,439,388
8,000–10,000	17,263	1,525,956
10,000–15,000	17,971	2,157,214
15,000–20,000	6,932	1,189,608
20,000–30,000	5,568	1,339,698
over 30,000	5,423	3,412,657

4. For certain purposes, it is more convenient to take as a measure of richness, the *logarithm* of income rather than income itself. Having chosen our unit of income, for instance, £1, we can find the measure of richness by looking up the logarithm of the number of units in an income: for instance, the measure of richness of a man with an income of £100 would be $\log_{10} 100$, which is equal to 2, and the measure of richness of a man with income of £1,000 is 3. We may give this measure of richness a special name 'income-power', because it expresses the power to which 10 must be raised in order to tell us the number of units in the income.

For example, a man with income-power 4, in England, means a man with income of £10^4, that is, with an income

The distribution of income between persons

of £10,000, and a man with income-power 2·3 has income £10$^{2·3}$, namely about £200.

We have seen how to describe the distribution of persons and of income amongst various income-classes: an alternative device is to set out in a similar table, the distribution of persons and of income between different income-power classes.

Table 1 can very rapidly be converted, if we have access to a table of logarithms.

TABLE 2. *Sweden: individuals and their incomes as declared in 1931, classed according to their income-power*

income-power class (unit = 1 kroner)	number of persons	aggregate income (hundred kroner)
Under 3·000	1,072,953	5,878,849
3·000–3·301	785,616	10,732,244
3·301–3·477	385,930	9,264,270
3·477–3·602	184,273	6,218,446
3·602–3·699	74,366	3,260,427
3·699–3·778	37,470	2,022,225
3·778–3·903	35,837	2,439,388
3·903–4·000	17,263	1,525,956
4·000–4·176	17,971	2,157,214
4·176–4·301	6,932	1,189,608
4·301–4·477	5,568	1,339,698
over 4·477	5,423	3,412,657

For reasons which we shall discuss in the next section, a great part of our theoretical discussion will be concerned with the distribution of persons and of income among income-power classes, rather than directly with their distribution among income classes. It is therefore important to recognise that a description of the distribution among income-power classes is in itself a description of distribution among income-classes, since income-power is simply a special measure of money-income. Any table, giving the distribution of persons or of income between income-power classes, can be converted at once into a table giving the distribution between income classes, if it is remembered that the class of people with income-power between X and Y is the same as the class of people with income between £10^X and £10^Y (where £ stands for the unit of currency).

For example, comparing Tables 1 and 2, we find that the class of people with income-power between 3·778 and 3·903 is the same as the class with income between $10^{3 \cdot 778}$ kr and $10^{3 \cdot 903}$ kr, that is with income between 6,000 kr and 8, 000 kr.

5. We may now consider the advantages to be gained by using the unfamiliar measure income-power in our theoretical discussions, rather than the familiar measure, income.

It so happens that the opportunities for a change of given *proportion* in income are more nearly the same for rich and poor, than are the opportunities for change of given *amount* of income. For instance, while it may be true that a bricklayer has as good a chance of doubling his income as has a millionaire, it is certainly not true that a bricklayer has as good a chance as a millionaire of increasing his income by as much as £10,000. Since we know that equal increases in income-power are the same things as equal *proportional* increases in income, we may express the fact that opportunities for a change of given proportion in income are more nearly the same for rich and poor than are opportunities for a change of equal amount of money-income, by saying that opportunities for changes of equal amount of *income-power*, are more nearly equal for rich and poor than are opportunities for equal change of money-income.

Since the nature of income distribution will be found to depend largely on the opportunities available to individuals for changing their position on the income-scale, it will be more convenient to discuss the way in which opportunities of changing income-power determine the distribution among income-power groups than to discuss how the opportunities of changing money-income determine the distribution among income-groups. The opportunities for changing income-power are far more nearly uniform than are the opportunities for changing money-income.

Secondly, it is found in practice that frequency distributions of people and income between income-power classes fit far better than do the distributions among income-classes to 'types' of frequency distribution familiar to statisticians. The properties of the distributions can accordingly be more easily discussed and summarised, if we consider them as distributions among income-power classes, rather than among income-classes. Moreover, a diagram illustrating the distribution of income between income-power classes will be found to give us a far more illuminating bird's-eye view of the state of income-distribution, than will a diagram of the distribution of income between income-classes, when plotted on the ordinary scale.

It is of interest to notice thirdly that income-power is a better measure of the opportunities which income provides, than is the crude measure money-income. It is more nearly true that equal increases in income-power, i.e. equal *proportional* increases in money-income, confer equal increases of opportunity for enjoyment, than that equal increases of money-income provide equal increases of opportunity for enjoyment for rich and poor. For instance, it is more true to say that an extra £1,000 per annum will give as much enjoyment to a man with £10,000 a year, as will an extra £10 a year to a man with £100 a year, than to say that an extra £10 a year to a man with £10,000 a year, will give as much enjoyment as it would give to a man with only £100 a year.

This is mentioned only as a point of possible interest: our argument will not depend upon its truth. It must be admitted that the statement will be capable of no *precise* interpretation or proof, and any individual must be at liberty to disagree with it.

6. In order to describe and chart a given distribution of incomes, our first step will be to draw up a table like Table 2 in §4 on p. 22, of the distribution of persons and of income between different income-power groups. Next, in order to illustrate this table, we may construct a couple of charts, measuring along each x-axis, income-power, and representing

i   The number of individuals with income-power between x_1 and x_2;

ii (In the other chart) Their aggregate income;

by areas lying between the ordinates of x_1 and x_2.

For instance, in Chart 1, the number of people with income-power between 3·301 and 3·477 is represented by the shaded area *ABCD*, and in Chart 2, the aggregate income shared by these people is represented by the shaded area *A'B'C'D'*.

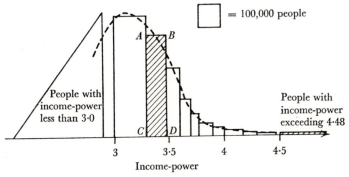

Chart 1   Stepped people-curve for Sweden: incomes declared in 1931

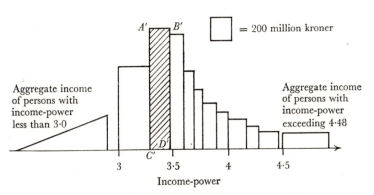

Chart 2   Stepped income-curve for Sweden: 1931

These charts can give us no more information than is contained in Table 2 on p. 22; for instance, although they will tell us the number of people with income-power between 3·477 and 3·602, they cannot tell us the number of people with income-power between 3·5 and 3·8. If our information

25

had been more detailed than that contained in Table 2, we should, of course, have been able to construct a chart which would have told us the number of people with income-power between *any* pair of limits, representing it as an area lying between the corresponding pair of ordinates. In this case, we should expect the top of the area representing people to be bounded by a smooth curve, instead of by a series of steps.

7. We can indeed guess roughly how this smooth curve must lie, and in Chart 1, it has been dotted in: Charts 3 and 4 show roughly what we should expect the correct charts to be like, which would tell us the number of people with income-power between *every* pair of limits and their aggregate income. For example, we can see from Chart 4 that the aggregate income of people with income-power between 3·5 and 3·8 is represented by the area *PQRS*, and must be roughly 1,075 million kr.

Chart 4 gives us a very good view of the way in which income is distributed in Sweden. We see the financial power concentrated around the income-power level 3·4, corresponding to an income of 2,500 kr a year. A large proportion of income goes to these people with income near to 2,500 kr a year, which is equivalent to an English income of £125 a year or £2 10s a week. On the other hand Chart 3 shows that the strongest group *numerically* is that of people with income-power around 3·1, and this means people with income of only 1,250 kr, or £63 a year, i.e. £1 5s a week.

Chart 4 shows what a considerable proportion of income is used up in satisfying the people with income-power greater than 4·3 (income greater than 20,000 kr = £1,000), and Chart 3 shows, by way of contrast, how few these people are.

To the casual glance, Chart 4 is perhaps more informative than Chart 3, but on closer inspection it will be found that some of the properties of income-distribution which are of greatest economic interest appear most simply as elementary properties of the curve in Chart 3. These properties will be discussed in the next section.

Meanwhile, since charts of these types will be used very often in our theoretical discussions, in order to illustrate how a distribution of income is likely to be changed by a

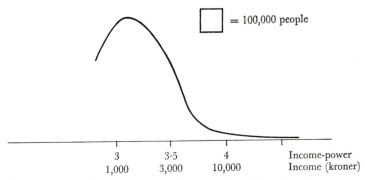

	3	3·5	4	Income-power
	1,000	3,000	10,000	Income (kroner)

Chart 3   Continuous people-curve estimated from Chart 1

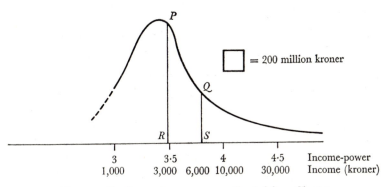

Chart 4   Continuous income-curve estimated from Chart 2

particular change in the economic conditions, it will be convenient to invent special names by which we may refer briefly to curves of the types shown in Charts 3 and 4. We shall refer to curves of the type in Chart 3 as 'people-distribution-curves', or 'people-curves', and to curves of the type in Chart 4, as 'income-distribution curves' or 'income-curves'.

8. By the usual elementary technique of the statistician, we can summarise the properties of a 'people-distribution-curve' as a series of measurements such as the mean, the mode etc. It is interesting to find that some of these measures correspond to features of the distribution which are of economic interest. To illustrate this contention, we may select for interpretation the five most obvious characteristics of the curve:

i   the mode,

ii the mean,

iii the median,

iv the standard deviation,

v   the skewness.

The mode of the curve means the top-point or maximum of the curve: this indicates the income-power level for which

i There are the most people per income-power class (*not* per income-class).

ii There is the most income flowing per unit of income-interval (*not* per unit of income-power interval).

For instance, Chart 3 tells us that there are more people with income-power between 3·05 and 3·15, than in any other income-power class of range 0·1; it also tells us that there is more income flowing to people with incomes between kr 1,200 and kr 1,300, than to people in any other income-class of range kr 100. (This must not be confused with the information given by Chart 4, that there is more income flowing to people with income-power between 3·35 and 3·45, than to the people in any other income-power class of range 0·1.)

The mean of the 'people-curve' tells us the average income-power of the people. This is of interest to those concerned with welfare economics: income-power is a better measure of opportunities of enjoyment than is income, so that the average welfare of a people is better indicated by their average income-power, than by their average income. For instance, if, in Sweden, the average income-power is 3·0, and the average income is kr 1,900 (among income-receivers in the case of each average), then as a measure of the average welfare of Swedish income-receivers, it is much better to take the average income-power 3·0, or kr 1,000, the corresponding income, than to take kr 1,900 the average income, or 3·28, the corresponding income-power. (One precaution must however be observed: *very* highly negative income-powers corresponding to *very* small incomes, i.e. absurdly small incomes, must not be counted, or must be counted only as, say 3 less than the modal income-power. For freak reasons, there may be people with zero or even negative incomes, and we must not count these people as infinitely wretched, by taking account in our average of their infinite negative income-power.)

If everybody had the same income, then the average income-power would correspond to the average income (i.e. would be its logarithm). When there is inequality, the income corresponding to the average income-power is always *less* than the average income. The ratio of the first quantity to the second provides an excellent index of equality. For instance, for Sweden, we could take as the index of equality $\frac{1,000 \text{ kr}}{1,900 \text{ kr}}$ or 0·53, if 3·1 really was the average income-power there. As an index of inequality, we may take 'one minus the index of equality...for Sweden, 0·47.

The index of inequality may be formally defined as follows: 'Let N be the number of income-receivers, and I their aggregate income, and M the mean of the people-curve, and i the index of inequality, then

$$i = \frac{I - N \mathbf{10}^M}{I}.$$

The advantage of this particular index of inequality is that it is a rough measure of the proportion of income wasted, so far as welfare is concerned, because of inequality of distribution. If Bernouilli's hypothesis* were fulfilled, so that

---

* Bernouilli's hypothesis is that the marginal benefit of a given proportional increase in income is the same for persons with different incomes.

income-power could be regarded as an exact measure of welfare, our index would be an exact measure of the proportion of income thus wasted. If, as many believe, the marginal benefit of a given proportional increase of income is less for rich than for poor, then our index of inequality must always understate the waste of income involved. These are however digressions from our theme.

The median of the people-curve tells us the income-power, and hence the income, of that income-receiver than whom just one half of the income-receivers are richer.

The standard deviation of the people-curve is a measure of the extent to which people are spread out over different income-power classes: it thus serves as an alternative index of inequality, and has more than once been proposed as such; it is, however, tiresome to compute, and does not obviously correspond to any intelligible economic concept. Inequality is of course not a simple one-dimensional homogeneous concept, and one distribution may for some purposes best be regarded as more unequal than another, whereas for other purposes it should be regarded as the more equal: the type of index required must depend on the purpose for which the enquiry is made. The index of inequality, i, given above is the best if we approach the problem from a human point of view; if we had some particular technical motive for our enquiry into inequality, other aspects of inequality might need more emphasis, and a different index might be more suitable. For instance, if the type of inequality represented by a few very rich people were of outstanding relevance to our enquiry, we might use as an index, the reciprocal of Pareto's 'alpha'. We should prefer to use the suggested index of inequality, i, were it possible to compute it: but often only rich people are included in the statistics; we then use instead the reciprocal of Pareto's 'alpha'.

The 'skewness' of the people-curve is a measure of its lop-sidedness. It is positively skewed if it stretches predominantly far to the right, and vice versa. We see that positive skewness means a powerful class of abnormally rich people, and that negative skewness means a numerous class of abnormally wretched people. More precisely, we may interpret the skewness to be an indicator of the extent to which one or other of these phenomena outshines the other in degree. The people-curve for Sweden seems to have slight negative skewness, although it is difficult to detect any skewness at all: this suggests that there is not a particularly powerful class of abnormally rich people in Sweden, but that there may possibly be quite a number of abnormally poor people. Since the information available about distribution among the poor is so scanty, these conclusions are very unreliable. In practice, it is hardly ever possible to estimate the skewness of the people-curve.

9. It is rather difficult to read the 'tails' of the people-curve and the income-curve, because they run so close to the x-axis. For this reason, it is often convenient to draw the stepped people-curve and income-curve on a one-way logarithmic scale. Special paper for this is quite cheap, and with the aid of a slide rule, the step curves in Charts 1 and 2, can quickly be plotted onto logarithmic paper, straight from table 2. Charts 5 and 6 have been compiled in this manner. It is easy to see that the people-curve and the income-curve must then run roughly as shown by the smooth curves. These can be more accurately obtained by methods suggested in Appendix 1.

These curves are very convenient, because their forms are unaffected by uniform proportional increases in population in all income-classes, or by uniform proportional increases in income by all people. Their form is independent of the unit of income, or of the proportion of people covered by the income-tax data. We shall accordingly make use of these curves in our theoretical discussions, and we may invent names for them.

We shall call the people-curve and the income-curve, when plotted on logarithmic scales, the 'people-ratio-curve' and the 'income-ratio-curve'. The origin of this nomenclature is the fact that on the logarithmic scale, equal ratios are represented by equal distances: the logarithmic scale is often referred to as the ratio-scale.

10. That completes the list of devices which we shall use for describing and charting income-distributions actual and theoretical. The four devices follow fairly naturally from the form in which the data are usually found in official publications, and from the fact that income varies over too

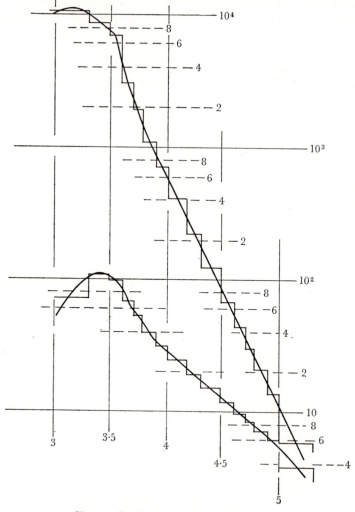

Chart 5   People-ratio-curve for Sweden, 1931

Chart 6   Income-ratio-curve for Sweden, 1931

wide a range to be acceptable as the *x*-co-ordinate in our charts. We choose instead income-power as our measure of richness, and we plot from the statistics, the distribution of persons (the people-curve) and of income (the income-curve), between income-power classes. For some purposes we shall plot the number of persons and of incomes on logarithmic scale, to obtain the 'people-ratio-curve' and the 'income-ratio-curve'.

In the following pages, we shall illustrate the use of these devices, by reading the curves obtained for a number of countries at the present day [1936], and noting how their properties vary in some respects, and yet are remarkably uniform in other respects. In the following chapters we shall enquire into the causes which determine the nature of such distributions.

11. In most countries there exist [in 1936] no reliable statistics of the distribution of incomes amongst any people except the unusually rich. For instance in the United Kingdom the only really reliable figures for distribution of income relate to the incomes only of those people who have to pay super-tax, namely those people who have incomes of over £2,000; these constitute about one quarter of one per cent of the population.

However, in 1919 a special enquiry was made and this made available statistics of income-distribution for incomes down to £130; unfortunately the year was an exceptional one and prices had been changing rapidly; the figures for different kinds of incomes have been obtained at different dates, when the price-level had reached different heights, and the whole set of data is highly unreliable.

For the United States we have Macaulay's estimate for 1919, and other estimates for 1929: these give information about income-distribution for all ranges of income, and are probably reliable as a rough guide.

In Germany figures have been published for the years 1913, 1924 and 1928, which give a rough picture of the distribution among the well-to-do; these figures are reliable, but the income-classes treated are few and wide.

The distribution of income between persons

In Australia, the census of 1915 made available detailed information about the distribution of income amongst rich and poor: naturally, the information about the distribution among the rich is more detailed and more reliable. For India and Canada, we have yearly income-tax data which may not be very reliable; these only tell us about income-distribution among the rich.

France publishes annually income-tax figures which give some picture of the distribution amongst the rich and the well-to-do: it is difficult to estimate the reliability of these figures.

The best figures available are probably those for the Scandinavian countries, Sweden, Norway and Denmark. In Sweden special enquiries were made in 1920 and 1930 into the distribution of capital and the distribution of wealth; this made available a double classification, which shows the numbers of people with capital in each of various ranges, who obtain income in each of various ranges. Denmark publishes similar figures obtained annually; Denmark also supplies separate data for each town and rural district. Norway gives, for 1931, separate figures for town and country, and for men and women in each. Holland publishes annual data of income-distribution which extended back over a long period.

I had also [in 1936] the data for New Zealand, Czecho-Slovakia, Austria, Italy and one set of data for the rich in U.S.S.R. in 1926. None of these data can be regarded as very reliable. Some further data were published by Pareto relating to districts in Germany. No doubt many other such statistics exist which have not come to my notice.

12. In the case of eight countries, we have some information regarding distribution among comparatively poor people. Without enquiring too closely into the reliability of these figures, let us compare the distributions by comparing their income-curves.

In Charts 7 to 14 are set out the income-curves for the following countries:

Description and charting of income distributions

i   United Kingdom 1938–9 (substituted in 1972 for the unreliable 1919 income-curve);

ii United States 1929;

iii Australia 1915;

iv Sweden 1931;

v   Czecho-Slovakia 1932;

vi Norway 1930;

vii Holland 1935;

viii Denmark 1925.

A casual glance at the eight income-curves illustrated in these charts is sufficient to verify that none of them are

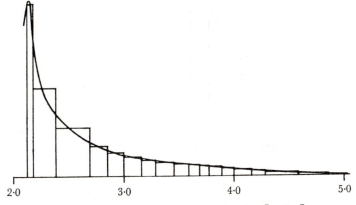

Chart 7   Income-curve for United Kingdom, 1938–9

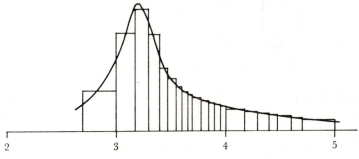

Chart 8   Income-curve for United States, 1929

violently asymmetrical. Indeed, the symmetry displayed by most of these curves is remarkable, considering the unreliability of the data from which they are compiled; this may be taken as justification of our decision to regard income-

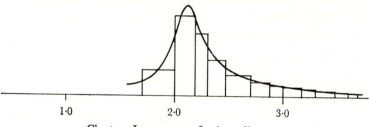

Chart 9   Income-curve for Australia, 1915

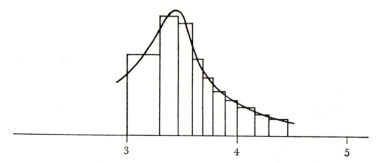

Chart 10   Income-curve for Sweden, 1931

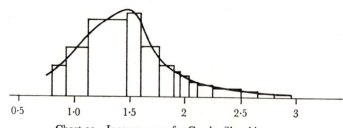

Chart 11   Income-curve for Czecho-Slovakia, 1932

power as the most significant measure of richness. If we had plotted these distributions on an income-scale, the resulting curves would of course have been violently asymmetrical; the fact that by plotting on an income-power base we obtain a symmetrical distribution, verifies the contention that the distribution is the resultant of forces acting uniformly on the income-powers, rather than on the incomes, of rich people and of poor people.

Curves with broad flat tops indicate great inequality of distribution among wage-earners and the lower middle

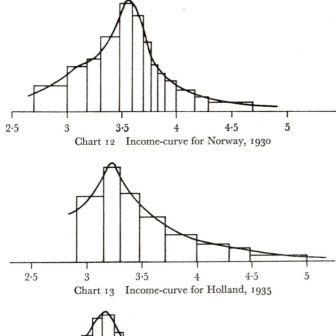

Chart 12   Income-curve for Norway, 1930

Chart 13   Income-curve for Holland, 1935

Chart 14   Income-curve for Denmark, 1925

class: e.g. such a state of affairs is suggested by the curves for Norway 1930; the opposite state of affairs is suggested by the curve for Australia 1915, where wages seem to have been concentrated at £2 10*s* to £3 a week.

Curves with long thick tails stretching out to the right

37

suggest a powerful rich class: e.g. the curve for U.S.A. 1929. In Denmark there appears to be a very small proportion of abnormally rich people.

13. In comparing the distributions in different countries by comparing their income-curves, we are hampered by the dependence of the shape of these curves on our choice of units: we have attempted to overcome this difficulty by arranging that each curve should have roughly the same height: however, this does not entirely remove the difficulty.

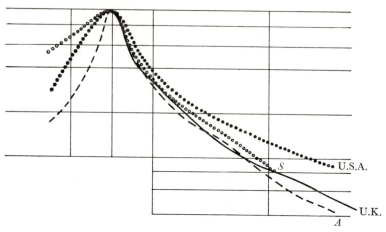

Chart 15   Income-ratio-curves for U.K. 1938–9, U.S.A. 1929, Australia 1915 and Sweden 1931

In order to supplement our information, we may look at the corresponding income-ratio-curves. These are shown in Charts 15 and 16, where they are drawn on top of one another.

These curves would have been a shock to Pareto, for according to his theory, they should be straight lines. As a matter of fact the *tails* of some of these curves are rather straight, and this is a fact for which we shall seek to account in our theory later in the book. For instance, these charts dispel finally any impression we may have drawn from Charts 7 to 14, that the distribution of income among income-

power classes might be a 'normal' distribution: for if the
distribution were normal, the income-ratio-curves would
all be parabolas, whereas, quite clearly, none are parabolas:
for instance, most of their tails are much too straight.

We have divided up the chart into four sections: the poor,
the normal, the well-to-do and the rich. We may refer to
the dividing lines as the 'poverty' line, the 'comfort' line and

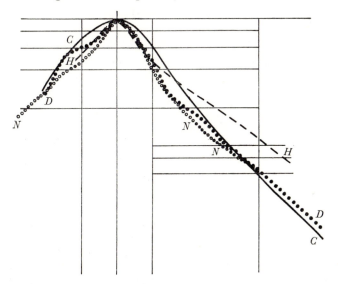

Chart 16   Income-ratio-curves for Czecho-Slovakia 1932, Norway, 1930,
Holland 1935 and Denmark 1925

the 'luxury' line. In the England 1939–40 distribution,
these correspond to the income-levels £70, £280 and £2,000:
for Sweden, 1930, they correspond to 1,000 kr, 4,000 kr and
28,000 kr (1 kr = 1 shilling).

We may distinguish three kinds of inequality:

i   That due to a large proportion of people being poor
(relative to the normal).

ii   That due to a large proportion of income flowing to
the well-to-do (relative to the normal).

iii   That due to a large proportion of income flowing to the
relatively rich.

The distribution of income between persons

Three types of inequality will be characterised respectively by the income-ratio-curve registering high values in (i) the poor region, (ii) the well-to-do region and (iii) the rich region.

Taking in turn the three criteria of inequality, we obtain for the eight countries the following comparisons. (The entries in the column relating to 'relatively poor people' should be regarded as particularly unreliable.)

TABLE 3. *Classification of eight countries according to degree of inequality judged by three criteria*

degree of inequality	criterion of inequality		
	high proportion of relatively poor people	high absorption of income by the well-to-do	high absorption of income by the rich
high	Czecho-Slovakia 1932 Sweden 1931	Czecho-Slovakia 1932 Holland 1935 Denmark 1925 U.S.A. 1939	U.S.A. 1929
medium	Denmark 1925 Holland 1935 Norway 1930 U.S.A. 1929	Sweden 1931 Norway 1930 U.K. (1939–40)	U.K. 1939–40 Holland 1935 Sweden 1931 Australia 1915
low	Australia 1915	Australia 1915	Czecho-Slovakia 1932 Denmark 1925 Norway 1930

N.b. The entries in this table have been re-assessed and do not quite correspond with the original version.

APPENDIX: CHANGES SINCE 1936

1. In this appendix, the charts shown in Chapter 3 will, where possible, be brought up to date, in order to give some impression of the changes in various countries over the thirty intervening years in personal income-distribution as portrayed in official statistics.

For comparison with the Charts 7 to 14, which showed pre-war income-curves for eight countries, Charts A.1. to A.8. give income curves for eight countries (not quite the same eight as before) in the late 1960s. Charts A.9. to A.12 compare the income curves for Great Britain in the financial years 1938–9, 1949–50, 1954–5 and 1966–7.

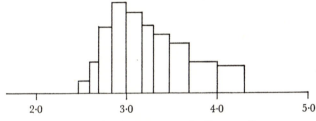

Chart A1   Income-curve for Japan 1968

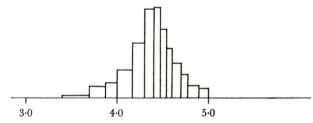

Chart A2   Income-curve for Sweden, 1968

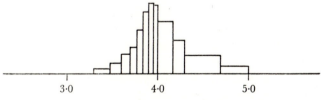

Chart A3   Income-curve for Holland, 1966

2. To illustrate the changes shown by the statistics of income-distribution in certain individual countries, Charts A. 13 to A. 18 give for each of six countries pairs of income-curves, solid for a pre-war year and dotted for a year in the 1960s. Chart A. 19 compares the income-ratio-curves for Great Britain in the 4 years 1938–9, 1949–50, 1954–5 and 1966–7.

3. Charts A. 20 and A. 21 bring up to date Charts 15 and 16, except that Czecho-Slovakia is no longer shown whereas West Germany and Japan, which did not appear in Chart 15 or 16, do so in Chart A. 20.

TABLE A. 1. *Classification of nine countries according to degree of inequality during 1965–8 as judged by three criteria*

	criterion of inequality		
degree of inequality	high proportion of relatively poor people	high absorption of income by the well-to-do	high absorption of income by the rich
high	W. Germany 1965	W. Germany 1965 Japan 1968 U.S.A. 1967	W. Germany 1965 Japan 1968
medium	Japan 1968 U.S.A. 1967 U.K. 1967	Holland 1966 U.K. 1967	U.S.A. 1967
low	Holland 1966 Sweden 1968 Australia 1967–8 Norway 1967 Denmark 1967–8	Sweden 1968 Australia 1967–8	U.K. 1967 Holland 1966 Sweden 1968
very low		Norway 1967 Denmark 1967–8	Australia 1967–8 Norway 1967 Denmark 1967–8

For comparison with Table 3, Table A. 1 has been compiled, using exactly the same criteria as before. However, since the post-war statistics for certain countries exhibit far higher equality at the wealthy end of the scale than any of the pre-war statistics, a new category of 'very low inequality' has been added to accommodate these countries.

Description and charting of income distributions

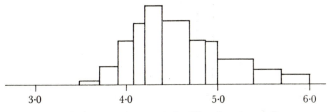

Chart A4   Income-curve for West Germany 1965

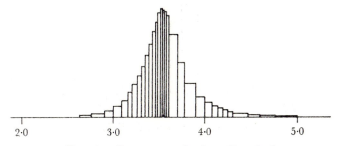

Chart A5   Income-curve for Australia 1967–8

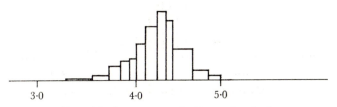

Chart A6   Income-curve for Denmark 1967-8

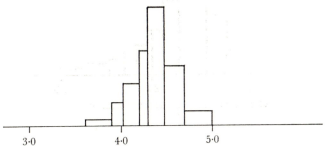

Chart A7   Income-curve for Norway 1967

43

The distribution of income between persons

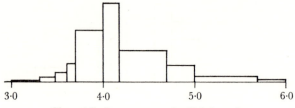

3·0 4·0 5·0 6·0

Chart A8   Income-curve for U.S.A., 1967

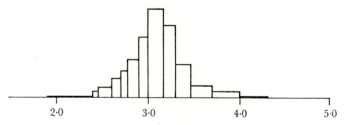

2·0 3·0 4·0 5·0

Chart A9   Income-curve for U.K. 1967

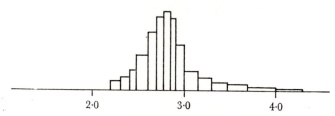

2·0 3·0 4·0

Chart A10   Income-curve for U.K. 1954–5

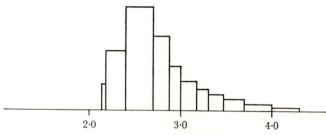

2·0 3·0 4·0

Chart A11   Income-curve for U.K. 1949–50

44

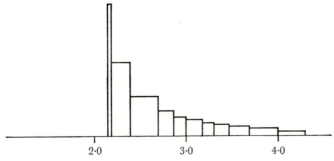

Chart A12   Income-curve for U.K. 1938–9

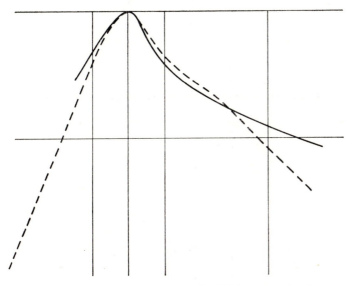

Chart A13   Income-ratio-curves for U.S.A. 1929 and 1967

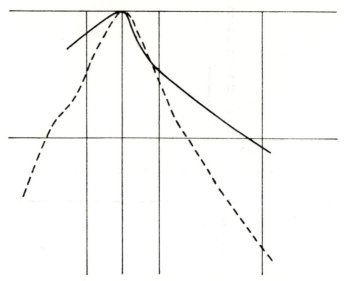

Chart A14   Income-ratio-curves for Sweden: 1931 and 1968

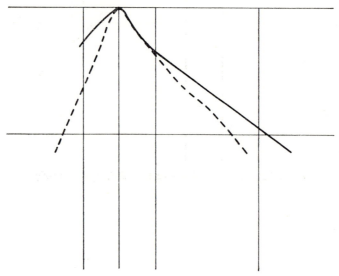

Chart A15   Income-ratio-curves for Holland: 1935 and 1966

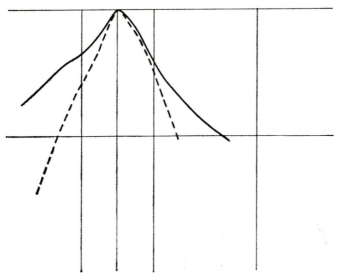

Chart A16   Income-ratio-curves for Norway: 1930 and 1967

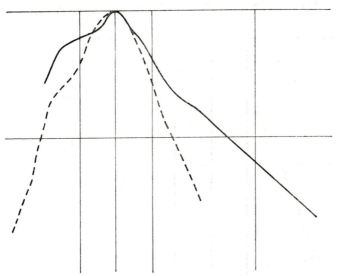

Chart A17   Income-ratio-curves for Denmark: 1925 and 1967-8

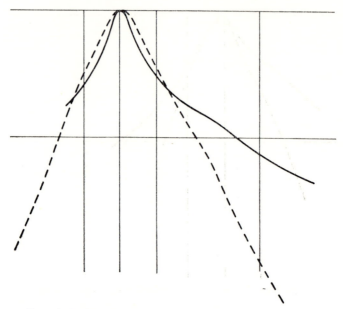

Chart A18 Income-ratio-curves for Australia: 1915 and 1967–8

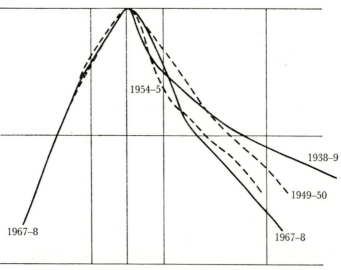

Chart A19 Income-ratio-curves for U.K.: 1938–9, 1949–50, 1954–5 and 1967–8

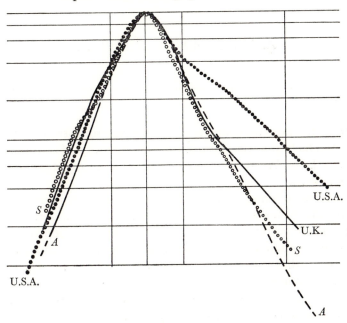

Chart A20   Income-ratio-curves for U.K. 1967, U.S.A. 1967,
Australia 1967–8, and Sweden 1968

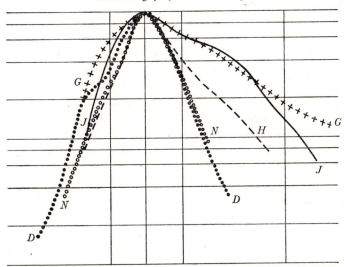

Chart A21   Income-ratio-curves for Norway 1967, Holland 1966, Denmark
1967–8, West Germany 1965 and Japan 1968

4. The sources of income

1. In the last two chapters we have made some study of the actual facts of income-distribution and the ways of expressing those facts. We now proceed to seek for an explanation of these facts.

We have found that the incomes of different individuals are not all more or less the same, but differ widely. The difference between the incomes of different individuals would commonly be explained in terms of the difference between their various *qualifications* for obtaining income.

There are many sorts of qualification for obtaining income, and the kinds will be different in different communities with different laws and customs. Let us consider for instance some of the qualifications which are useful in England today for obtaining income.

One qualification for obtaining income is the possession of the skill, energy and opportunity to perform work for an employer in return for a wage: we may sum up these assets in the phrase 'ability to work'. The coalminer owes his income to his ability to hew coal, and the director of a colliery owes his income to his ability in his office.

A second useful qualification for obtaining income is the possession of property, because this can be hired out to businessmen. For instance, the position of people who draw income in the form of dividends on industrial shares is essentially that of owners of 'shares' in an industrial property who hire it out to businessmen. Again a land-owner may use his land as a qualification for obtaining income, by hiring it out to farmers.

In such ways, the entire income of any individual may be attributed to his possession of various qualifications for obtaining income, and the difference between the incomes of different individuals may be expressed in terms of the difference between their qualifications.

2. It has indeed been usual for economists to adopt such an approach to the problem of distribution. They usually refer to the qualifications for obtaining income which people possess as being 'factors of production', because most of these qualifications owe their effectiveness to the fact that they help somebody to produce something which he can sell. These factors of production, or qualifications for obtaining income, are divided by economists into four great types:

ii Possession of the *ability to work*,

ii Possession of property of the type *capital*,

iii Possession of property of the type *land* and

iv Possession of peculiar bargaining power, or other economic advantage due to the presence of economic *frictions*: these advantages are called *monopoly advantages*.

Economists also allow for the existence of a fifth qualification for obtaining income, namely the good fortune to benefit by unforeseen change; this they call

v *Windfalls*.

The distinction between capital and land need not yet detain us: we may be content to remark that the category land includes certain other assets besides those commonly understood to be land, and that the distinctive property of such assets is that it is difficult for man to increase the total supply of them available.

3. We are now in a position to appreciate the likeness of economic life to a vast game of cards, in which there is dealt to each individual a hand composed of cards in the four great suits *ability* to work, *capital*, *land* and *monopoly advantage*, to which may perhaps be added later a joker representing *windfall*. His score, the income which he draws, depends on the value of the combination of cards in his hand,

that is to say, upon his combination of ability, capital, land, monopoly advantage and good fortune.

During the game, the players are free to exchange the majority of their cards for money, which serves as a counter. For instance, capital and land can be bought and sold, and again, by spending money on education or training, an individual can improve his ability to work.

Certain cards on the other hand cannot be bought and sold. For instance biological qualities are obtained at birth, and subsequent expenditure of money will have very little effect on them: qualities like strength and dexterity, good memory and nimbleness of thought are of great economic value to their owner, but they cannot ordinarily be bought or sold.

Those cards, or qualifications for income, which can be sold will have a price, and the keenness of buying and selling will be such as to make the price of any qualification proportional to the additional income which that qualification would yield to a potential buyer. In real life, the price of any piece of property or course of training will be proportional to the money-value of the net advantage which these would yield to a potential purchaser.

Moreover even those cards which cannot be bought and sold will bear to their owners a value which is proportional to the extra income of advantage with which they provide them.

At any moment we may attach to each little qualification for income that a man may possess, a certain 'marginal' value, which will be proportional to the extra income which that qualification brings to him.

4. The distribution of income in a community will depend partly on the deal of the cards, i.e. on the aggregate amounts and the distribution of ability, of capital, of land, of monopoly advantages and windfalls, and partly on the relative values set on ability to work, capital, land, monopoly advantages and windfalls.

In our study of the distribution of income, we must discuss

the causes which settle the aggregate amounts of each of these assets, and their relative prices and rewards, but we must study also the distribution of each or all of these qualifications among individuals.

5. We have seen that income is drawn in virtue of qualifications which can be classified into various types. In order to construct a theory of the distribution of income, it is most natural to construct separate theories to account for the distribution of each type of qualification, and of the income drawn from each. If we then regarded every individual as drawing his income predominantly from one type of qualification or another, we could compound our separate theories to explain the distribution of income from all sources.

In the next section we shall map out the lines on which such a theory might be developed, and in the following section, we will consider under what circumstances such a theory would be most convenient, and under what circumstances it would not be convenient.

6. Suppose that we have to construct a theory to explain the distribution of income in South America. Our first step would be to divide up the continent into various districts, each of which was fairly homogeneous and self-contained. For instance, we might take separately each political area, and further subdivide these into industrial areas and agricultural areas, provided that these were sufficiently distinct and that there was little mobility between them. For each area, we should divide up income into:

i income from ability to work,

ii income from capital,

iii income from rent of land,

iv income from monopoly advantages,

v income from windfalls, speculation etc.

We should construct a theory of the distribution of income from work, based on the supply of ability and on the opportunities available for its profitable employment; the

53

type of distribution to be expected would depend on the agricultural nature and the industries of our area.

Our theory of the distribution of capital would take into account the property laws of the country, the system of inheritance, the opportunities available for large-scale farming or large-scale business etc.

Our theory of the distribution of income from land would take account of the systems of land-tenure and the uses to which land could be put and so forth.

We should construct similar theories to find the distribution of income from other sources, and then we should estimate the distribution, in the area, of income from all sources, by some sort of adding-up process. For each area, we should obtain a similar set of theories, and we should obtain the distribution for the whole of South America by adding together the distributions for the separate areas.

7. This method would be appropriate, when political or geographical barriers prevented movement from one area to another, or the frequent substitution by individuals of one type for another of qualifications for obtaining income.

It would be inappropriate if the barriers between different areas were ineffective, or if the shift from possession of one type of qualification to another were easy.

For example, if we considered separately the distributions of income in Surrey and in Sussex, we should get into difficulties unless we took account of the fact that unequal distribution of income in Sussex would be likely to cause unequal distribution in Surrey, because people move to and fro between the counties. Similarly, if we considered separately the distribution of income from Consols and the distribution of income from War Loan, we should get into difficulties unless we took account of the fact that people sometimes move out of Consols into War Loan or something else.

The difficulty is that qualifications for obtaining income are very largely substitutes for each other, so that unequal distribution of any one of them may cause unequal distribution of those which may easily be substituted for it: we cannot learn the whole truth by studying the causes acting on the distribution of each qualification separately, without considering also the interdependence of the distributions of different kinds of qualifications.

In a modern European country where transport facilities are excellent, and where ample opportunities exist for choice whether to invest in training, enterprise, or safe shares, the difficulty is so pronounced that it becomes absurd to divide up qualifications for obtaining income into more than two or three water-tight compartments.

For many purposes, it is wisest to treat qualifications for obtaining income as homogeneous, and to have regard only to their aggregate value. For the effect of economic influences upon a man's income from a certain type of qualification will depend very often less on his stock of that particular qualification than on his stock of all qualifications. For instance, the effect of income-tax on my stock of securities will depend more upon what my aggregate income is, than on how large is my stock of securities. Again, it is easier to predict the effect on a man's aggregate income of a legacy of a set of jewels, than to predict the effect it will have on his income from land: for the man may convert the jewels into so many different qualifications for obtaining income.

The fact that different types of qualification can be interchanged means that changes in the relative values of different qualifications may have far less *permanent* effect in the face of other modifying forces. For instance, a huge once-for-all increase in the payments by editors for short stories might affect distribution appreciably in the first instance; but this effect would eventually be wiped out, because most people would soon find that it was impossible to get stories published unless they had invested large sums in courses of short-story writing and in the services of various agents who would commend their short stories to editors. Such costs would rise, until the yield on the investment of being able to get one's short stories printed would be no higher than that on other forms of investment. The well paid short-story writers would be losing an income on the capital which had to be sacrificed to their 'training'. We see that when different types of qualification can be interchanged, a redistribution of one type, ability, tends to produce a redistribution in the opposite sense of another type, capital, which will eventually cancel the effect on the aggregate distribution of incomes.

In so far as certain qualifications cannot be bought, a change in their value or reward *will* have permanent effects on the distribution of incomes. For instance, supposing that only good mathematicians can become actuaries, a permanent increase in the pay of actuaries is likely to have a permanent effect on the distribution of incomes, even in the face of permanent shaping forces like death duties. Again, since unskilled labourers do not sink much capital into their training, and do not have much opportunity for economising on education and training in order to accumulate capital or land, a permanent raising or lowering of the wages of unskilled labour is likely to have a permanent effect on the distribution of incomes. Indeed the very fact that there exists a fairly uniform distribution of ability to perform unskilled work coupled with trade union policy to demand uniform wages, acts as a permanent force attracting incomes towards the level corresponding to the wage paid to unskilled labour: this is because unskilled labourers do not vary the amounts of their money which they spend on securities and on training. Superimposed on the forces of change like inheritance and death, thrift and chance, which would alone produce a fairly smooth distribution curve, there is this force permanently dragging incomes towards the customary wage for unskilled labour, and this produces a hump in the distribution curve, which is otherwise smoother.

In the higher income-levels, where property and ability are far more easily interchanged, the permanent forces drawing incomes towards particular income-levels are very weak in comparison with the other permanent forces, and the result is that over these ranges there are no bumps in the distribution curve, and also over these ranges a sudden change in the reward of one qualification, say in the rents of land, will have far less permanent effect on distribution in the face of other permanent forces of change, although it will have considerable immediate effect.

8. We have seen that the effects of sudden changes in the relative prices of different types of qualification upon the distribution of the higher incomes may not be permanent; yet a study of the causes determining the relative prices of the different types is still important: for the changes in these relative prices will have large initial effects on the distribution of high incomes, and on the distribution of low incomes they may have large permanent effects. We have seen for instance that the relative price of the ability to perform unskilled labour to that of other qualifications for obtaining income has a very big permanent influence on the distribution of income, because it determines forces permanently acting to attract incomes towards a certain level.

The study of the relative prices or rewards of the different types of qualification is already well developed by economists; the subject is known as 'the distribution of income among the factors of production', and to this subject we shall turn in Chapter 6.

9. Before turning to study the classical theory of distribution between factors, and to adapt it to our own particular purpose of studying distribution of incomes between persons, it will be well to sharpen our definitions of factors of production, or of types of qualification for obtaining income and to subdivide further these types, and indeed to regroup them for our purposes.

Accordingly the next chapter is devoted to definitions and the explanation of the classification of qualifications for obtaining income: having cleared this ground we can then proceed to discuss what determines the aggregate supplies and the relative prices and rewards of the various types. Having done that we shall then pass on to the main task of deciding what determines the distribution among persons of these various types, and of the aggregate incomes obtained from combinations of them.

5. Detailed classification of income-sources

1. The variations between the incomes of different persons can be expressed in terms of the difference between their qualifications for obtaining income. We have seen that these qualifications can be classified into five main groups, namely:

i   possession of ability,

ii   possession of capital,

iii   possession of land,

iv   possession of monopoly advantage,

v   possession of good fortune, or windfall sources of income.

In order to analyse the forces determining the relative values and the distribution of different types and sub-types of qualification, we should require more precise definitions of ability, capital, land, monopoly and windfall and we should require to define certain sub-classes within these main classes of qualification. Finally, we regroup these sub-classes according to an alternative scheme in which certain distinctions relative to the determination of individual distribution will be emphasised.

2. The possession of 'ability' will refer to the possession of personal qualities which enable a man to obtain a wage in any position of service or responsibility. The wage-earner may be regarded as hiring out his ability to an employer and we may regard his wage as being due to, or drawn from, his ownership of ability to work.

Wages for different kinds of work are found to vary, and since the wage paid to a director is usually higher than that paid to an errand boy, we may say that the director owns more ability than the errand boy. Indeed, as a rough measure of ability, we may take the yearly wage which that level of ability ordinarily earns, and speak of a director having twenty times as much ability as an errand boy, if his wages are twenty times as big as those of the errand boy.

It will be noticed that the sense in which we use the term 'ability' is purely that of 'ability to earn income': this is an unusual use of the word, and its use in this sense is merely a matter of convenience.

Ability may be inborn in a man, or else it may be acquired by effort, or thirdly it may be bought for money. A man may have the ability to get a high civil service income because he was born a genius, or because he worked very hard for the examinations, or thirdly, because an expensive education and expensive coaching for the examinations fitted him for the civil service post, although his genius and his industry were only moderate. The role of expensive training in producing ability is an extremely important one in the modern world.

Accordingly it will be convenient to distinguish two kinds of income from work:

i Income due to inborn ability.

ii Income due to ability purchased (by training) or to ability acquired by work which would otherwise have been earning income directly. As an example of this last type of ability, we may consider that of an accountant who obtained his training by working for a far lower wage than he might have obtained in some other occupation.

Income from work may be regarded as the hire paid for ability: inborn ability cannot be bought, but certain abilities can be bought, and these latter abilities are sometimes called 'human capital', because they are analogous to 'capital' or income-earning property, a source of income which we may next discuss.

3. The simplest form of income from property that can be discussed may be typified by that of the owner of a piano, who hires it out for people to amuse themselves with, and receives in this way more than enough money to pay for the

tuning of the piano and any other repairs necessary to keep it from deteriorating.

We see how close the analogy is between income from purchased ability, and income from property, when we consider that instead of buying the piano for hiring out to musical people, the man might have spent his money on learning to sing, in which case he could have hired out his voice, instead of the piano, to the musical people, by arranging for them to pay to come and hear him sing.

A more usual method of obtaining income from the ownership of property is the following: a property, such as a blast furnace, may be quite useless when left to its own devices, but may be found to be very useful when controlled by men: accordingly, it is sometimes possible to obtain an income from the ownership of a blast furnace, by hiring the ability of a lot of men to work the blast furnace, and selling the produce of the joint effort of the men and the blast furnace. After allowing for the cost of raw materials and repairs to the blast furnace, there may be considerable profit left over: if it is now possible to hire the ability of the men controlling the blast furnace for a sufficiently low wage, there may be some income left over for the owner of the blast-furnace.

In real life, owners of blast furnaces, factories, land and other productive equipment often do find it quite possible to secure incomes for themselves in this manner; indeed, this possibility is in many cases the chief stimulant to the erection of factories, and to the improvement of land, and were it not for these possibilities, it is very doubtful whether factories and other productive equipment would not be allowed, under the present organisation of society, to fall into disrepair.

A more complicated way of making an income out of a piece of property is to hire it out to somebody else, so that he can make an income out of it in the manner described above.

If a particular piece of property enables its owner to obtain a very large income, it is natural that other people should try to copy him, and should try to construct similar pieces of property for themselves. If they succeed in doing this, they may quite conceivably reduce the man's income from his property. For instance, suppose that a man constructs a machine which will amuse millionaires, and that he finds that he can hire this out for a very large sum to a millionaire; now suppose that all his friends construct similar machines and try to hire them out to other millionaires, then they may find themselves unable to do so owing to a scarcity of suitable millionaires. In their anxiety to earn *some* incomes from the machines they may very well lower the price at which they offer to hire out their machines, and sooner or later the owner of the original machine may have to offer his millionaire reduced terms, in case he should hire somebody else's machine instead.

But now suppose that it was not a machine which the man hired out to the millionaire, but a beautiful piece of country, which was so lovely that nobody could possibly hope to construct one like it, then the position would be different. No longer would there be a danger that his friends might underbid him, for no longer could they hope to find anything which would tempt the millionaire away from his amusement in country of such unique quality.

4. This example suggests an important economic distinction between property which can be reproduced, like machines, and property which cannot be reproduced, like acreage of land or genuine old masters. Accordingly we shall distinguish between property which can and property which cannot be reproduced, and shall refer to them as

i Capital,

ii Land.

In practice the line of division between the two types of property is not quite precise, because there may be some types of property which can be reproduced, but only in very small quantities and with difficulty, and on the other hand there may be property which cannot be reproduced, but for which close substitutes can be found. In particular cases, mere convenience may dictate whether a certain piece of property is to be regarded as capital or as land.

5. The income yielded on certain types of property depends largely on how much the property could be sold for: the income from such property may change very greatly, and changes in its value may have considerable effects on distribution. This is because any increase in the price of the property will thereby increase the income from the property, and hence will also increase the demand for the property; this in turn will raise the price again, and a small initial rise in demand may by such a process cause a large rise in price.

The most important example of this type of property is money. Money is useful in all sorts of ways, amongst which that of being held in readiness for purchases is important. Hence the owner of money is qualified to obtain an income by hiring it out. Since an increase in the price of money in terms of goods will automatically increase in the same proportion the amount of useful purchasing for which it can be held in readiness, we see that any increase of the price, in terms of goods, of money, is likely to increase in almost the same proportion the amount of goods which people will be prepared to exchange for money: hence, the only limit to a rise in the price of money, once it has been set off, is the point at which people find again that they have enough money to satisfy their requirements for holding money.*

As a second example, we may consider land which is held because in emergency it could be exchanged for food. Then the value in terms of food of the insurance thus provided will increase in proportion to the price of land in terms of food, if the price rise is expected to last: hence an initial increase in demand for land may cause a very big increase in the insurance income yielded by land, and in the income that the owners obtain by letting out the land on long lease.

6. We may now consider monopoly advantage, the fourth class of qualification for obtaining income. We may distinguish between the following three types:

i   shared monopoly advantage,

---

* Modern readers in 1973 may find it more illuminating to consider the case of a decrease in the price of money in terms of goods.

ii conditional monopoly advantage,

iii complete monopoly advantage.

7. By shared monopoly advantage, we shall mean an advantage shared by several persons who compete to obtain income, which, owing to some economic friction, is not available to any potential competitor. The possession of such an advantage may enable the competing persons to draw extra income above the true competitive level, even though they may compete fully against each other.

As one example of shared monopoly advantage, we may consider the possession of good connections. To be in touch with well-informed business opinion, and to be able to introduce business to one's firm because one is on speaking terms with influential men, can be a fruitful source of revenue, just because these capabilities can be possessed by only a few people. Shared monopoly advantage of this type shades off into purchased ability, when we consider the circle of business friends as having been acquired at school, club or university.

As another example of shared monopoly advantage we may consider a group of competing retail shops in the main street of a city. These shops may find that owing to their position, even though they compete keenly with each other, they are selling at higher prices than less favourably placed shops, and are drawing larger profits. Moreover, since all these good sites are already filled, fresh competitors are not drawn into the street, and their profits will remain high.

Such a 'shared monopoly advantage' is practically indistinguishable from 'land'. For instance, the favourable situations for shops in our example may be regarded as pieces of land with a high yield for shop building. In other cases, the analogy between 'shared monopoly advantages' and 'land' may not be quite so obvious, but in all cases shared monopoly advantage will yield income according to the same principle as land yields income, and for purposes of analysis, such advantages will be regarded as a peculiar kind of land.

8. By 'conditional monopoly advantage' we shall mean advantage possessed exclusively by one individual interest but which could be obtained by other individuals also if they chose to expend labour and capital in obtaining them. 'Goodwill' is a commonly met type of conditional monopoly advantage. At a given moment, a firm may have won such a reputation for its product, that it can afford to charge very high prices without fear of losing many customers to rivals who charge low prices: yet if a competitor cares to expend labour and capital upon improving the quality of its products and upon advertising them, it may be able to build up an equal reputation, and to share the advantage. Hence a firm will not be able to obtain a high yield on capital invested in acquiring 'goodwill', without causing rival firms to invest their capital in goodwill also, until the yield is brought down to a more normal level.

As another example of conditional monopoly advantage we may consider the advantage of a firm which has obtained sole rights in selling an ingenious labour-saving device for the housewife: for the time being it may charge high prices, but by the expenditure of labour and capital, other firms will be able to invent and put on the market substitutes for this device.

As a third example we may consider a firm which has purchased a machine for polishing its products and so rendering them more attractive to simple customers. This will not for very long enable it to charge very much higher prices than its rivals, for they too will then buy similar machines. Even so, the price is likely to remain raised sufficiently to cover the payments for depreciation and interest upon the machine.

In practice, it may be hard to distinguish between conditional monopoly advantage and capital, and it will in fact be found convenient to regard conditional monopoly advantage as equivalent to a special kind of capital, for purposes of analysis of the forces determining its value, amount and distribution.

9. By complete monopoly advantage we shall mean the exclusive possession by an individual interest of an advantage which others can be prevented from sharing. This type of monopoly is rare, but where it exists it may enable very large incomes to be procured.

Such an advantage may be gained by the deliberate collaboration of all the sellers in a given market, provided that this is supported by a campaign to ruin or buy up competitors outside the 'ring', or by the discouragement of new competitors by successful concealment of high profits.

It may also be gained by a financier who acquires some control over the policies of a large number of competing firms and co-ordinates them in such a way as to obtain large dividends for himself; this gentleman also must be careful to keep out rivals.

Complete monopoly advantage may be derived by a careful use of an exclusive combination of knowledge and experience, available to one group of interests alone, for gaining income, for instance on the stock exchange.

The banks derive income from their complete monopoly advantage in being allowed to expand credit. Banks have also been accused of deriving a more sinister form of monopoly advantage from their power over concerns dependent upon them for credit, by directing their policy so as to augment the banks' own income.

10. 'Windfall advantage' simply means any advantage gained by the occurrence of something unforeseen, which enables a man to obtain more income. For instance, a man might obtain income because of an unforeseen offer by an American to buy one of his uglier pictures for ten thousand pounds.* Farmers might obtain income from an unforeseen stimulus (such as increase of population) to the demand for agricultural produce. In 1931, when gold rose in price, this must have caused windfall gains to those who had at their disposal golden trinkets.

* Modern readers should substitute 'a million dollars'.

11. Let us now reassemble our classification of the types of qualification for obtaining income. It may be set out as in the accompanying scheme:

i Ability   1 inborn
                    2 purchased
ii Capital ⎫   ⎛ Yield
iii Land   ⎭   ⎪ Income due to
                                   ⎨ exchange-
                                   ⎝ value

iv Monopoly   1 Shared
                    2 Conditional
                    3 Absolute
v Windfall

We see that these fall again into three classes:

i Qualifications which are not bought and sold.
ii Qualifications which are bought and sold but which cannot be built up by expenditure of labour and capital.
iii Qualifications which are bought and sold and which can be built up by the expenditure of labour and capital.

If we were to group the sub-types of qualification for obtaining income into these three classes, we should obtain the following scheme.

I Non-marketable qualifications.
  a. Inborn abilities;
  b. Windfall advantages.

II Marketable qualifications of which more cannot be constructed.
  a. Land;
  b. Shared monopoly advantage;
  c. Complete monopoly advantage.

III Marketable qualifications of which more can be constructed.
  a. Purchased ability;
  b. Capital;
  c. Conditional monopoly advantage.

66

Detailed classification of sources

For our purpose of discussing the distribution of income between persons, the distinctions between these three classes of qualification are particularly important. The distribution between persons of qualifications in class I alone cannot be modified by market transactions: again, the supply of qualifications of any type in class III alone will be influenced by market prices. The value of qualifications in class III alone will be influenced by their cost of reproduction. The importance of these distinctions will become clear in the argument of the next chapter.

6. The amounts, relative values and distribution of qualifications for obtaining income

1. The principles which determine the amounts and relative values of different qualifications for obtaining income are already fairly well-known and in this chapter we shall only remind ourselves very briefly of these. The problem to which little answer has yet been given is how are determined the personal distribution of individual qualifications or of their aggregate value.

2. The aggregate amounts of non-marketable qualifications, and of marketable qualifications which cannot be reconstructed, will not rise in response to the lure of high profit (except insofar as the marketable qualifications can be imported from other communities). In general, their aggregate amounts will be determined by such forces as nature and chance. These are the main forces which determine the aggregate amounts of inborn abilities, windfall advantage, land, shared monopoly advantage and complete monopoly advantage.

3. The aggregate amounts of the qualifications which can be constructed will depend on their original supply and on the construction of them which has taken place since. Their relative values will depend chiefly on their relative costs of construction; in the short run, it will depend also on the demand for these qualifications. Every year, 'investment' will be pushed forward into the accumulation of capital equipment, purchased ability and monopoly advantage, and when change of demand raises the price of a particular

type of qualification above its cost of construction, that type of qualification will be the more rapidly constructed than others, and the law of diminishing utility will cause its value to fall back into line with its cost, when its amount has been sufficiently expanded. The distribution of accumulation between different kinds of qualifications, productive equipment, training and monopoly advantage, will be like that of a rising tide which finds its own level up creeks and gulleys: in every channel for accumulation, capital will flow until the yield or marginal efficiency there is on a level with that in other channels.

The process of investment and the rate of interest will depend not only on the will to accumulate, but also on the opportunity: this will depend on the banking policy and on the psychology of the people; when these are unsuitable, the opportunity may be reduced and unemployment may be caused.

The value of any qualification for obtaining income will be proportional to the income which a 'marginal' unit will provide: the rate of interest will be equal to the ratio of the annual income to the value of the qualification, which, we have seen, will usually be equal to the cost of construction, when the qualification *can* be constructed.

Where the qualification can *not* be constructed, its value will still be determined in the same way by the marginal income, and this will depend on the demand for the use of the qualification. If the qualification is marketable, it will be so distributed that the marginal income which it yields to each person is roughly the same.

4. These rules enable us to tell the effect of important economic changes on the amounts and values of different qualifications. Increase of population will increase the amount of inborn ability and reduce its relative value per unit: it will send up the demand for agricultural produce and raise the value of land, drawing up some above the margin of cultivation: similarly, it will raise the value of

certain monopoly advantages and create others; the rate of interest is also likely to be raised at the same time as the marginal efficiency of capital.

Accumulation is a force tending to lower the rate of interest, by lowering the relative value of those qualifications which can be constructed. It is likely to raise the value of the other qualifications, especially that of land, as the qualifications which can be constructed are less easily substituted for land than for other qualifications.

On the other hand, new inventions, technical progress and the advantages of large scale may raise the rate of interest and the relative value of productive equipment which can be constructed. The discovery of new ways of investing in monopoly advantage and particular types of ability may also have the effect of raising the rate of interest. Inventions which economise the use of land are likely to reduce its value, because the demand for its produce will not greatly expand when its price is lowered.

The improvement of transport and communications will alter the relative values of different types of monopoly: it is likely to increase the ease with which large interests can co-operate, and to lower the cost of construction of monopoly advantage. The more accumulation takes the form of accumulating monopoly advantage, the higher will be raised the value of those abilities which are required for this type of accumulation: accumulation of monopoly advantage and accumulation of the ability required for obtaining monopoly advantage will proceed hand in hand.

5. These are a few of the most obvious generalisations which can be made about the forces which change the amounts and relative values of different qualifications for obtaining income. They have been more fully discussed elsewhere, and it would distort our emphasis to say more of them here than the summary given below in Table 4.

Qualifications for obtaining income

6. It is the distribution between persons of the qualifications which primarily interests us.

Consider the three types of qualification:

i   Non-marketable qualifications;

ii Marketable qualifications of which more cannot be constructed;

iii Marketable qualifications of which more can be constructed.

TABLE 4. *Table of influences acting on the amounts and relative values of various qualifications for obtaining income*

class of qualification	main influences
1 ability	population, eugenics and heredity; climate and care of health, standard of living; educational facilities, industrial environment; social mobility between occupations and classes; demand for ability by institutions; trade union policy, employers' associations; custom – a legacy from the past
2 capital	amount and character of past accumulation depended on: population and supply of land and natural resources; laws relating to property; date of becoming industrialised; thrift of the population; inequality of distribution; state investment, taxation etc. banking policy
3 land	amount of land available, both above and below the margin of cultivation; demand for the use of land; facilities for foreign trade and the level abroad
4 monopoly advantages	means of conveyance of persons, goods and information; legal restrictions; superstition, laziness and convention; economies of large scale; ease of collaboration of interests; extent of gangster methods; influence of business on politics
5 windfalls	imperfect foresight; conflicting expectations; wars and acts of God

Inborn ability is typical of the first category: the possession of the soil and of limited markets are typical of the second category: the possession of factories and of a reputation for quality are typical of the third.

Consider the ways of the rich. Their predominant economic characteristic is their anxiety to save. It is they who launch out into new industrial ventures and convert their natural gifts into blast furnaces and railways. Indeed, the richer and more ambitious a man becomes, the greater preference will he have for the new forms of wealth which he can build up for himself over those which he can purchase from an existing stock. Naturally, qualifications when they are constructed will in general pass first into the possession of the rich. Accordingly, we should expect a particularly unequal distribution of the marketable qualifications which can be constructed.

After a time, the unequal distribution of the marketable qualifications which have been constructed will react on the distribution of other marketable qualifications, because people will sell the one and buy the other. Hence we should expect the distribution of marketable qualifications which cannot be constructed also to be markedly unequal, but not to such a great extent.

Finally, consider the distribution of non-marketable qualifications. Here there is no reason to suppose a very unequal distribution: it is a chance distribution, and upon the inequality of this distribution depends the inequality of distribution of qualifications later constructed. But since we have seen that it is primarily the rich who acquire newly-constructed qualifications, the inequality of distribution of non-marketable qualifications will cause a far *greater* inequality of distribution of the marketable ones.

In this way, we can account for the following facts:

i The distribution of income from non-marketable qualifications is not very unequal.

ii The distribution of income from marketable qualifications, more of which cannot be constructed, is more unequal.

Qualifications for obtaining income

iii The distribution of marketable qualifications of which more can be constructed is yet more unequal.

iv Those qualifications of type (iii), such as monopoly advantage, whose acquisition is made cheaper by the possession of large income, will be the most unequally distributed.

7. The distribution of income from a homogeneous source

1. Let us now consider more carefully what will determine the distribution of income from a particular type of qualification. For simplicity let us suppose that the type of qualification is homogeneous and cannot be substituted for other types. The distribution of income will then depend on how much of the qualification each individual possesses.

2. The amount of the qualification possessed by any individual will depend on

i How much he possessed a year ago.

ii How much he has acquired since then or lost since then.

Taking a longer view, the amount possessed by any family depends on how much they had a century ago, and how much they have acquired or lost since then.

3. The question whether the distribution is going to be equal or unequal evidently depends

i On whether families can lose or gain large proportions of their stock of the qualification, i.e. if the chance element is high.

ii On whether the possession of a large stock of qualifications makes it easier to get more, or less easy.

If the chance element is high we should expect a high degree of inequality – because a few lucky people would always have gained large amounts three or four times running. If the fact of having a lot of the qualifications made it easier to acquire more, we should again expect a high degree of inequality.

74

Distribution of income from a homogeneous source

As an example of the first point, we should expect the distribution of income from gambling at Monte Carlo to be unequal. As an example of the second, we should expect the distribution of farm-land to be unequal, if there were economies of large-scale farming so that the large farmers would be able to buy more land out of their profits.

4. Now let us consider the distribution of the aggregate income from all qualifications. This will depend on how good are the qualifications each individual possesses for obtaining income: this will depend on how much he had a year ago, and on how much he has lost or gained since then. His aggregate income will largely depend on his start in life and on the use he has made of that start.

Any person who has been 'dealt' a set of qualifications by nature and his parents, may be considered as spending his life trading with these qualifications, exchanging some for other qualifications, in order to increase their aggregate value and his income.

By exchanging qualifications, he will increase his stock of some qualifications and will reduce his stock of others, but the aggregate value of this stock of all qualifications will remain less affected by these exchanges than will the value of the individual stocks of particular qualifications. When the man dies he will hand over to his sons stocks of other qualifications for obtaining income besides inborn ability. These stocks may be mainly in the form of capital, land, monopoly advantages, or expensive education, but the aggregate value of them is likely to depend largely upon the aggregate value of the father's own stock of qualifications for obtaining income.

Hence, some sort of continuity can be traced between the aggregate values of the father's stock of qualifications and the aggregate value of his son's stock of qualifications, although little continuity can be traced between the father's stock and the son's stock of each single qualification for obtaining income.

5. In order to discover the forces determining the nature of the distribution of income, i.e. the nature of the distribution of the aggregate value of all qualifications for obtaining incomes, we shall accordingly have to study carefully these links between past and present distribution that are provided by this tendency for the aggregate value of qualifications to preserve a continuity.

It will be convenient to withdraw emphasis from the distribution between different qualifications for obtaining income, and to discuss only the changes in each individual's total value of qualifications and in his total income from them all. We have seen that there are likely to be many links between the income of a man in one year and his income in the next year, and many links between the income of a father and of his son and between the income of a man and of his heir, whereas there will be fewer links between a man's portions of any one particular qualification at different dates, since he may exchange one qualification for another.

Our new approach will be to express a man's income this year as being due to what his income was last year and to things that have since happened to change it. We shall explain the distribution of income of this year as being due to what the distribution of income was last year, and to things which have since happened to alter the distribution. Finally, we shall explain this year's distribution in terms of change for many years back, and to some form of distribution in the distant past.

6. Our emphasis will be on the forces of change, that is to say, on causes which act to change the incomes (or to change the richness of qualifications for obtaining incomes) of different individuals. These, we shall maintain, are the forces which in the long run determine the distribution of income in a country, whatever it may originally have been.

This, surely, is what the practical man would suppose: inequality is due to the forces which allow incomes to increase when they are already large, and to decrease when they are already small. It needs little perspicacity to discover that inequality is due to the action of the rule 'to him that hath shall more be given, and from him that hath not shall be taken away even that which he seemeth to have'. If this rule were strictly obeyed, income would of course become more and more unequally distributed, and the fact that inequality is not found to be increasing, although the poor can save far less easily than the rich, shows that there must be some force acting to counteract this tendency.

We have discussed in earlier chapters some of the forces which change incomes. We have found that there is a force drawing incomes in towards the customary rate of wages paid to unskilled labour; because, if a man by good fortune earns rather more than this, yet the chances are that his son will not share the good fortune, and the family income will be sucked down again when the father dies. Other forces of change which we have discussed are changes in the amounts and changes in the relative rates of reward of different qualifications for obtaining income. These changes are important and we have seen that they may have large effects on the distribution of income.

7. We shall find occasion to draw a distinction between two kinds of causes of change:

1 *Impulsive* causes of change, which act once only.
2 *Forces* of change which act continuously.

For an example of an *impulsive cause*, or *impulse* of change, we may consider a sudden new invention which takes place once and for all, and which causes immediately a huge redistribution of income, both by presenting many people with monopoly advantages and by altering the rate of interest. Most of the causes of change which we have so far discussed fall into the category *impulse* of change, because they are causes which act once and for all to change incomes.

As an example of a force of change, we may consider again the case of the existence of the fairly uniform unskilled wage rate, which acts continuously to suck in incomes towards this income (thus balancing the tendency for the outflow from the dense region of incomes to exceed the inflow from the thin region of incomes outside it).

As another example of a force of change, we may consider the effect of taxation, which is to decrease continuously the flow of saving by the rich.

The effect of these two types of causes of change will be different upon distribution of income. In the short run the impulse of change will have more effect than the force of change, but in the long run the force of change will smooth away the effect of the impulse.

8. The effect of forces of change and impulses of change on the distribution of income will be like that of forces and impulses applied to a system of bodies, in which there is some friction: the forces acting on the system will determine its equilibrium position, but the action of an impulse may at first be to disturb the positions of the bodies far more than do the forces, yet given time the forces will bring the bodies towards their equilibrium position, and this will be independent of the impulses which they may have received. The bodies may never reach equilibrium, because fresh impulses are applied at frequent intervals, yet the forces have more effect on the position of the bodies than do impulses which took place long ago, and eventually they will have more effect on the position of the bodies than will impulses which are now being applied.

In the economic system of the distribution of incomes, after each disturbance or impulse of change such as a new invention, the distribution of income is likely to settle back again to something like equilibrium under the action of constant forces of change. In the long run, it is the constantly acting forces of change which are the most important in determining the distribution of income. Some of these we have already discussed, for instance the continuous tendency for population to change and for capital to be accumulated, but a great many of the more important of these forces of change have yet to be discussed. A few such forces are: death duties, progressive taxation and systems of inheritance laws. It is on forces of change rather than on impulses of change, that attention will be concentrated in the next chapters.

9. We shall discuss the effects of forces of change in terms of an equilibrium distribution which they tend to produce: in fact the forces of change are themselves shifting and so the equilibrium is in fact never reached, even when there are no disturbing impulses of change. But the concept of equilibrium is a complex one, and we may pass to a new chapter in order to discuss it.

8. The equilibria of distributions of income

1. It will be found that in earlier chapters we learned to describe and to chart distributions of income, and we examined some actual distributions of income as given in available statistical publications. In later chapters, we discussed the influences which determined the amounts and rates of reward of various qualifications for obtaining income, but found that this approach did not enable us to say much about the distribution of incomes between persons, unless we could find out more about the distribution of qualifications between persons. We decided next to try to account for the properties of distributions of income by showing that they were determined by economic forces of change which acted on incomes; such forces as inheritance, which enables a family to keep on acquiring riches, and such forces as expensive education, which enable the rich to remain better qualified than the poor to earn large salaries.

2. In our attempt we shall be hampered by the fact that such influences are never remaining for long the same, but are changing along with institutions from century to century; as a result, the phenomenon which we have to explain is not a fixed but a changing one; the properties of the income-distribution are altering every year, along with the economic influences which determine the form of that distribution.

This is a difficulty which is met with by economists and engineers in many of their problems. To cope with it, they have invented the concept of equilibrium. In the study of mechanics, a body is said to be in equilibrium if it is at rest and if it is likely to remain indefinitely at rest, unless the forces acting upon it change. More broadly, a body might be described as being in equilibrium, if it were merely observed that it was remaining at rest.

Equilibria of distributions of income

The branch of the study called statics is almost entirely concerned with finding the equilibrium positions of bodies corresponding to various sets of forces supposed constant; having mastered the problem of determining these equilibrium problems, the student is then equipped to study more complicated problems concerning the movements of bodies which are not in equilibrium, and which are perhaps under the influence of changing forces.

The same system of approach has been suggested for economic problems; in the analysis of the 'stationary state' the student works out the 'equilibrium' level to which prices and the amounts of goods produced would settle, if all the economic forces remained the same and if they were left the time to work out their full effects.

We shall make use of the same concept of 'equilibrium' in our study of the forces which determine the distribution of incomes; we shall study the conditions under which the distribution would settle down to a stationary or 'equilibrium' distribution.

3. We are confronted with the preliminary problem of deciding how to define an 'equilibrium' distribution of incomes.

We may distinguish 4 degrees of equilibrium for an income-distribution. We may call these:

i   dead equilibrium
ii static equilibrium
iii quasi-static equilibrium
iv moving equilibrium.

4. *Dead equilibrium* need not detain us; it means the condition when every individual's income remains unmoved as time rolls on. We shall not study the conditions under which dead equilibrium would be possible.

5. *Static equilibrium* will mean a state of affairs where individual incomes may change, but where the aggregate

81

distribution remains unchanged, in the sense that the income-curve remains absolutely stationary as time moves on. In static equilibrium, individual incomes may change, but the number of incomes between any given pair of limits must remain unchanged. It will be noted that in static equilibrium both the total income and the total number of incomes must be constant.

In our theory of the distribution of income the equilibrium-distribution will play much the same part as the equilibrium position plays in the theory of mechanics. Under certain circumstances, it will be shown in a later chapter that the action of the given set of economic forces upon a given number of incomes must lead eventually to a unique position of static equilibrium.

This will be the case only under certain restricting conditions: for instance, the constant economic forces must be such as to allow the total income and the total number of incomes to be stationary. Obviously, if one of the forces which were constant were a tendency for the population to multiply at 1 % per annum, then static equilibrium would be impossible until this force were checked, because static equilibrium is incompatible with an increasing number of incomes.

6. *Quasi-static equilibrium* differs from static equilibrium, only in that it also allows *general* changes in income-power (i.e. equal increases of income-power for every income-receiver) and *general* increases in the number of income-receivers (i.e. an equi-proportional increase in the number of people in each income-class).

It will be remembered that the people-curve and the income-curve show the distributions between income-power classes of people and of incomes. The people-ratio-curve and the income-ratio-curve are the same curves plotted on logarithmic paper, which represents equal ratios by equal distances.

Owing to the ratio-property of the paper on which the income-ratio-curve and the people-ratio-curve are plotted, general increases of equal proportion in the number of people in each income-power class will simply have the effect of shifting the income-ratio-curve and the people-ratio-curve along the direction of the y-axis without altering their shape at all. Owing to the same property of the income-power scale, any combination of

i a uniform proportional increase in the number of people in each income-power class,

ii a uniform proportional increase in the income of each person,

will result merely in shiftings of the income-ratio-curve and the people-ratio-curve, without altering their shapes. Hence, we see that in quasi-static equilibrium, the form of the income-ratio-curve and of the people-ratio-curve must remain unaltered, although the curves may be shifting about in any direction. We shall find that when forces of change are 'steady', quasi-static equilibrium must be reached, even if population and income per head change.

7. *Moving equilibrium.* We may leave the explanation of the term moving equilibrium to Chapter 19 near the end of the book, where the concept will be discussed. It refers to a steadily changing distribution brought about by steadily changing forces. The term 'moving equilibrium' is used for want of any better label.

In practice, the distributions are never found to be even in quasi-static equilibrium. This is easily discovered by plotting the income-ratio-curves for the same country for a series of years. If the distribution was in quasi-static equilibrium, the income-ratio-curve would remain of the same shape even if it was shifting about the page from year to year. In this case, the slope at any particular point on the curve would remain the same from year to year.

What actually has happened to the portion of the English income-ratio-curve referring to surtax players is shown in Chart 17, where are plotted the changes of the slope of the curve in the U.K. during 1915 to 1933, at portions corresponding to

The distribution of income between persons

(1) incomes between the 200th and 800th richest person,

(2) incomes between the 800th and 3,200th richest persons,

(3) incomes between the 3,200th and 12,800th richest persons,

(4) incomes between the 12,800th and 51,200th richest persons.

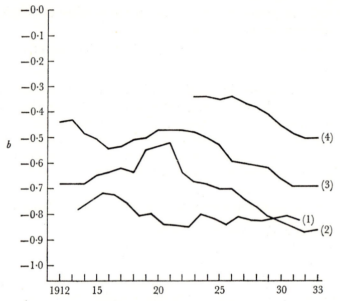

Chart 17   Changes in the slopes *b* of 4 segments of the income-ratio-curve for U.K. high incomes 1912–33

If we take moving averages so as to eliminate random disturbances due to impulses of change, we find that the slopes of the four parts of the curve remain distinct, showing that the curve retained its characteristic concavity, over these portions, through the period, but that for each portion of the curve, steepness has been increasing fairly steadily since 1920 (except for the *very* rich), thus indicating increasing equality, whereas before 1920 this was not the case.

These curves do suggest that the form of the income-ratio-curve is changing fairly systematically and smoothly, and

84

that an analysis is needed which will predict gradual smooth change in step with gradually changing circumstances.

Before advancing to such a theory, we shall however consider more elementary models of the real world, wherein the forces remain steady until static or quasi-static equilibrium is attained. We shall examine the effect of the introduction of new forces into such model worlds, and we shall find afterwards that their effects will be not much different when they are introduced into a world where there is 'moving equilibrium'.

APPENDIX: SHIFTS IN DISTRIBUTION
OF HIGH INCOMES IN THE UNITED
KINGDOM 1924–67

1. This appendix extends the consideration of the changes in the distribution of income among super-tax payers in Great Britain up to the late 1960s. The analysis has still to be limited to what appears in the official statistics.

These statistics suggest a very considerable reduction of the inequality among such taxpayers over the last forty or fifty years, and perhaps the simplest way to show this is to

TABLE A. 2. *Comparison of numbers of incomes over £50,000 and over £5,000 1924–5 and 1967–8*

year	numbers of incomes	
	over £50,000	over £5,000
1924–5	601	27,428
1967–8	683	193,305
Percentage increase	13·6	604·8

compare the changes in the number of persons recorded as having incomes exceeding £50,000 with the corresponding changes for over £5,000. Table A. 2 gives the comparison and it will be seen that whereas in 1967–8 there were only a few more persons recorded with incomes over £50,000 than were so recorded in 1924–5, yet the number recorded with income exceeding £5,000 had multiplied by about seven over the same period. Of course, the purchasing power of the pound had diminished considerably over the same period. However, when a rough correction is made to allow for the change in the price level, as is done in Table A. 3, much the same contrast still appears. Whereas in 1967–8 the number shown with incomes over £100,000 was only about one thirteenth of the number shown with incomes over the comparable level of £50,000 at the earlier date, the number shown in 1967–8 with incomes over £10,000 was nearly three-fifths of that shown with incomes over the comparable level of £5,000 in 1924–5.

2. In order to show in greater detail the changes indicated by the statistics over the period, Table A. 4 gives estimates at 12-year intervals of the levels of the 200th, 800th, 3,200th,

TABLE A. 3. *Comparison of numbers of incomes recorded as over £25,000 and over £2,500 in 1924–5, and recorded as over £100,000 and over £10,000 in 1967–8*

	numbers of incomes recorded as	
year	over £25,000	over £2,500
1924–5	2,058	71,093
	over £100,000	over £10,000
1967–8	159	42,334
as % of above number for 1924–5	7·7	58·9

TABLE A. 4. *Changes between 1927–8, 1939–40, 1951–2, and 1963–4, in the incomes of ranks 200, 800, 3,200, 12,800 and 51,200*

Year ...	1927–8	1939–40	1951–2	1963–4
Rank	Estimated level of income in thousands of pounds per annum			
200th	81	69	52	84
800th	40	33	29	42
3,200th	19	16	17	24
12,800th	8·3	7·5	9·4	14
51,200th	3·3	3·2	4·9	7·7

12,800th and 51,200th largest incomes, based on a procedure of interpolation on the Pareto curves. Whereas the estimated money-value of the 200th income *fell* by over one third between 1927–8 and 1951–2, and was still in 1963–4 only just above the 1927–8 level, that of the 51,200th income rose in ratio 3:7 over the same 36 years.

3. On the basis of more detailed estimates of the kind shown in Table A. 4. it has been possible to bring up to date the

statistics illustrated in Chart 17 above in Chapter 8. These are summarised in Table A. 5 and are illustrated in Chart A. 22 which traces the slopes of the four segments of the income-ratio-curve over the whole period from 1913–14 to 1966–7: these curves shown in Chart A. 22 have been smoothed by taking centred 3-year averages of the relevant slopes.

4. For readers who are more accustomed to measure equality amongst the rich by Pareto's 'alpha', the slope of

TABLE A. 5. *Level and annual rates of change of b over each of 3 12-year periods 1927–63 for each of four segments of the income-ratio-curve for the U.K.*

year or 12-year period ...	1927–8	1939–40	1951–2	1963–4	1927–39	1939–51	1951–63	1927–63
income-range by rank	estimated values of $|b|$				estimated annual increase of $|b|$			
200–800th	0·88	0·82	1·49	0·98	−0·005	0·055	−0·04	0·003
800–3,200th	0·74	0·97	1·57	1·56	0·02	0·05	−0·001	0·023
3,200–12,800th	0·60	0·71	1·18	1·56	0·01	0·04	0·03	0·027
12,800–51,200th	0·35	0·48	0·89	1·25	0·01	0·035	0·03	0·025
200–51,200th	0·64	0·745	1·28	1·34	0·01	0·045	0·005	0·019

TABLE A. 6. *Levels and annual rates of change of α* over each of 3 12-year periods 1927–63 for each of four segments of the Pareto curve for the U.K.*

year or 12-year period ...	1927–8	1939–40	1951–2	1963–4	1927–39	1939–51	1951–63	1927–63
income range by rank	estimated value of $|\alpha|$				estimated annual increase of $|\alpha|$*			
200–800th	1·97	1·85	2·41	1·99	−0·010	0·047	−0·035	0·001
800–3,200th	1·83	1·95	2·51	2·41	0·010	0·047	−0·008	0·016
3,200–12,800th	1·69	1·84	2·34	2·54	0·012	0·042	0·017	0·024
12,800–51,200th	1·51	1·63	2·09	2·44	0·010	0·038	0·029	0·026
200–51,200th	1·75	1·82	2·34	2·345	0·006	0·043	0·001	0·017

* α is here recorded as a positive number according to the usual convention, although since the Pareto tail slopes down to the right it might seem more correct to record α as a negative number.

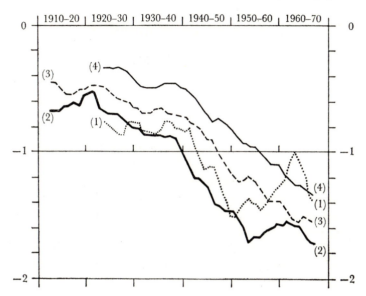

Chart A22   Changes in the slope *b* of 4 segments of the income-ratio-curve for
U.K. high incomes: 1912–66

the more conventional cumulative distribution curve of
income plotted on 2-way logarithmic paper, Table A. 6
gives estimates of the changes of the slopes over the same
periods of the 4 corresponding segments of the Pareto curve.
Alpha is numerically greater than *b* by about 1·0 but
apart from this the story told is roughly the same apart from
small differences of detail.

9. Income determined by independent causes

1. The study which we have made in the last chapter has shown us that there is a certain amount of stability in the *form* of income-distribution from year to year, although the number of incomes may be changing, and although the average size of incomes may fluctuate violently with changes in the price level or with changes in productivity. The main characteristics of the distribution, as expressed by the shape of the logarithmic curve of distribution, were found to change smoothly.

2. Whereas we have found this stability in the characteristics of the distribution, yet individual incomes, we know, are by no means steady in their movements. Our discovery has been that although individual incomes are fluctuating violently about, the net effect of all this movement is a mere reshuffling which leaves little trace on the main characteristics of the *distribution* of these incomes.

The contrast between the stability of the characteristics of the distribution and the instability of the individual incomes is heightened by the fact that by death some incomes are terminated or dispersed among the incomes of descendants, whereas by maturity new persons enter the ranks of the income-receivers every year: the income-distribution is like a tree whose stature and proportions may remain fairly stable for centuries, although sap is constantly stirring within the tree, and although each spring a large part of the tree is newly grown, and each autumn a large part of the tree dies.

We shall find that in order to explain the stability of the whole distribution we must understand the nature of the forces which cause individual incomes to change: if we can show that these forces are such as to cause the increase of some incomes to be balanced by decrease in other incomes in such a way that the net effect is a mere reshuffling then we shall in fact have accounted for the stability of the whole distribution.

3. First, let us try to explain what sort of distribution we should expect the actual economic conditions to produce, for if these conditions then remained stable, it would not be astonishing that the distribution also remained stable.

The amount of any individual's income is the resultant of a number of causes. It will depend on his age, on his property, on his education, his connections, his intelligence and his good fortune: it will depend on a hundred and one details of his own career and of the careers of his ancestors. If we could assume that none of these causes were important compared to all the rest put together, and if we could assume that the individual's income could be divided up into little bits, each of which depended on one only of these causes, and that all the causes were independent, then we should have some reason to suppose that the distribution of incomes would follow the Gaussian law. It can be shown that the distribution of any property will obey this law, provided that the property is measured as the sum of a lot of independent small quantities.*

4. The type of distribution of incomes which would follow the Gaussian law is a symmetrical type, and we have seen that actual distributions of income are not at all symmetrical.

The reason is that we are not entitled to assume that incomes are the sum of a lot of little bits, each of which is due to a specific small cause, and independent of the size of the other little bits.

For instance, two of the causes which determine a man's

---

* This statement is not true without further qualification or explanation of the adjective 'small' in this context [1972].

income are his business ability and his opportunities for doing business; yet it would be absurd to say that his income can be divided into little bits, one of which is due to his business ability and another of which is due to his opportunities for doing business, and to suppose that the size of the one bit was independent of the size of the other; evidently, the extra income derived by the man from a conjunction of business ability and business opportunities will be far in excess of the sum of the extra incomes he would obtain from either alone. The income of a farmer may depend partly on the size of his farm and partly on the price of farm produce, yet the extra income caused by an extra high price will not be independent of the size of his farm.

5. The Gaussian law cannot be expected to apply to incomes, but may it not apply to the distribution of income-power? An extra high price for agricultural produce may after all increase the incomes of all farmers by the same proportion, even though it does not increase them by the same amounts. Perhaps it is true that the size of a person's income depends on a number of small causes each of which has a *proportional* effect whose magnitude is largely independent of the proportional effects of the other causes; if this were true, it would then follow that an individual's income-power (the logarithm of his income) consisted of little bits, each due to a particular cause, the size of each bit of income-power depending only on its own cause, and not on the size of other bits. In this case we should expect people to be normally distributed between income-power classes, and the people-curve to be Gaussian.

If there is this Gaussian distribution the equation of the distribution of income can be shown to be of the form

$$y = A e^{-\frac{1}{2}z^2},$$

where

$$z = B + C \log x$$

and x denotes income.

This equation of distribution of income is the same as

that proposed by Gibrat in *Les Inégalités Economiques*.' He also proposed the more complicated form

$$y = A e^{-\frac{1}{2}z^2},$$

where

$$z = B + C \log (x - x_0).$$

The latter form contains an extra arbitrary constant x_0 and consequently a far better fit can be obtained from it for any set of actual income data; yet it is difficult to find any theoretical justification for the inclusion of the constant x_0, and we may confine our attention to the simpler suggestion that the distribution will be of the form $y = A e^{-\frac{1}{2}z^2}$, where $z = B + C \log x$, so that there is a Gaussian distribution of income-power.

6. We have seen that the most plausible set of conditions which would lead to a Gaussian distribution of income-power is that in which income-power was the resultant of a large number of small causes, the proportional effects of which upon income were independent of the magnitude of the other causes.

A man's income is determined by a number of causes, some of which have been operative during his own lifetime and some of which have been operative during the lifetime of his ancestors, but which have through inheritance reacted on his own income. In order to satisfy the condition that the proportional effect of each small cause should be independent of the magnitude of each of the others, we need in particular the condition that the proportional effect of taxation and public relief upon a man's income should be independent of the amount of his income; we need also the condition that a man's prospects of being able to survive with his income reduced in a given proportion should be the same whatever may be his income.

In practice, it is evident that the very poor stand to lose less money-income through the incidence of taxation that will the rich: indeed they will lose a far smaller proportion of income. This is however a relatively trivial objection, and might cause only a slight distortion of the distribution of income-power from the normal form.

It is a far more serious objection that it is impossible for people to survive if their income falls below a certain point; hence if a force is acting to decrease an income which is already very low, either that force must be counteracted, or else it will succeed in eliminating altogether the income. Hence it is not true that the proportionate effects of forces on small incomes will be the same as their proportionate effects on larger incomes: there comes a point at which incomes can be driven down no further.

This objection is a practical rather than an *a priori* reason for rejecting the hypothesis that the proportional effects of small forces on incomes are independent of one another; it is still possible to discuss an imaginary world in which the hypothesis is satisfied.

There is some profit in pursuing this discussion, for it will show us that in such a world, the degree of inequality will be increasing at an appreciable rate; this is not often found to be the case with actual income distributions, and this provides another reason for rejecting the hypothesis of equal proportional effects when we are discussing the real world.

7. In *Les Inégalités Economiques* Gibrat suggests, as a measure of inequality, $1/C$, where the income distribution is

$$y = A e^{-\frac{1}{2}z^2}, \quad z = B + C \log (x - x_0)$$

and x denotes income and x_0 is some constant.

In the case where the proportional effects of small forces are independent, we know that the distribution of income-power is normal, and that in Gibrat's equation $x_0 = 0$, so that $z = B + C \log x$, and z is a linear function of income-power ($\log x$).

In this case income-power is distributed normally because any individual's income-power can be considered as the aggregate of a lot of little bits, the size of each of which is independently determined, some of these little bits being due to recent causes and some being due to causes in the distant past.

$1/C$, the measure of inequality, is the standard deviation of the distribution of income-power: if the small causes that determine the bits of income-power be denoted by c_1, c_2, c_3, ... and if the standard deviations of the amounts of the little bits of income-power be s_1, s_2, s_3, ..., then it is well known that $1/C$, the standard deviation of the aggregate income-power, must be given by the equation

$$\left(\frac{1}{C}\right)^2 = s_1^2 + s_2^2 + s_3^2 + \dots.$$

Now, as time passes, we know that the individual incomes change under the action of further small causes: let us suppose that these causes are c_{n+1}, c_{n+2}, ..., c_k in the course of a decade, and that the standard deviations of the amounts of income-power which they add to (or subtract from) the original incomes are s_{n+1}, s_{n+2}, ..., s_k, then the standard deviations of the total change in income-power resulting from the small forces acting during the decade will be S, where

$$S^2 = s_{n+1}^2 + s_{n+2}^2 + \dots + s_k^2$$

and C will have changed, so that if before we had

$$\left(\frac{1}{C}\right)^2 = s_1^2 + s_2^2 + s_3^2 + \dots + s_n^2$$

we have now

$$\left(\frac{1}{C'}\right)^2 = s_1^2 + s_2^2 + \dots + s_k^2$$

$$\therefore \left(\frac{1}{C'}\right)^2 = \left(\frac{1}{C}\right)^2 + S^2.$$

This shows us that under the hypothesis considered, the square of the index of inequality $1/C$ will in any period increase by the square of the standard deviation of change in income-power during that period.

Simultaneously, we should expect the slope of the income-ratio-curve to become less and less (numerically) as the distribution of income spread out towards the edges. But we have seen (cf. Chart 17, Chapter 8), that in England the reverse has been taking place: the income-ratio-curve has since 1920 been becoming steadily steeper over three distinct ranges, indicating conclusively that a declining proportion of the income subjected to super-tax is flowing to the very rich.

The fact is that if small causes really were independent of the size of income, the distribution of income would spread outwards towards extremes of poverty and of richness, in such a way that inequality would increase at an intolerable rate: after a century or two, a large proportion of the incomes would have become extremely small, unless the progress of the community's standard of life was so rapid as to make only gains of income possible, and decreases of income impossible; on the other hand, a few people would possess enormous fortunes, after this tendency had been allowed to work itself out for a century or more. Obviously, such a tendency must come up against checks: the very poor will fail to survive, or will be helped out of their extreme poverty by assistance of some kind or another; some force must operate to prevent small incomes from becoming still smaller incomes, and to bias the causes of change of the very small incomes in the direction of either increase or annihilation. Hence the small causes will depend for their effect upon the size of the income, and hence on the size of other small causes in the past: the hypothesis of the independence of the small causes is violated.

8. Gibrat escapes this conclusion by the following argument. It is true, he admits, that the whole of a man's income cannot be thought of as the resultant of a number of small causes whose proportional effects are independent of each other, yet this may be true of that part of a man's income which lies in excess of the minimum required to keep him alive. If x_0 be the required minimum income, then we know that no income can for long be less than x_0, and consequently we may regard the part x_0 of the man's income as guaranteed, i.e. certain to survive, and as immune from forces of change.

Only the part $(x - x_0)$ will be subject to change. Consequently, given the conditions of the independence of small causes acting to form the income $(x - x_0)$, we should expect a distribution of the form

$$y = A e^{-\frac{1}{2}z^2}; \quad z = B + C(x - x_0)$$

9. There are three objections to this reasoning. The first is that it is very difficult to see why the minimum part x_0 of the income x should be immune from those forces tending to increase income in some proportion, although it may be readily admitted that for incomes whose amount x exceeds x_0 by little, forces tending to *decrease* the part x_0 are likely to encounter some check. For instance, if the minimum income is £25, and there is some force tending to raise incomes as a whole in a certain village, then if this force raises an income of £60 to £95, it would surely be more natural to expect it to raise an income of £30 to £47 10s., i.e. in the same proportion, than to expect it to raise it only from £30 to £35: yet it is the latter case which would arise if the excesses of the two incomes over £25 were each to be increased in the same proportion.

The second objection is that if Gibrat's hypothesis were satisfied, we should expect the index of inequality for each distribution to be increasing in the same way as we showed that it must be increasing in the special case where $x_0 = 0$. In fact the index is not found to be increasing for many distributions of income.

The third objection is that when plotted on logarithmic paper, the tails of the distribution curves of income-power are found to be far straighter than they would be if Gibrat's hypothesis were satisfied.

Finally, we may note that when Gibrat tries to fit a curve of his type to actual income data he often finds that the value obtained for x_0 is far in excess of what is known from other information to be the minimum possible income. This shows that if he chose x_0 the actual minimum possible income, he would not be able to find a curve which would fit the income data very well. This bears out the contention that the hypothesis of independence of the proportional effects of small causes acting on income in excess of x_0 is not approximately satisfied in these cases.

10. Hence we are led to abandon the hypothesis that the proportional effects of small causes acting upon income are independent of one another.

In the next chapter we shall develop a theory which assumes that the proportional effects of economic influences on groups of incomes depends largely on the size of the incomes in the group.

10. Forces of change

1. We have seen that the nature of the income-distributions found in actual life cannot be explained on the hypothesis that incomes are the resultant of a lot of small causes, whose proportional effects on income are independent of each other. The main objection to this hypothesis is that certain checks are brought into play so soon as an income has become very low, to prevent it from becoming lower still. It is not true that the causes acting to change incomes have proportional effects independent of the size of income, because certain checks prevent those causes from succeeding, which would lower still further the very low incomes.

2. We must construct a theory which will take into account the fact that the economic influences changing income act with different proportional effect upon different incomes at any one level, and upon different groups of incomes at different levels.

At any moment, a man's income depends on what it was a year ago, and on influences which have since acted to change it: similarly, the distribution of income at any moment depends on what the distribution was a year earlier and on economic influences which since have acted to alter individual incomes.

3. It is accordingly convenient to have some standard method of measuring the effects of causes which have acted during a year to change individual incomes. The rough method which we shall adopt is this: we shall consider separately each income-level for which the proportional effects of economic causes upon individual incomes differ significantly from their proportional effects upon incomes of other amounts. Considering any particular level I, let I'_1 be

4-2

The distribution of income between persons

the average increase of incomes (initially) of amount I, during one year, as the result of all economic influences: then we shall take

$$I_1 = I_1'/I$$

as our first measure of the effects of the economic influences on incomes of amount I. We shall usually measure I_1 in thousandths so as to avoid having very small quantities. Thus if incomes of £800 fall on the average by £4 during the year,

$$I_1 = \frac{-4}{800} \times 1,000 = -5,$$

for incomes at the level £800.

4. As a second parameter we shall choose a measure of the extent to which economic influences affect differently the different incomes initially of any amount I. Thus if I_2' is the variance of change (mean square deviation from mean of changes) of incomes (originally) of amount I, in one year, we shall take as our second parameter

$$I_2 = I_2'/I^2$$

and measure I_2 in thousandths.

Thus, if the variance of change of income originally of amount £800, were £²2,000 during one year, we should take as our second parameter

$$I_2 = \frac{2,000}{640,000} \times 1,000 = 3 \text{ approx.}$$

5. These two parameters will not tell us everything about the change during one year of the incomes initially of amount I. In order to know this we should have to know the exact form of the function $p(r)$, where $p(r)\,dr$ is the proportion of incomes of amount I originally, which increase by between Ir and $I(r+dr)$. I_1 and I_2 are the mean and variance of r, and we could describe $p(r)$ fully by

$$I_1, I_2, J_3, J_4, \ldots,$$

where J_3, J_4 are certain other parameters (measuring the abnormality of the distribution of shift of income-power).

It is explained in Appendix 3, p, 232, that for rough purposes J_3, J_4, ... can be treated as zero since they are likely in practice to be small. The reason for this is considered in the next paragraph.

6. If we consider the group of incomes initially of amount I, we may regard them as being acted upon during the year by a complex of economic influences, whose absolute effects upon income are causally interwoven. We could however probably classify these these influences into a number of groups, some large and some small, such that the *proportional* effects on income of each group of influences could be regarded as independent.

If the groups were many and if each group were small, the shifts of income power caused by all influences together would be approximately normally distributed: the parameters J_3, J_4, ... are measures of the *abnormality* of the distribution of shift of income-power, and in this case they would be all close to zero.

In practice, not all the groups of influences will be small, and the distribution of shift of income-power due to the aggregate of causes may be appreciably abnormal. When this is the case, the abnormality of the distribution of shift will be built up of the abnormalities of the distributions of shifts due to each large group of influences; in so far as they are of opposite kinds for different groups of influences these may cancel out.

In any case, our best estimate of the abnormality of the distribution of shift of income-power is *zero*, unless there is some particular reason why the abnormality in the case of a particular large group of causes can be estimated as other than zero.

J_3 measures the skewness of the distribution of change of income-power, and it may be possible to estimate this in exceptional cases. J_4, J_5, ... are never likely to have an appreciable effect on the distribution of income. The further consideration of the use of J_3, J_4, ... is deferred until Chapter 12.

7. To the parameters I_1, I_2, J_3, ..., at any income level, we give the name 'forces of change'. By saying that the forces of change are constant, we shall mean that for each income-level I_1, I_2, J_3, ... remain the same from year to year.

Our method of examining the effect of a given set of economic influences will be to discover what distribution of income would be brought about by the corresponding sets of forces of change, if these forces remained constant.

8. To measure the effects of a particular economic influence, we may define the parameters i_1, i_2, j_3, ..., where these are the changes in I_1, I_2, J_3, ... caused by the introduction of the new influence.

To examine the effects on distribution of a new influence with parameters i_1, i_2, j_3, ... on top of old forces I_1, I_2, J_3, ..., we shall find the difference between the distributions which would be brought about by the two sets of forces of change I_1, I_2, J_3, ... and $I_1 + i_1$, $I_2 + i_2$, $J_3 + j_3$, ...

In the next chapter we discuss the question whether it is possible to estimate the magnitudes of I_1, I_2 for each income level in any country and whether we can estimate the quantities i_1, i_2 for any particular economic influence.

11. Particular causes of change

1. In the last chapter we defined the forces of change I_1 and I_2 to be the average (proportional) change of income and the (proportional) variance of change of income for the incomes at any level during one year. I_1 and I_2 would be sufficient to describe the forces acting on the incomes of given amount to a fair degree of accuracy, provided that we could divide economic influences up into a fairly large number of independent groups. For a more accurate account we should require estimates of a further quantity J_3, 'skewness', and for very accurate description we should need to know J_4, J_5, ... as well.

2. In order to make a rough estimate of I_1 and I_2 for the income-level £2,000, we should act as follows. Consider a group of men who have income £2,000 each this year. What will their average income be next year? Suppose we estimate £1,990. Then the force of change I_1 is discovered by the formula

$$I_1 = \text{1,000} \times \text{average proportionate change}$$
$$= \text{1,000} \times -\frac{10}{2,000}.$$
$$\therefore \quad I_1 = -5.$$

Similarly we might guess I_1 for each income-level.

3. In order to work out I_2 we could act as follows: consider the 25 % most fortunate and the 25 % least fortunate of these people whose income are each £2,000 this year. What will be the gap between their incomes next year?

Suppose we guess: the lucky 25 % will have £2,100 and over: the unlucky 25 % will have £1,900 and less. Then the gap between them, which we may call q, is £200. By a well known formula* in elementary statistics, we may estimate the variance of change as $\frac{9}{16}$ of $q^2 = \pounds^2 22,500$. Hence I_2 works out at

$$I_2 = 1000 \times \frac{22,500}{4,000^2} = 1\cdot4.$$

4. The method of working out i_1 and i_2 for any particular economic influence is very similar. Consider the effects of income-tax at 5s. in the $\pounds$ on incomes of $\pounds2,500$. These taxes may use up income which would otherwise have been invested in securities or education or other qualifications for obtaining income. Consequently they will cause a permanent reduction in income.

The taxes absorb $\pounds625$ of income. On the average, perhaps $\pounds425$ would have been consumed and $\pounds200$ invested in qualifications for obtaining incomes.

Let us suppose that the yield on these qualifications would have averaged 6 %, then on the average, income next year will be lessened by 6 % of $\pounds200$ because of the taxes on this year's income of $\pounds2,500$. Hence we may write

$$i_1 = 1,000 \times \frac{-12}{2,500} = -4\cdot8.$$

In order to work out i_2, the variance of the effect, we have to estimate the gap between the 25 % most fortunate and the 25 % least fortunate. On the average $\pounds12$ is lost because of the tax: we may guess that 25 % lose $\pounds2$ and less and that 25 % lose $\pounds20$ and more. Then the gap, q, is $\pounds18$ and the variance $\frac{9}{16}q^2$ is $\pounds^2 182$ so that $i_2 = 1000 \times \dfrac{182}{2,500^2} = 0\cdot03$, for incomes of $\pounds2,500$.

Similarly, we might estimate i_1 and i_2 for each income level; for higher incomes i_1 would be larger numerically, because the rich consume a smaller proportion of their incomes and invest a larger proportion in acquiring qualifications for more income. A larger proportion of the tax would

---

* A crude unreliable method of estimating variance, but one appreciated by non-mathematicians.

be likely to take the place of purchases of new qualifications, and a smaller proportion would displace consumption.

5. A special method for estimating i_2 is required, when only a certain proportion of people are affected at all by the change.

Consider the effect of recurring annual charges on the 5 % of people in each income-class politically most vulnerable (Jews, Pacifists etc.). Then the correct way to estimate i_1, i_2, is as follows:

Take a particular income-class (£450 say), and work out the average loss of income in a year *for the group affected* (the vulnerable people, in our example). Suppose the average loss is £50.

Then by the ordinary rules we should have i_1

$$i_1 = 1,000 \times \frac{-50}{450} = -111$$

but since only 5 % of people fall into this group, we must divide the estimate for i_1 by 20 to obtain $i_1 = -5\cdot55$.

Similarly, to obtain i_2 we work out the gap q for the group affected. Of the group, suppose 25 % lose only £10 and 25 % lose over £90, then $q = 80$ and $\frac{9}{16}q^2 = 3,600$, so that by the ordinary rules

$$i_2 = 1,000 \times \frac{3,600}{(450)^2} = 18 \text{ approx.,}$$

but since only 5 % of the people are in the group, we obtain instead

$$i_2 = \tfrac{18}{20} = 0\cdot9.$$

6. In order to make the estimates of the proportional effects upon income of particular influences in each year, we should need a complicated apparatus of thought. The provision of such an apparatus must form the basis of a separate enquiry*, and for the purposes of this theory, it has been considered convenient to take as our data the hypothetical results of such an enquiry. Given any cause of change such as

* Not yet undertaken.

income-tax, thrift campaigns, special scholarships for the poor, free medical treatment, free milk etc., we shall assume as *given* the rough effects it has per annum on the incomes of each given amount. We shall assume for instance a knowledge of the proportion affected, when this is small, and of the average annual increase of those affected, and also of the gap between the changes of 25 % most fortunate and the 25 % least fortunate of those affected.

Although we shall generally assume such information to be given, and thus avoid the temptation of an interesting field of research, whose too hasty cultivation would lend a spurious impression of precision to our results, yet we may suggest briefly the orders of magnitude* for the forces of change for particular influences, which such research might possibly reveal.

7. For causes which increase all incomes over a wide range by the same proportion, i_1 will be constant over this range and i_2 will be zero.

For causes which have very different effects on the incomes of different people, even though their incomes are equal, i_2 is likely to be relatively large.

For instance, for a trend fall in the price-level or a trend increase in productivity, we should expect i_1 to be fairly constant over wide ranges of income, and i_2 to be small, but for the changes brought about by opportunities for gambling in stocks and shares, we should expect i_2 to be large and i_1 to be relatively small.

8. Let us consider a numerical example of the forces due to gambling on the stock exchange. Let us suppose that for each income-level above £10,000, 2 % gamble seriously, and that on the average they win enough to form the source of extra income equal to 0·1 % of their present income.
Then

$$i_1 = (1/50) \times (1,000/1,000) = 0·02.$$

* Deliberately, however, we have *later* chosen I_1 and I_2 rather small, so as to exaggerate the effects of *new* measures on income distribution and ease their expression in the form of charts.

But now consider the 25 % most lucky: they may win enough to form the source of an extra income equal to 11 % of their present income; the unlucky 25 % may lose enough to deprive them of 10 % of their present income. The gap is 21 %.

Hence i_2 works out as

$$i_2 = (1/50) \times 1{,}000 \times (9/16) (0 \cdot 21)^2 = 0 \cdot 50.$$

9. Consider the effect of a fall by $(\frac{1}{5})$ % of itself per annum in the rate of return of industrial capital. Suppose that this results in a similar decline in the yield of one half of the qualifications for obtaining income possessed by people with incomes of £5,000. Then for these people there will be an annual loss of income of £5 due to these causes: hence for these causes and for this income-level,

$$i_1 = -1.$$

10. We shall eventually regard the causes of differences between the incomes of men and of their heirs as causes of change of income, and we shall extend the concept of forces of change $I_1, I_2, J_3, \ldots$, to cover the effect of these causes also.

The effect of death duties will be to decrease I_1, especially for the very rich, if the death-duties are progressive. Let us suppose that the effects of death duties removing x % of a man's property are to reduce permanently the income of the heir by $\frac{1}{4}x$ %. Then I_1 must be reduced by $2 \cdot 5\, x/L$, where L is the average interval of years during which the income passes from one subjection to death-duties to another.

Suppose that for incomes of over £10,000 we estimated that $L = 40$ years, and x % $= 40$ %, then the effect of the duties must be to reduce the force of change I_1 by $2 \cdot 5$.

11. Contrast this effect with that of death duties contrived to cut down everybody's capital to £20,000. By cutting down the capital by x %, we cut down the income of the heir permanently by $\frac{1}{4}x$ %, let us again suppose. Let us further assume that by the time the duty has been acting for some

while, people usually manage to acquire amounts of capital £5x, by the time they die, if their income is by then £x.

Then when £x > £4,000, the effect of the duties will be to cut down income from £x to £($\frac{3}{4}x$) + £1,000. Thus we have an average loss of income of £($\frac{1}{4}x$) − £1,000 and

$$i_1 = -(250x/L) + (1,000,000/L).$$

Taking L as 40 years again, we obtain the following table for i_1:

TABLE 5. *Values of* i_1

income	£4,000	£5,000	£10,000	£20,000	£100,000
i_1	0	−1·25	−3·75	−5	−6

12. Finally, let us consider the effect of various changes in inheritance law upon the forces of change.

As our standard system let us take one where every man dying leaves all his power to earn income to one particular heir, his 'son', and assume that at income-levels over £200 the effect is always that the son's average chance is to have an income of about the same as his father's in the long run.

13. Compare with this a system by which the son may inherit no property. Since the chief advantage of having rich parents is that they invest in all sorts of useful qualifications *other* than property, with which one can obtain income, this system will not be quite so drastic as might first be supposed. Perhaps it will cut down permanently the income of the heir at various income-levels by the following amounts:

TABLE 6. *Reduction of incomes*

£200–£500	£500–£2,500	£2,500–£50,000	over £50,000
12%	16%	20%	25%

These may be underestimates of the effect. If they are correct, and we take 40 years again as our interval between deaths, i_1 works out as shown in Table 7.

TABLE 7. *Values of* i_1

£200–£500	£500–£2,500	£2,500–£50,000	over £50,000
−3	−4	−5	−6·25

14. Now consider a system by which a father divides his property equally among his sons and a bachelor leaves his to his nearest of kin (assumed to be the son of a man in his own income-class). The average change of income is likely to be zero, provided that there is on average one son each. But there will be considerable variation owing to the difference in size of different families. Consider the 25 % unlucky sons in large families: they only get 50 % or less of the property and their ill-fortune permanently lowers their income by $12\frac{1}{2}$ %: however 25 % lucky ones get a 150 % share of property or even more: their income is increased permanently by $12\frac{1}{2}$ %. The gap is 25 %. Taking the generation again as 40 years,

$$i_2 = 0\cdot9.$$

Hence the effect of the variation in the size of families is to increase I_2 by about 1.

15. Now consider a system by which all property is left to eldest sons.

We shall get an odd sort of distribution, perhaps like this.

TABLE 8. *Distribution among heirs*

multiple of property	0	1	2	3	4	5
increase of income (%)	−25	0	25	50	75	100
proportion of heirs (%) receiving this	53	20	10	10	5	2

The variance of (proportional) change of income works out as 0·112, so that taking a generation of 40 years

$$i_2 = 2\cdot8.$$

We see that this type of inheritance system has a considerable effect in increasing I_2.

16. We may now summarise these results in the form of a table showing the differences in the values of I_1 and I_2 which would be caused by the various systems of inheritance and death-duties.

TABLE 9. *Table showing the effects of inheritance systems on I_1 and I_2*

system number	Effect on I_1					Effect on I_2
1 (standard)	nil					nil
2	for incomes over £2,500: −2.5					nil
3	at income £4,000	£5,000	£10,000	£20,000	£100,000	
	effect is nil	−1·2	−3·8	−5·0	−6·0	nil
4	at income £250–	£500–	£2,500–	over		
	£500	£2,500	£50,000	£50,000		
	effect is −3	−4	−5	−6·2		nil
5	at all incomes	nil				−0·89
6	at all incomes	nil				+2·8

explanation:

system number	system
1	(standard system) sons allowed to share their father's inheritance, and anything left by his childless friends in his income-class
2	death-duties of 40 % on property of those with income over £2,500
3	death-duties cutting down property to £20,000
4	abolition of inheritance of property
5	mutual insurance among the individuals in any and each income-class, arranging to divide out equally the property of those dying between their sons
6	convention by which only the eldest son inherits property.

17. The examples given earlier in the chapter led to the answers shown in Table 10.

These examples were illustrative and were not based on serious estimates of the effects of the influences selected for analysis. We shall use some of these illustrative figures to provide the basis for further examples showing the effect of these influences on the equilibrium distribution of income.

Particular causes of change

TABLE 10. *Summary table relating to four examples*

	influence	range of incomes	effect on I_1	effect on I_2
1	5s. in the £ tax	at £2,500	-4.2	$+0\cdot03$
2	annual £50 levy on the most vulnerable 5% of people	at £450	$-5\cdot55$	$+0.9$
3	gambling on stock exchange	over £10,000	$+0\cdot02$	$+0\cdot5$
4	fall of rate of return on industrial capital by 1/500th of itself every year	at £5,000	$-1\cdot0$	0

12. Equilibrium under constant forces

1. In Chapter 10, we explained at some length what were meant by the forces of change acting on the incomes in a given group. I_1 was the average proportional increase of income for the group, and I_2 was the variance of the proportional increase; I_1 and I_2 being measured in thousandths. By saying that the forces of change remain *constant*, we shall mean simply that these two quantities I_1, I_2 for each income-power class remain constant as time passes, and that any measures J_r such as skewness, of the abnormality of the effects of all causes on the income-powers in the class, also remain constant.

2. We shall examine the possibility that, under the action of constant forces of change, the distribution of income must always settle down to an equilibrium distribution, and that the same distribution of income must be reached whatever the original distribution may have been.

3. It is broadly true that under the action of constant forces of change an equilibrium distribution must sooner or later be approached, but it is not universally true, and in order to prove it true we have to insert provisos, in order to exclude certain trivial and ridiculous cases where the equilibrium obviously could not be approached.

For instance, if the number of income-classes was infinite, and we started off with a hypothetical distribution with, say, 2^{-r} incomes in the rth class, then to approach equilibrium, some incomes might have to come back, so to speak, from infinity, and this would take an 'infinite' time. Accordingly we must make a provision that the number of possible income-classes is finite.

Secondly, we might get the sort of situation where the

forces of change made everybody who had more than a certain amount £1,000 in one year have less than it in the next, and everybody who had less than £1,000 in one year have more than it in the next. Under such conditions, except from a very special initial distribution, obviously it would be impossible to approach equilibrium.

In order to preclude this possibility, we may make this assumption: that if, for any income-class, $f(x)$ denotes the number of people changing income by x in one year, then $f(x)$ is 'not nought' throughout some finite range including $x = 0$, however small. In other words, in each income-class, some must stay where they are, and some change by just a little each way.

The sort of situation which these provisos are fashioned to exclude are obviously trivial and out of relation to anything which is likely to happen in the real world, and the provisos themselves are also fairly obviously realistic. Accordingly we need make no apology for tacitly assuming these provisos fulfilled throughout the rest of the book, except where they must obviously be modified because of some change in the problem which we are examining.

In order to make equilibrium of *this* sort possible, we must obviously insert some condition which makes it impossible for the number of income-receivers to change, and in order to make the analysis very simple, we may suppose that all income-receivers are immortal, and that no new ones ever arrive. This assumption will not be retained for very long: it is introduced here in order to avoid the necessity for a more complicated definition of the forces of change as yet.

4. Assuming income-receivers to be immortal, it is shown in Appendix 2 that under any set of constant forces of change (except the trivial exceptions ruled out above), an equilibrium distribution of income must eventually be reached; this will be a static-equilibrium distribution of income, in which the number of incomes in each individual class will remain constant.

Apart from the assumption of immortality, this is a

perfectly general result. We need to make no assumption about the causes of change of income-power being independent, or the causes of change being small or numerous.

The result opens up a whole field of approach to the problem of analysing the causes of particular forms of income-distribution, for it provides a concept analogous to the economist's stationary state, in which the forces of the moment have been given time to work out their full effects.

We shall learn to find the equilibrium distribution corresponding to any given set of forces of change, and we know then that the actual distribution must become more and more like the equilibrium distribution, except in so far as the forces of change alter, or impulses of change (see Chapter 7, p. 77), not included in the forces of change, disturb the distribution away from the equilibrium.

5. In order to do this, we need to know that the equilibrium distribution corresponding to any given set of forces of change is unique, and does not depend at all on the initial distribution, once we know the number of income-receivers. This is proved in Appendix 2, Theorem 2.

This result gives precision to the common-sense expectation, not however obviously true, that under the action of new economic forces the character of income-distribution (itself the resultant of *past* economic forces) will eventually be transformed so as to reflect the new economic influences, until all trace of the old economic forces has been eradicated from the income-distribution.

Given sufficient time and the absence of disturbing impulses of change, there is a unique distribution of income to which any given set of forces of change must lead.

6. The fact that there is only one equilibrium-distribution of income to which a given set of forces of change can lead, when acting on a given number of incomes, provides us with a fairly simple method of finding out this equilibrium distribution, once we know what are the forces of change and how many incomes there are.

Equilibrium under constant forces

The equilibrium distribution is the only distribution of income among the given individuals which will remain unchanged under the action of the given forces of change. In order to find out which income-distribution is the equilibrium distribution, we have only to find out which distribution will remain unchanged by the forces of change. If the forces of change are of a fairly simple type, i.e. if the causes of change acting on neighbouring income ranges are fairly similar, it will be found possible to discover the equilibrium distribution by a method of trial and error. For having found any distribution by trial and error which will remain unchanged by the forces of change, we shall know that this is the *unique* equilibrium distribution of income, to which the given forces of change *must* lead, whatever may have been the initial distribution of income.

7. It will be remembered that we defined the forces of change to be the set of values I_1 and I_2, where I_1 represents the average proportional increase of income in one year and I_2 is the (proportional) variance of these shifts (I_1 and I_2 being measured in thousandths).

It is natural to suppose that over any set of consecutive (neighbouring) income-classes, these forces of change will be more or less the same, and that as we pass along the income-scale, we should find these parameters I_1, I_2, etc. altering 'continuously' (i.e. smoothly); we shall assume that this is the case.

We have seen in Chapter 11 how we could estimate the forces of change I_1 and I_2 for any given income-level, if we only had a fairly rough knowledge of the effects of economic influences on individual incomes at that level. Our next task is to discover what form of distribution of income could remain in equilibrium under the action of constant forces of change whose parameters I_1, I_2 are known to have given values at each of a set of income-levels.

For this purpose, we may consider incomes as being classified into a number of income-classes, each of the same proportional extent (e.g. of 1 %), and we may also regard these classes as being income-power classes, each of the same *absolute* extent (since income-power means the logarithm of income).

8. Consider the condition that the amount of income flowing to people in a particular income-class should remain the same, when the forces of change are the same for income-classes close to the given income-class as for that class. One possible position of equilibrium would be that there is initially the same amount of income flowing in each income-class, and that for each income-class the average change of income during a year is zero. For if p_r denotes the proportion of the people in an income-class, C_r, who pass out of it during a year into our given class, and q_r represents the proportional increase of their incomes, it is easy to see that the proportional increase in the amount of income flowing to the given income-class during the year will be $\sum_r p_r q_r$ summed for all r. The condition for equilibrium is that this sum $\sum_r p_r q_r$ should be zero.

But it is also obvious that

$$I_1 = \sum p_r q_r,$$

since this is the average proportional increase of incomes by the individuals moving out of any income class.

We see then, that when initially there is the same aggregate amount of income flowing to the people in each income-class, i.e. when the income-curve and the income-ratio-curve are horizontal, then there can only be equilibrium when $I_1 = 0$.

9. But actually, two complications may occur and prevent such equilibrium.

i The income-ratio-curve may not be horizontal (i.e. different aggregate amounts of income may flow to different income-classes).

The existence of *variance* in the changes of income from each class will then mean that more income will overflow out of the classes with much aggregate income to those with little, than will overflow in the reverse sense.

Thus there will be a displacement of income downhill along the income-ratio-curve, towards the classes where little aggregate income is found.

ii I_1 may not be zero, so that there will be a flow of income to higher income-classes (if I_1 is positive) or to lower income-classes (if I_1 is negative).

For equilibrium, these two tendencies must cancel out: if I_1 is positive, the income-ratio-curve must slope downwards to the left in order to keep income from flowing away towards the higher incomes; for equilibrium to be possible, I_1 and the slopes of the income-curve and the income-ratio-curve must all be of the same sign.

10. For equilibrium, the first tendency has to be balanced by the second. Now the *first* tendency evidently will be the stronger,

i the greater is the slope b of the income-ratio-curve, and the consequent disparity of aggregate income of different income-classes,

ii the greater is the variance I_2 causing overflow of income each way from income-classes.

The *second* tendency will be the stronger the greater is I_1, the average (proportional) increase of income from each income-class.

As an equation expressing the condition for equilibrium we should expect something like

$$bI_2 = CI_1,$$

or perhaps
$$bI_2^a = CI_1^{a'},$$

where C, a and a' are constants.

11. It is shown in Appendix 3 that for a condition of equilibrium at any income level

$$bI_2 = 2I_1$$

is a correct rough rule.

We can check that the dimensions of this equation are correct, because if i denotes the dimension of income and j denotes the dimension of income-power,

$$b \quad \text{has dimensions} \quad \frac{i}{ij} = j^{-1},$$

$$I_2 \quad \text{has dimensions} \quad j^2,$$

$$I_1 \quad \text{has dimensions} \quad j.$$

The equation set in the form

$$b = \frac{2I_1}{I_2}$$

provides us with a rough rule for estimating the slope of the income-ratio-curve at every income-level, provided we can make estimates of the effects of economic influences on individual incomes at each level; for then, as shown in Chapter 11, we can obtain estimates of I_1 and I_2 for each level, and so make a rough estimate for b at each level, as $b = 2I_1/I_2$.

12. This rule is rough for two reasons:

i It is inexact unless I_1 and I_2 are the same for all neighbouring classes from which incomes flow into the given class.

ii It is inexact unless the forces measuring 'abnormality', $J_3, J_4, \ldots$ are zero.

Inexactness due to the first cause is discussed in Appendix 3. It is not likely to be very serious.

Inexactness due to the second cause would be eliminated if we know in what ways the distribution of change of income-power was abnormal.

If we know the average change of income and the variance of change of income for the individuals who at the beginning of the year had incomes at a level I, then we know H_1, H_2, the averages at the end of the year of their incomes and of the squares of their incomes. Suppose that we know also $H_3, H_4, \ldots,$

Equilibrium under constant forces

the averages at the end of the year of higher powers of their income.

Now let us plot the points

$$(0, \log H_1),\ (1, \tfrac{1}{2} \log H_2),\ (2, \tfrac{1}{3} \log H_3),\ \ldots,\ (N-1, \tfrac{1}{N} \log H_N)$$

and pass through them a curve of degree $N-1$.

If N is large this will cut $y = \log I$, in the point $(-b, \log I)$, where b is the slope of the equilibrium income-ratio-curve. This is proved in Appendix 3, §12. The curve will be a straight line with positive slope, if the independent causes of change of income-power are all small; any abnormality in the effects due to a large group of causes will be expressed as curvature of the line. The slope of the curve will be everywhere positive.

As an example of this method of finding b, the slope of the income-ratio-curve, consider the calculation of b from the following data.

Of a group of incomes initially of amount £1,000, it is found that after one year they are distributed as follows:

TABLE 11. *Frequency distribution of incomes which were £1,000 in previous year*

income class (£)	proportion of incomes (%)	average (£)
under 850	10	820
850–920	10	890
920–60	10	945
960–85	10	975
985–97	10	992
997–1,010	10	1,003
1,010–35	10	1,020
1,035–80	10	1,055
1,080–150	10	1,090
1,150 and over	10	1,190

then, using £1,000 as unit of value, H_1, H_2, H_3 and H_4 work out as 0·9980, 1·0056, 1·0228 and 1·0499. Plotting the points $(0, \log_{10} H_1)$, $(1, \tfrac{1}{2} \log_{10} H_2)$, $(2, \tfrac{1}{3} \log_{10} H_3)$, $(3, \tfrac{1}{4} \log_{10} H_4)$ and fitting a cubic through them, it will be found that it cuts the x-axis in the point $(0·43, 0)$, giving $-0·43$ as the value for b correct to 2 decimal places.

If we work out I_1 and I_2 from the data in Table 11, we find

$$I_1 = -2\cdot0, \quad I_2 = 9\cdot6$$

and the rough formula $b = 2I_1/I_2$ now gives us

$$b = -0\cdot42,$$

so that we find that the accuracy of the rough formula is quite good in this case.

The distribution in this example is not carefully chosen so as to give a good result; it is not made particularly normal; the writer just invented a distribution which seemed likely, bearing in mind however

i   that it was likely to be fairly symmetrical,

ii   that it was an empirical fact that b usually lay between o and -2 so that I_1 should lie between o and $-4I_2$ for income of about £1,000.

13. We shall always use the rough rule for finding b in future, bearing in mind that when sufficient information is available we can find b more accurately by the graphical method described above.

This simplification is only dangerous where we find that b lies outside the range o to -2: since we find empirically that for incomes above the average, b does lie in the range o to -2, this means in effect, that our rough formula $b = 2I_1/I_2$ can become dangerously rough only when we are considering the incomes of the poor. Even for their incomes however, the formula becomes seriously rough only when the effects of the large independent groups of causes of change on income-power are appreciably abnormal.

13. The form of distribution under constant forces

1. In order to illustrate the application of the rules suggested in the last chapter, we may attempt to discover the distribution that will be brought about under an hypothetical set of conditions, when these conditions remain constant.

2. Let us consider English income receivers to consist of four groups:

i   Rich people with over £2,000 income.

ii Well-to-do people with from £200 to £2,000.

iii 'Normal' people with between £80 and £200.

iv Poor people with less than £80.

3. Consider now a group of rich people with incomes at some given level £10,000. Suppose that after a year their average income has changed from £10,000 to £9,970 and that whereas 25 % of them now have incomes increased to more than £10,500, yet 25 % have incomes decreased to less than £9,400. Then the 'gap' between £10,500 and £9,400 being £1,100 we find that the variance of change of income is

$$\tfrac{9}{16} \times (£1,100)^2 = £^2 680,000$$

and we find that the forces I_1 and I_2 are given by

$$I_1 = -3, \quad I_2 = 6 \cdot 8.$$

In so far as the economic influences acting on the incomes of rich people are likely at all (rich) income-levels to be similar (in their proportional effects), we may take $I_1 = -3$ and $I_2 = 6 \cdot 8$ as estimates of the forces of change for *all* rich income-levels.

Now consider a group of well-off people with incomes of £1,000. After a year their average is £996, let us suppose: 25% have income less than £925 and 25% have incomes over £1,070: the gap q is then £145, and we find

$$I_1 = -4, \quad I_2 = (9/16)(141)^2/1,000 = 11.8.$$

Consider next a group of poor people with incomes of £60; suppose that after a year, their average income will have risen to £63 owing to the fact that some will have found employment again; but 25% find their incomes shrunk to below £55 and 25% find their incomes risen above £73 10s. Then

$$I_1 = 50 \quad \text{and} \quad I_2 = 53.$$

We find from these estimates the following values for I_1 and I_2 and for b, the slope of the income-ratio-curve.

TABLE 12. *Values of I_1, I_2 and b*

income level (£)	I_1	I_2	b
60	50	53	1.9
1,000	−4	11.8	−0.7
10,000	−3	6.8	−0.9

In order to calculate the equilibrium level of b, for normal incomes, it is better to consider directly the conditions of industrial demand, and the policy of trade unions with regard to wages. Those rigid influences determine the distribution of income among 'normal' income-levels and the distribution determines the forces rather than vice versa, at these income-levels: this point is explained more fully in Chapter 21.

Suppose then that we estimate in such manner the equilibrium distribution of incomes between £80 and £200. For instance we estimate that most income per £ of income-interval will flow at the income-level £90; suppose we also estimate that there will be only half as much income flowing to people with incomes between £182 and £200 as to those with incomes between £130 and £143.

These two facts tell us further that $b = +1$ at the income

level £90, and $b = -2$ on the average, between the levels £140 and £185.

We have, then, the following values of I_1, I_2, the forces of change, and b, the slope of the (equilibrium) income-ratio-curve, at various income-levels.

TABLE 13. *Values of I_1, I_2 and b (extension of Table 12)*

income level (£)	income power	I_1	I_2	b
60	1·78	50	53	1·9
90	1·95	.	.	1·0
140–85	2·24–2·26	.	.	−2·0
1,000	3·00	−4	11·8	−0·7
2,000 and over	3·30+	−3	6·8	−0·9

We can now construct Chart 18, to estimate b at all income-power levels. From this estimate, we can construct the income-ratio-curve, in Chart 19, and, from this we plot the income-curve in Chart 20.

That part of the income curve which refers to normal incomes was not obtained by application of the formula $b = 2I_1/I_2$, but we assumed some knowledge of this part of the curve from information about industrial demand for labour and trade union policy.

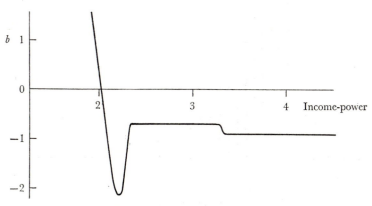

Chart 18 Equilibrium value of slope b as function of income-power

The distribution of income between persons

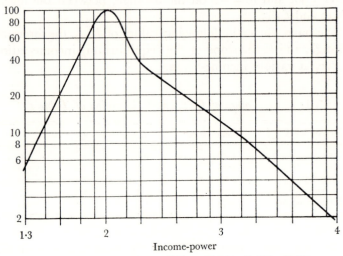

Chart 19   Equilibrium income-ratio-curve

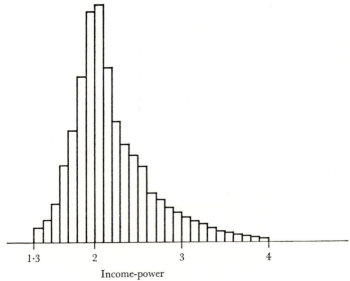

Income-power

Chart 20   Equilibrium income-curve

The form of distribution under constant forces

The parts of the curve for low and high incomes were obtained by application of the formula, $b = 2I_1/I_2$, to our estimates of the effect of economic influences during a year, on incomes of £60, £1,000 and £10,000.

4. The fact that the branches of the income-ratio-curve are comparatively straight follows naturally from the supposition that the average proportional increase of income, I_1, and the variance of proportional increase, I_2, are likely to be roughly similar for all income-levels in the rich class, and for all incomes in the well-to-do class, and that within the poor class the forces of change I_1, I_2, are also likely to be roughly the same at different income-levels.

5. The reason that I_1 is likely to be negative for the well-to-do and rich is this: the fact of being rich or well-to-do is due to the possession of exceptionally good qualifications for obtaining income: speaking loosely, we may say that it is due to exceptional luck. Sometimes, good luck of this sort will last: a brilliant man may have a brilliant son, or a rise in the value of a commodity may prove to be permanent; but more often than not, the good luck comes eventually to an end: a brilliant family becomes decadent, or the leading firm eventually falls to second and then to third place.

The ranks of the small rich class are continuously recruited from the well-to-do class, and to make room the least successful rich people move down to the well-to-do's. On the average this means a loss of income to those initially rich. A shuffling between a rich class and a poor class, must mean on the average a reduction of income for those initially rich, and an increase of income for those initially poor. In real life, such a shuffling is constantly taking place, and in consequence, for the rich, I_1, the average proportional increase of income per head, is negative, whereas for the poor it is positive.

* Compared to that for the whole community.

125

14. The effects of particular measures on the equilibrium distribution

1. The introduction of new economic measures will alter the equilibrium distribution of income, by altering the forces of change I_1 and I_2 for each income-class, and so altering the slope of the income-ratio-curve at each point and the shape of the income-curve.

We have seen how to calculate the alteration in I_1 and I_2 brought about by a new economic measure, by estimating the average increase of income caused at each income-level, and the gap between the increases of income caused to the 25 % most fortunate and that caused to the 25 % least fortunate, at each income-level. We have learnt also to work out the change in the slope of the equilibrium income-ratio-curve, brought about by any change in I_1 and I_2. We are now in a position to show what modification in the equilibrium distribution will be caused by any initial economic measure, if we can make rough estimates of its effects on individual incomes, in the manner suggested in Chapter 11.

2. The effect of a new influence must partly depend on what influences already are acting, and on what initial equilibrium distribution results from them. We shall use as our standard, the forces I_1 and I_2 and the distribution found in the last chapter, for illustrating the effects of particular measures upon distribution. Before proceeding to this exercise, we may establish certain generalizations about the effect of any new measures upon any equilibrium distribution.

3. An income-ratio-curve usually consists of two branches on either side of a hump. Let us consider four types of measure.

i   Those which steepen the left-hand branch.

ii Those which steepen the right-hand branch.

iii Those which flatten the left-hand branch.

iv Those which flatten the right-hand branch.

Chart 21 illustrates the effect which the four types of influence will have on the income-curve, and we see that

1 The first type decrease inequality by reducing the numbers of the very poor.

2 The second type decrease inequality by reducing the numbers of the very rich.

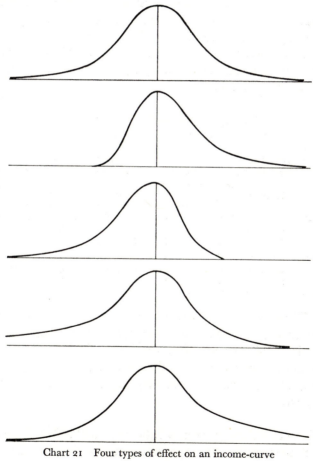

Chart 21 Four types of effect on an income-curve

3 The third type increase inequality by augmenting the numbers of the very poor.

4 The last type increase inequality by adding to the numbers of the very rich.

Now, where b is the slope of the income-ratio curve, we have seen that

$$b = (2I_1/I_2) + e,$$

where I_1 and I_2 are the average proportional increase and the variance of proportional increase (usually measured in thousandths) at each income-level and e is an error depending on the abnormality of the distribution of income-power; e will in general be small.

We can reclassify economic measures according to their effects on the forces of change, I_1, I_2, acting on rich and poor. This we do in Table 14.

TABLE 14. *Classification of economic measures*

influences acting on the incomes of	effect of influence on incomes	effect on I_1	effect on I_2	effect on slope of income-ratio-curve	classed above as type	effect on equality of distribution
poor	increase	+	.	steeper	1	greater
	decrease	−	.	less steep	2	less
	scatter	.	+	less steep	2	less
rich	increase	+	.	less steep	3	less
	decrease	−	.	steeper	4	greater
	scatter	.	+	less steep	3	less

These results verify common-sense, but we have made this advance beyond common-sense, that we can estimate the magnitude of the final effect on distribution, provided that we can estimate the magnitude of the new influences, and of those already acting, in the way suggested in the last two chapters.

4. In actual fact, most new influences will affect I_1 and I_2 simultaneously for all ranges of income, so that its effects on

the distribution must be found as the sum or balance between the effects suggested in the above table.

We can however make the broad generalisation, that any new economic influence, by affecting different people's incomes differently, is likely to add to the sources of inequality, but that this effect may be partly or wholly offset if the influence makes it easier for the poor to get richer or for the rich to become poorer.

5. Now let us consider the effect of particular economic measures upon the distribution of income discussed in the last chapter and illustrated in Charts 18, 19 and 20.

Let us suppose that initially we have static equilibrium under constant forces of change, and rigid demand for labour as illustrated in Table 13 of Chapter 13, §3, reproduced below.

TABLE 15. (*Table 13 reproduced*)

income level (£)	income-power	I_1	I_2	b
60	1·78	50	53	1·9
90	1·95	.	.	1·0
140–85	2·14–2·26	.	.	−2·0
1,000	3·00	−4	11·8	−0·7
2,000 and over	3·30	−3	6·8	−0·9

The resultant equilibrium distribution was shown in Charts 18–20 on pp. 123–4, and its principal properties are summarized in Table 16.

We shall investigate what modifications are introduced into this distribution by each of the following measures.

i A uniform rate of taxation of 5*s* in the pound on incomes above £200.

ii State expenditure on health of poor children.

iii Progressive income tax.

iv Opportunities for gambling on the Stock Exchange.

v A continuous annual fall by (1/5) % *of itself*, of the rate of return on industrial capital.

6. Let us suppose that an uniform tax of 5*s.* in the pound is imposed on all incomes over £200, and that the spending of the proceeds does not further disturb the distribution of income.

In order to determine the effects of the tax, we must know how it will affect people's purchases of shares or of other qualifications for obtaining income.

We assumed in §4 of Chapter 11 that for people with incomes of £2,500, 32 % of the tax was paid out of saving and 68 % out of consumption, and that the yield on the qualifications saved would have been 6 % on the average. By these assumptions, we showed that for the income-level £2,500, I_1 would be reduced by 4·8, because of the tax; the effect on I_2 would be small.

TABLE 16. *Equilibrium distribution of income shown in chart 20*

income-range (£)	percentage of income	percentage of persons
under 25	3·4	21
25–50	8	20
50–80	14	20
80–100	12	12
100–200	30	20
200–400	13	5
400–1,000	10	1·6
1,000–2,000	4	0·3
2,000–4,000	2·5	0·1
4,000–10,000	1·6	0·0
10,000–20,000	0·7	
20,000–40,000	0·4	
40,000–100,000	0·3	
100,000 and over	0·3	

For higher incomes a larger part of the tax is likely to be paid out of savings, and for lower incomes a smaller part of the tax. Hence the effect on I_1 will probably be larger for higher incomes and smaller for smaller incomes. We should have to make separate estimates for the effect on I_1 at each income range.

Let us assume that as a result of such estimates we obtain the following table.

TABLE 17. *Effect of tax*

income-level	£200	£500	£1,000	£2,500	£10,000
effect of tax on I_1	0	−2	−3	−4·8	−6

then the changes in I_1, I_2 and b will be those given in the table below.

TABLE 18. *Effects of tax at 5s. in £ on I_1, I_2 and b*

income level (£)	before tax			after tax		
	I_1	I_2	b	I_1	I_2	b
200	.	.	−1·5	.	.	−1·5
500	−4	11·8	−0·7	−6	11·8	−1·0
1,000	−4	11·8	−0·7	−7	11·8	−1·2
2,500	−3	6·8	−0·9	−7·8	6·8	−2·3
10,000	−3	6·8	−0·9	−9	6·8	−2·6

The effect of the tax on the slope of the income-ratio-curve at various income-levels is illustrated in Chart 22 (*a*). This enables us to find the effect on the income-ratio-curve, as shown in Chart 22 (*b*). Finally the modification in the equilibrium income-distribution is shown in Chart 23, which summarises it.

These charts relate only to the change in the equilibrium distribution of income *gross* of tax. To obtain the income-curve for income *net* of tax, we must shift to the left, by $\log_{10}\left(\frac{4}{3}\right)$, that part of the curve which relates to the incomes liable to the tax.

7. Let us next investigate the effect of state expenditure on the health of poor children, assuming that the money is raised in some manner which does not further disturb distribution.

Let us suppose that the effect of this expenditure is to increase the efficiency of the poor in such a way, that in every year, 10 % of those with income less than £60 a year are affected, and for these 10 %, the average increase of income caused is a permanent increase of 5 %. Then assuming the effects to be fairly uniform on the 10 %, we may neglect any effect on I_2, and consider the total effect of the measure to be an increase in I_1 of $1,000 \times 0.05 \times 0.1 = 5$ for the income-levels below £60.

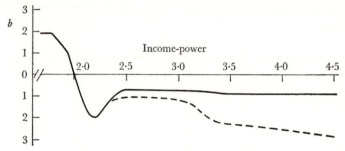

Chart 22 (*a*) Effects of taxation on the slope of the equilibrium income-ratio-curve

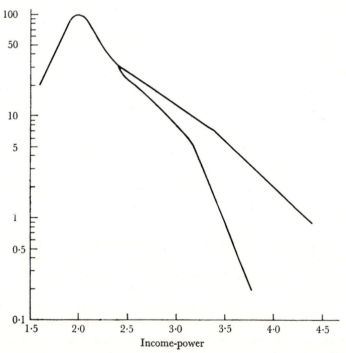

Chart 22 (*b*) Effects of taxation on the equilibrium income-ratio-curve

Hence for these incomes I_1 is increased from 50 to 55 and b is increased from 1·9 to 2·1, I_2 remaining unchanged. The corresponding shifts in the curves shown in Charts 19 and 20 are illustrated in Charts 24 and 25. We find that the percentages of income between £40 and £100, between £25 and £40 and under £25 are reduced considerably.

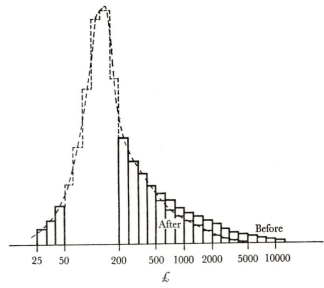

Chart 23   Effects of taxation on the equilibrium income-curve

8. We have discussed in Chapter 11, p. 106, the possible effects on the forces of change of the introduction of gambling on the stock exchange. We estimated that for incomes over £10,000, I_1 would be reduced by 0·02 and I_2 would be increased by 0·5. Hence the effect of abolishing such opportunities would be to increase I_1 by 0·02 and to reduce I_2 by 0·5 for incomes over £10,000.

Hence I_1 would still be almost equal to -3, and I_2 would be decreased from 6·8 to 6·3 for incomes over £10,000.

b, the slope of the income-ratio-curve, would consequently be steepened from $-0·9$ to $-0·95$ for incomes over £10,000.

The distribution of income between persons

9. Now let us suppose that a measure is introduced which hinders the formation of monopolies by powerful financiers. It is estimated, perhaps, that every year 1 % of those with incomes over £50,000 will be so hindered in their business careers by these measures, that on the average they will increase their incomes during the year by 10 % less (of their income) than they would otherwise have done. Moreover, of those with incomes between £10,000 and £50,000, ½ % are affected in the same way.

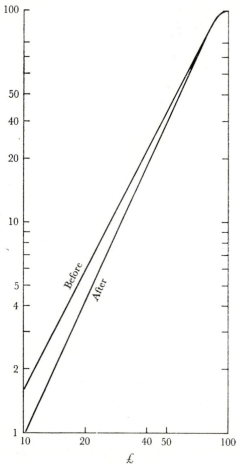

Chart 24 Effects of health measures on equilibrium income-ratio-curve

Effects of particular measures

Of those with incomes below £10,000 a negligible proportion are affected.

Then for those with incomes over £50,000, I_1 is reduced by 1, and for those with incomes between £10,000 and £50,000, I_1 is reduced by 0·5. Hence we have the changes of I_1, I_2 and b shown in Table 19.

Charts 26 and 27 show the corresponding shifts in the relevant portions of the income-ratio-curve and the income-curve. We find that the distribution of income going to those

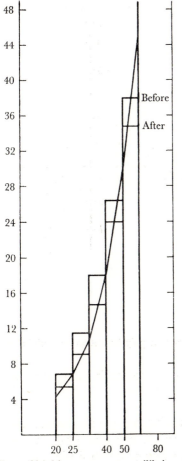

Chart 25   Effects of health measures on equilibrium income-curve

TABLE 19. *Effects of monopoly legislation*

income level (£)	before measure			after measure		
	I_1	I_2	b	I_1	I_2	b
10,000–50,000	−3	6·8	−0·9	−3·5	6·8	−1·03
over £50,000	−3	6·8	−0·9	−4·0	6·8	−1·17

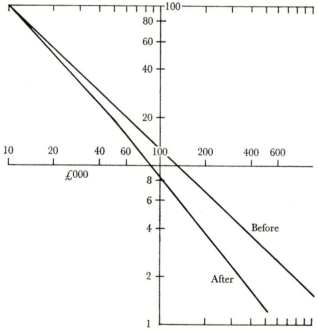

Chart 26   Effects of monopoly legislation on equilibrium income-ratio-curve

with incomes over £10,000 is changed in the manner shown in Table 20.

10. In the next chapter, we shall abandon our assumption that income-receivers are immortal, in order that we may investigate the effect of death duties and systems of inheritance.

Effects of particular measures

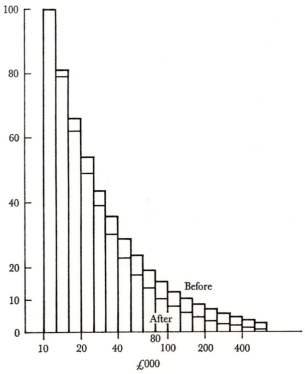

Chart 27   Effects of monopoly legislation on equilibrium income-curve

TABLE 20

	proportion of income (%)	
income range (£)	before measure	after measure
10,000–25,000	56·2	62·5
25,000–50,000	20·3	20·4
50,000–100,000	10·9	9·5
100,000 and over	12·6	7·6
all over 10,000	100·0	100·0

15. Effects of inheritance and death-duties on the equilibrium distribution

1. Our research has so far been conducted on the assumption that no income-receiver ever dies and that no individual is ever recruited to the ranks of the income-receivers. We shall now abandon that hypothesis, and investigate the effects of death and of inheritance upon the equilibrium distribution of income-power.

2. Let us first consider a very simple case, and suppose that during the time when an individual receives any income at all his income never varies, so that the only causes of change of distribution of income-power are causes which operate when individuals die, and other individuals inherit their power to obtain income.

In order further to simplify our picture, we may suppose also that when an individual dies, he bequeaths power to earn income to one individual and one individual only, who up to this time has not been an income-receiver. This ensures that the number of income-receivers shall remain constant.

In order to make the exposition even clearer, we may suppose also that the length of time during which an individual receives income is always exactly 40 years.

These simplifying assumptions will be abandoned in due course.

3. Let us now consider the nature of this world which we have invented. At any moment we may suppose income-power to be received by a large number of individuals, whose names are Brown, Robinson, Snooks, etc., no two names being exactly the same. Brown perhaps owns vast property

and obtains much income-power, whereas Robinson is his servant and earns little, and Snooks begs, and gets hardly any income-power at all.

Any fluctuations in the income-powers of these individuals are for simplicity ignored, and we consider, as it were, the average of their income-power over the 40 years during which they have it.

Now let us glance away whilst 40 years elapse; when we look again we find Brown replaced by a successor who has inherited his power to obtain income: we may without offence refer to the newcomer as 'young Brown': similarly, in the place of Robinson and Snooks, we find individuals to whom we may refer as young Robinson and young Snooks.

Perhaps young Brown is not so rich as was his predecessor, because young Brown has taken to drink or to intellectual pursuits; Robinson earned a passable wage, but young Robinson is a dullard and only earns pennies for opening gates; his income-power is very small indeed, smaller in fact that that of young Snooks, who earns a decent living as an employee in a factory which has recently sprung up in the district in which he lives.

Turn now to the third generation: very young Brown is an assistant lecturer with little income-power; very young Robinson's income-power comes out of poor-law funds, but very young Snooks is the prosperous manager of the local branch of a cotton weaving concern, and his income-power is as great as was that of the original Brown of a hundred years ago.

4. We have examined one little bit of the whole system of the varying fortunes of different families; it is as though we had followed three threads for three moments, in one of very young Brown's most up-to-date looms. It is of such threads that the whole pattern is built up, which constitutes the distribution of income-power in this imaginary world.

Every generation of 40 years, there is a reshuffle: young Brown's income-power depends largely on what was Brown's income-power, and very young Brown's income-power depends on young Brown's income-power. The distribution of income between families today depends on the distribution 40 years ago, and on influences which make the incomes of individuals today differ from those of their ancestors of 40 years ago.

5. There is a close analogy between the way in which the distribution between families is moulded by the influences that act in each generation to shuffle sons into different income strata from those occupied by their parents, and the way in which distribution between persons is moulded by the influences that act each year to change the incomes of individuals.

Accordingly, we might take as our unit of time the generation and, neglecting the changes of income during life, define I_1 and I_2 (each measured in thousandths) as the average proportional increase of income between father and son, and the variance of proportional increase. We should interpret 'income' as meaning some sort of average income taken over the years when each individual received income.

We should then show how the slope of the income-ratio-curve must at each point be given by

$$b = 2I_1/I_2$$

for equilibrium to be possible under the action of the constant forces.

We could then investigate what changes in I_1 and I_2, and hence in b, would be caused by particular systems of inheritance and death duties, and discover the effects that would be produced by them upon the distribution of income.

6. It is however more satisfactory to consider at the same time influences acting to change the incomes of the living, and those acting to change incomes between a man and his heir. Retaining our unit of time, the year, we may abandon our assumption that each income-receiver is immortal and make instead the following simplifying assumption.

We assume that when in any income-class n men die, they will share between them n heirs.

7. Our definition of the forces of change must now be modified.

Suppose that at the beginning of the year there are N individuals in a given income-class, and that during the year n die, leaving n heirs: then we define I_1 and I_2 exactly as before, except that in measuring the average income of the N individuals one year later, we replace the n incomes of the dead men by the n incomes of their heirs.

Thus if I was the original income and if one year later the average income of the $N-n$ survivors and the n heirs is $I\left(1+\dfrac{I_1}{1,000}\right)$, then I_1 is one force of change; similarly if the variance of the distribution of the N incomes is then $I^2 I_2/1,000$, I_2 is the other force of change.

We can then make use of all our old results. Under the action of constant forces of change, I_1, I_2, there will eventually be reached an equilibrium distribution in which the slope of the income-ratio-curve at each point will be given roughly by the formula
$$b = 2I_1/I_2.$$

8. Now let us consider again the effects of

i   Death duties limiting capital to £20,000.

ii   Death duties removing 40 % of all property for people with incomes above £2,000.

iii   Abolition of inheritance of property.

iv   Mutual insurance among the fathers in each income-class, arranging that when they die their property should be shared equally among all their sons.

v   A system by which all property goes to the eldest son or next of kin.

We may suppose that initially there was a system by which sons were allowed to inherit only from their own fathers and from their father's friend in his income-class who died childless. We can then examine how the equilibrium distribution is affected when one of the above six systems is imposed. As our initial position, we may take that discussed in Chapter 11, and assume the forces of change initially to be those set out in Table 21.

TABLE 21. *Values of I_1, I_2 and b in standard system*

income level ($£$)	income-power	I_1	I_2	b
60	1·78	50	53	1·9
90	1·95	.	.	1·0
140–85	2·14–2·26	.	.	−2·0
1,000	3·00	−4	11·8	−0·7
2,000	3·30	−3	6·8	−0·9

Since the effect of the measures discussed will be to alter the forces of change, I_1, I_2, only for incomes of £250 and over, we need only consider estimates of I_1 and I_2 originally for this range.

In so far as the forces of change acting on the incomes of all well-to-do people are likely to be similar, we had best assume (as in Chart 18 of chapter 13 §3) that for the range £250–£2,000, I_1, I_2 have the values given for the income-level £1,000, and that for all higher income-levels they have the values given for the income-level £10,000. We then have this situation initially:

TABLE 22. (*Additions to Table 21*)

income range ($£$)	income-power range	I_1	I_2	b
250–2,000	2·4–3·3	−4	11·8	−0·7
2,000 and over	3·3–	−3	6·8	−0·9

9. We obtained in Chapter 14 the following table showing the effects of the various measures on I_1 and I_2, given a particular initial system of inheritance.

By combining Tables 22 and 23, we may compile Table 24 showing the values which the forces of change I_1 and I_2 will have at various income-levels, after the various systems of inheritance have been imposed on the given initial situation.

TABLE 23. *Table showing the effects of inheritance on I_1 and I_2*

	system	effect on I_1	effect on I_2
I	(Standard) Sons allowed to share their father's property, and anything left by his childless friends in his income class	o	o
2	40 % death duties on property for incomes over £2500 income (£)	−2·5	o
3	Death duties cutting down property to £20,000 4,000 / 5,000 / 10,000 / 20,000 / 100,000	o / −1·25 / −3·75 / −5 / −6	o
4	Abolition of inheritance of property 250–500 / 500–2,500 / 2,500–50,000 / 50,000	−3 / −4 / −5 / −6·2	o
5	Mutual insurance among those in each income-class, dividing out equally among their sons the property of those dying	o	+0·9
6	Convention that only the eldest son should inherit property	o	+2·8

TABLE 24. *Values of I_1 and I_2 after imposition of various systems of inheritance*

system number ...	I	2	3	4	5	6
income level (£)			value of I_1			
250–500	−4	−4	−4	−7	−4	−4
500–2,000	−4	−4	−4	−8	−4	−4
4,000	−3	−5·5	−3	−8	−3	−3
5,000	−3	−5·5	−4·25	−8	−3	−3
10,000	−3	−5·5	−6·75	−8	−3	−3
20,000	−3	−5·5	−8	−8	−3	−3
50,000	−3	−5·5	−9	−9·2	−3	−3
			value of I_2			
250–2,000	11·6	11·6	11·6	11·6	12·5	13·6
2,000 and over	6·8	6·8	6·8	6·8	7·7	9·6

The distribution of income between persons

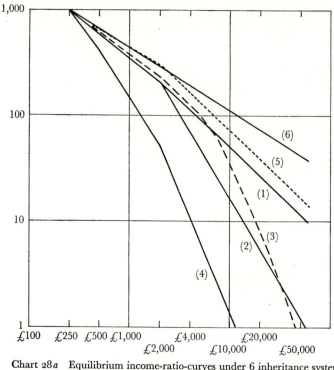

Chart 28a Equilibrium income-ratio-curves under 6 inheritance systems

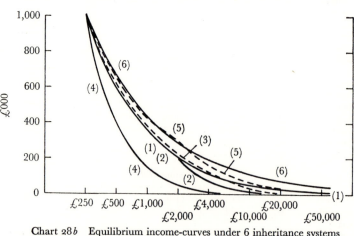

Chart 28b Equilibrium income-curves under 6 inheritance systems

By use of the formula, $b = 2I_1/I_2$, we can now construct a table to tell us the slope of the income-ratio-curve at the various income-levels under the different inheritance systems.

TABLE 25. *Table showing the slope b of the income-ratio-curve at various income-levels, under various systems of inheritance*

system number ...	1	2	3	4	5	6
income level ($£$)			value of b			
250–500	−0·75	−0·75	−0·7	−1·3	−0·65	−0·6
500–2,000	−0·75	−0·75	−0·7	−1·5	−0·55	−0·6
4,000	−0·9	−1·6	−0·9	−2·25	−0·9	−0·6
5,000	−0·9	−1·6	−1·25	−2·25	−0·9	−0·6
10,000	−0·9	−1·6	−2·0	−2·25	−0·9	−0·6
20,000	−0·9	−1·6	−2·25	−2·25	−0·9	−0·6
50,000	−0·9	−1·6	−2·65	−2·7	−0·9	−0·6

On the basis of these data, it is easy to construct the equilibrium income-ratio-curves shown in Chart 28a. From these are constructed the income-curves shown in Chart 28b, illustrating the modification in the distribution of income introduced by the various measures.

16. The limitations imposed by the assumption that forces are constant

1. The analysis of static equilibrium which we have developed bears a very close resemblance to the economist's analysis of the stationary state, and it is open to the same objections, and to some others besides. In this chapter we shall consider these objections and suggest the lines along which our subsequent analysis must develop in order to meet them.

2. In the economist's stationary state, conditions remain unchanged, and in particular the amount of capital equipment remains unchanged. The effect of a new invention, of an increase in population, or of a shift in tastes, are analysed by comparing the two stationary states which are possible before and after the change. Since, it is argued, the position in the real world is always moving towards the position of stationary equilibrium corresponding to the economic influences then acting, the ultimate effect on the position in the real world, of some permanent change in conditions, must be roughly equal to the change in the position of stationary equilibrium due to the change.

A natural objection to this method of analysis is that one of the most important influences acting in the real world is the existence of a method by which rich people can perform net saving without hoarding: this method prevents the monetary stock from being withdrawn from active circulation and the draining away of 'effective demand' into hoards. The method consists of spending money to construct capital equipment; in a stationary state this method is assumed absent, because capital equipment is taken as given. Hence in comparing two stationary states, we are comparing two imaginary worlds in which an important influence is absent; it may be that this absence has a more pronounced effect in one stationary state than in the other, so that by comparing them we get a false indication of the comparison between corresponding positions in the real world, where the opportunity for net saving exists.

3. The corresponding objection to our concept of static equilibrium distribution is this. We assume constant forces of change, and this rules out the possibility of increase of income per head after a certain point: in the real world income per head is constantly increasing as a result of those same influences which our constants, I_1 and I_2, are intended to measure. We see that if the economic influences were really to remain constant, I_1 and I_2 would have to change in order to allow income per head to increase. The behaviour of I_1 and I_2 corresponding to a steady advance in income per head is not that they should remain constant, but that they should move up the income-scale in step with the increase of income per head.

TABLE 26. *Forces of change in 1860*

income level (£)	I_1	I_2
25	24	16
50	20	20
100	−20	20
200	−15	20
400	−10	16
800	−10	15
1,600	−10	15
3,200	−10	15

For instance, if income per head has doubled since 1860, and if in 1860 we had the values for I_1 and I_2 shown in Table 26, and if economic influences had remained much the same, except for a general industrial progress, the forces of change would not still be the same in 1936, but would be those shown in Table 27, having shifted upwards in response to the increase of income per head which they had caused.

TABLE 27. *Forces of change in 1936*

income level ($£$)	I_1	I_2
25	.	.
50	24	16
100	20	20
200	-20	20
400	-10	20
800	-10	16
1,600	-10	15
3,200	-10	15

4. When the forces of change move up in this way so as to allow a steady increase of income per head, we may say that they are 'steady', to distinguish the condition from that of 'constancy' which so far we have discussed. In the next chapter, we shall abandon our assumption of constant forces of change and examine the effect of steady forces.

5. Another objection to constant forces of change, as we have defined them, is that they allow no increase of population and no variation of fertility as between rich and poor. Both these phenomena exist in the real world and they may have important effects on distribution. We shall introduce these complications in Chapters 17 and 18.

6. In the real world forces of change are not likely to be either constant or steady, and it may be that this fact has a significant bearing upon the effects of any measure designed to modify the distribution of incomes. In Chapter 19 we shall examine a world where the forces of change alter smoothly and systematically, and find that the effects of measures will be roughly the same as if the forces of change had been steady.

7. We have seen that by increasing income per head the forces of change, by the mere fact that they alter distribution, may react to change the forces themselves; but this phenomenon may occur for other reasons than the change in income per head. Increased inequality may affect the rate at

which people wish to save; this may affect either the rate of investment or the trend level of unemployment or the rate of interest, or all three, and so react to alter the forces of change.

Chapter 21 is devoted to a discussion of the bearing of this upon results obtained on the assumption of constant steady or independently determined forces of change.

8. Accordingly we now abandon our assumption that the forces of change are constant.

17. Increasing income per head

1. Suppose that we have a static equilibrium distribution of income-power with forces of change I_1 and I_2. Now suppose that our currency appreciates in ratio $1+k$ per annum, relative to roubles, and that a Russian professor in London works out, I_1', I_2', the forces of change in England, *using roubles as his unit of account.*

Evidently
$$I_1' = I_1(1+k) + 1{,}000k$$
$$I_2' = I_2(1+k)^2$$

and b the slope of the income-ratio-curve is given by
$$b = 2I_1/I_2 = 2(1+k)\ (I_1' - 1{,}000k)/I_2'.$$

2. From the point of view of the Russian professor, there would not be static equilibrium for income-distribution in England, but quasi-static equilibrium, with constant population but *increasing* income per head. He would deduce, rightly, that the condition for quasi-static equilibrium with constant population, but income per head increasing in proportion $(1+k)$ per annum is that the income-ratio-curve should at each point have slope:
$$b = 2(1+k)\ (I_1' - 1{,}000k)/I_2'. \tag{1}$$

This rule applies quite generally. In any country where income per head increases in ratio $1+k$, but total population remains constant, the condition for quasi-static equilibrium is that the slope of the income-ratio-curve should be
$$b = 2(1+k)\ (I_1 - 1{,}000k)/I_2,$$

where I_1, I_2 are the forces of change at each income-level.

3. Let us define a steady set of forces of change in a land with constant population, to be a set of forces which move up the income-scale so as to allow increasing income per head. Thus if $(I_1(x), I_2(x))$ and $(\bar{I}_1(x), \bar{I}_2(x))$ are the forces of change at income-level x in two consecutive years, and if the forces (I_1, I_2) move up the scale from x to $x+xk$ between the two years, the condition for steady forces of change is evidently

$$I_1(x) = \bar{I}_1(x+xk),$$
$$I_2(x) = \bar{I}_2(x+xk)$$

if the rate of increase $(1+k)$ remains constant from year to year. If the rate of increase of income per head changes from $1+k$ to $1+\bar{k}$, then the condition would be

$$I_1'(x) = \bar{I}_1'(x+xk),$$
$$I_2'(x) = \bar{I}_2'(x+xk),$$

where

$$\left.\begin{aligned}I_1'(x) &= (1+k)\,I_1(x) + 1{,}000k, \\ \bar{I}_1'(x) &= (1+\bar{k})\,\bar{I}_1(x) + 1{,}000\bar{k},\end{aligned}\right\}$$

and

$$\left.\begin{aligned}I_2'(x) &= (1+k)^2\,I_2(x), \\ \bar{I}_2'(x) &= (1+\bar{k})^2\,\bar{I}_2(x).\end{aligned}\right\}$$

4. It is proved in Appendix 2, that under the action of steady forces of change, a unique quasi-equilibrium distribution of income must be reached. We can use equation (1) to find the properties of this quasi-equilibrium distribution, provided that for any year we know k, the proportionate rate of increase of income per head, and I_1 and I_2, the forces of change at each income-level.

Consider the country discussed in Chapter 13, pp. 121–3, where we found the following values for I_1 and I_2 at various income-levels:

TABLE 28 (*Table 13 repeated*)

income level ($£$)	I_1	I_2	b
60	50	53	1·9
90	.	.	1·0
140–185	.	.	−2·0
1,000	−4	11·8	−0·7
2,000 and over	−3	6·8	−0.9

Now suppose that instead of these being constant, they are steady with an increase of income per head of 1 % per annum. Then instead of calculating b, the slope of the income-ratio-curve, from the equation $b = \dfrac{2I_1}{I_2}$, we must now calculate according to

$$b = 2(1+k)\,(I_1 - 1{,}000k)/I_2,$$

where $\qquad k = 1 \% = 0\cdot01.$

Hence we obtain for our values of b

TABLE 29. *Values of b allowing for increase in income per head*

income level (£)	b
60	1·5
90	1·0
140–185	−2·0
1,000	−2·4
2,000 and over	−3·86

From these new figures we get an entirely different picture of the equilibrium distribution. This is shown in Charts 29 (*a–c*), which are obtained in exactly the same way as Charts 18–20 were obtained in Chapter 13.

We see what a very false impression was gained from our supposition that forces of change were constant, if in fact they were steady with an increase of income per head of 1 % per annum.

5. This comparison might lead to the conclusion that an increase of income per head caused an increase in equality; this would be a wrong conclusion. The increase of income per head does not directly affect the degree of inequality or the form of the quasi-static equilibrium distribution. The introduction of an economic influence increasing income per head does alter I_1 and I_2 and k, and it does alter the corresponding *static* equilibrium distribution, but it does *not*

alter $\left\{\dfrac{I_1 - 1{,}000k}{1+k}\right\}$ or $I_2/(1+k)^2$, and the form of the quasi-static equilibrium distribution is therefore not directly affected. Changes in individual income corresponding to a general increase of income per head are not relevant to the problem of distribution: our formula

$$b = 2I_1/I_2$$

wrongly took them into account. Our new formula

$$b = 2(1+k)\,(I_1 - 1{,}000k)/I_2$$

succeeds in ignoring them.

The correct interpretation of the difference in Charts 18–20 and 29*a–c* is not that an increase of income per head causes that difference, but that if we ignore the fact that income per head is increasing, we distort the significance of

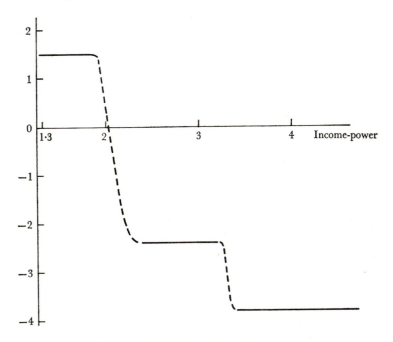

Chart 29   Allowance for increasing income per head
(*a*) Equilibrium values of *b*

153

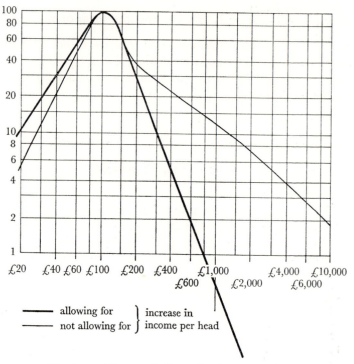

Chart 29   Allowance for increasing income per head
(*b*) Equilibrium income-ratio-curve

I_1 and I_2, and attribute to special influences acting at a special income-level effects which are in reality due to a general cause acting at all income-levels.

In so far as cyclical fluctuations do affect incomes at all levels to the same extent, they are irrelevant to the problem of income-distribution, and should not affect the slope of the income-ratio-curve. Our formula $b = 2I_1/I_2$ would have taken account of them, but our new formula

$$b = 2(1 + k)\,(I_1 - 1{,}000k)/I_2$$

rightly ignores them.

6. In the next chapter we shall consider the analogous modifications that have to be introduced, if we are to take account of changes in population.

Increasing income per head

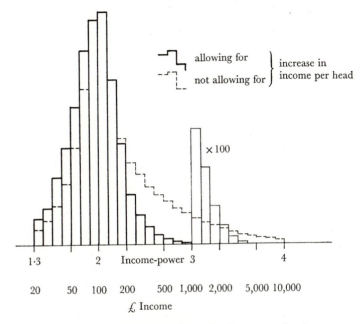

Chart 29   Allowance for increasing income per head
(c) Equilibrium income-curve

18. Increasing population and large families among the poor

1. In order to examine the effects of changing population on income-distribution, we must abandon our assumption that the number of heirs equals the number of those dying in each income-class. We now suppose that a man dying may bequeath qualifications for obtaining income to any number of persons who have never yet obtained income, or to no such persons.

Let us suppose that during a unit of time (the year) m of the N occupants of an income group die and bequeath qualifications for obtaining income to $m+n$ individuals who have not previously obtained income. Then, in place of the N original occupants of the income group, we see one year later $N+n$ individuals with various incomes. We may call n/N the 'fertility' at this income level. We must also modify our definition of the forces of change in view of the new circumstances.

2. Suppose that I was the income of each of the original N occupants. Then we may define I_1 and I_2 as follows:

$I\left(1 + \dfrac{I_1}{1,000}\right)$ equals the average income of the $N+n$ individuals, one year later,

$I^2 I_2/1,000$ equals the variance of distribution of income among the individuals then.

It will be seen that this fits in with our former definition of I_1 and I_2 when $n = 0$.

3. Consider the case where income per head remains constant but $h\left(= \dfrac{n}{N}\right)$, the fertility for every income-class, is the same and constant but not zero.

156

Then evidently if the slope b of the income-ratio-curve is everywhere given by

$$b = 2I_1/I_2$$

the amount of income flowing to people in each income-class will increase in proportion $(1 + h)$ per annum, and since h is the same for each income-level, there will be quasi-static equilibrium with constant income per head.

Hence, when h, the fertility, is the same at every income-level, and income per head is constant, the condition for quasi-static equilibrium is

$$b = 2I_1/I_2.$$

When h is not the same for all income-ranges, this condition breaks down.

4. Suppose that h_0 is the proportionate growth of the number of all income-receivers per annum, and suppose that h, the fertility, is different for different income-levels.

Then, where income per head is constant, the condition for quasi-static equilibrium works out at

$$b = \frac{2I_1}{I_2} - \frac{1,000(h - h_0)}{(b - 1)\,I_2}$$

provided $(h_0 - h)/(b - 1)$ is small.

5. As an example of the use of this formula, let us examine the effect of income-distribution of the following differences between the birth rates and death rates of rich and poor.

TABLE 30. *Birth and death rates for rich and poor*

	rich	poor	whole country
births per 1,000 income receivers	24	30	26
deaths per 1,000 income receivers	23	25	24

Let us suppose that in the absence of these differences, the forces of change would have been those given in Table 28.

TABLE 31. (*Table 28 repeated*)

income level ($\pounds$)	I_1	I_2	b
60	50	53	1·9
90	.	.	1·0
140–80	.	.	−2·0
1,000	−4	11·8	−0·7
2,000 and over	−3	6·8	−0·9

6. We see that the direct effect of low fertility among the rich is to decrease inequality by causing there to be less rich people, and that the direct effect of high fertility among the poor is to add to their numbers and so increase inequality.

But there is an indirect effect of low fertility among the rich to which more attention is usually paid. The indirect effect is that since there is low fertility, there will be fewer heirs to each man dying, and a larger share of property will go to each heir. For instance in our example, each year 24 rich heirs share the property of 23 dead rich men, whereas in the country as a whole 26 have to share the property of 24.

Hence the rich get $\frac{23}{24}$ of a share each on the average, whereas if their fertility had been normal, they would have got $\frac{24}{26}$. They therefore get 8 % more property than they would otherwise have had.

If we suppose, as in Chapter 11, that x % increase in property causes $\frac{1}{4}x$ % increase in income, we see that they will gain 1 % increase of income on the average.

Since the birth rate and death rate are roughly $\frac{1}{40}$, the generation will be 40 years; hence the effect on I_1 for the rich will be an increase of

$$1{,}000 \times 0\cdot01 \times \tfrac{1}{40}$$

equals an increase of 0·25.

This will partly but *not wholly* offset the decrease in inequality.

7. It is not however necessary to work out the effects of each cause separately. Let Kx % be the proportionate effect

upon income of $x\%$ increase in property inherited, at some income-level, then at that level, we need, for equilibrium

$$b = \frac{2I_1 - 1000(h - h_0)\left[(1/(b-1)) + K\right]}{I_2},$$

where I_1, I_2 are the values which the forces of change would have apart from the effect on the share of property inherited, due to fertility differing from the average for the country.

We see that the effect of low fertility among the rich will be to *decrease* inequality unless

$$K(1-b) > 1 \quad \text{for the rich.}$$

In England in 1933, $b = -0.5$, approximately, so that low fertility among the rich will increase or decrease inequality according as a 3% increase in the inheritance will permanently increase income by more or less than 2%. I should be inclined to the view therefore, that it would *decrease* inequality.

High fertility among the poor, on the other hand, is certain to increase inequality, both by increasing their numbers and by causing children in large families to be undernourished and therefore inefficient: k is likely to be small for the poor, so there will be no appreciable effect in connection with inherited proprty, but on the other hand high fertility may cause a pressure of juveniles on the labour market and cause a fall in the unskilled wage. This would lower I_1 for the poor and cause a more unequal equilibrium distribution.

19. Moving equilibrium under changing conditions

1. Our discussion has so far been concerned with the effect of constant or steady forces of change. But in the real world forces of change will be altering all the time, and sometimes we may be able to predict the nature of the alteration which is going to take place. For instance, we may be able to predict changes in the fertility of different income-power groups, and in the savings of the rich when these latter are caused by changes in the rate of interest. In such cases, we shall be able to predict no static or quasi-static equilibrium distribution of income-power.

2. Yet it would seem natural to suppose that under the action of steadily altering forces of change, the influence of the original distribution of income (at some arbitrary zero hour) should become less and less pronounced, so that the actual distribution approached more and more nearly to some standard sequence of income-power distributions independent of any original properties of the distribution.

3. This supposition is correct and it is proved in Appendix 2 that if we assume that the fertility of all income-classes is the same, then, under the action of any forces of change, altering in any fashion whatsoever, there will be an ideal sequence of income-distributions for successive years to which the actual distribution will conform more and more closely as time passes, and with which it must eventually be identical. We may call these ideal distributions the *dynamic equilibrium distributions* of income-power. The dynamic equilibrium distribution is unique only if we are told how the forces of change have been altering since time began; if, however,

we know how the forces of change have been altering for a long time back, the dynamic equilibrium distribution will be almost exactly determined. If we know only how the forces of change have been altering for a short time back then we must select an initial distribution to start from at the moment where our knowledge of the forces of change begins; this will introduce an element of arbitrariness into the dynamic equilibrium distribution, which will however become less and less the further ahead we look.

4. The theorem that there exists a unique dynamic equilibrium distribution of income-power at any moment holds good for nearly any system of altering forces of change, whether they be altering systematically and smoothly, or irregularly. Where the changes are irregular, it is naturally impossible to obtain any simple rules about the nature of the dynamic equilibrium distributions. Where the alterations are smooth and systematic we can make some estimate of the dynamic equilibrium distribution.

5. At any moment, given for each income-power range the three forces of change I_1 (1,000 times the average proportional change of income), I_2 (1,000 times the variance of this proportional change of income) and h, the proportionate increase of numbers, and if we know also the proportionate growth of population for the whole community, h_0, and the proportional increase of income for the whole community, k, we have learnt to estimate the quasi-static equilibrium distribution for the community, to which the actual distribution would settle down if the forces of change shifted uniformly along the scale of income-power. It might reasonably be expected that if the forces of change were altering only slowly and smoothly, the dynamic equilibrium distribution would be not much different from the quasi-static equilibrium distribution appropriate to the forces of change at any moment.

6. This expectation is indeed correct. It is proved, however,

in Appendix 2, that in so far as the form of the quasi-static equilibrium distribution is changing there is a tendency for the form of the dynamic equilibrium distribution curve to lag behind that of the quasi-static equilibrium distribution curve, and to resemble more closely at any moment the quasi-static equilibrium distribution curve of a time some years earlier. This result is confirmed by common-sense: for if the dynamic equilibrium distribution ever 'caught up' with the quasi-static equilibrium distribution, then it would stay with it and would not move on to the different quasi-static equilibrium distribution appropriate to the next year; thus it would get left behind in the movement along the sequence of quasi-static equilibrium distributions after all.

The dynamic equilibrium distribution is like a dog moving towards its master, the quasi-static equilibrium distribution, with velocity proportional to its distance from him. So long as the master moves systematically and smoothly, it is obvious* that the dog will always be behind him.

7. When the law of shift of the forces of change is particularly simple, it is possible by jugglery with symbols to estimate the moving equilibrium distribution at each moment; an exhibition of this process is given in Appendix 2, but the process is so imperfect that no useful general conclusions can be based upon it: each case must be treated by this method

---

* If it is not obvious, it can be confirmed by numerical examples chosen at random: for instance, let the dog start at $x = 0$ at time $t = 0$, when the master is at $x = 10$; let the master move 2 every unit of time and let the dog's velocity be one tenth of his distance from his master per unit of time; then for $t = 1, 2, 3$ etc. we obtain:

t =	0	1	2	3	4	5	6
Master M =	10	12	14	16	18	20	22
Dog D =	0	1·0	2·1	3·3	4·6	6·0	7·4
Distance M−D =	10	11	12	13	13	14	15

t =	7	8	9	10	11	12
Master M =	24	26	28	30	32	34
Dog D =	8·9	10·4	12	13·6	15·2	16·0
Distance M−D =	15	16	16	16	17	17

separately. We can, however, base some general conclusions on our knowledge that the moving equilibrium distribution follows the quasi-static equilibrium distribution. The more slowly the quasi-static equilibrium distribution changes its form, the more closely will the moving equilibrium distribution resemble it.

8. We know that the actual distribution of income-power will be approaching more and more near to the moving equilibrium distribution, except in so far as it is disturbed by impulses of change (by sudden causes of economic change which act for a short time only and are not counted as forces of change, cf. Chapters 12 and 20). We know also that the moving equilibrium distribution alters in such a manner as to resemble at any moment the quasi-static equilibrium distribution of some years earlier. Putting these two pieces of knowledge together, we find that the actual distribution is likely to alter so as to resemble the quasi-static equilibrium distribution of a few years earlier, except in so far as it is prevented from doing this by impulses of change which jerk it away from the equilibrium distributions.

Given sufficient knowledge of the forces of change this would be a very valuable result. We could quite easily estimate the form of the quasi-static equilibrium distribution in any year, and then, by comparing the actual distribution with it, we should know the way in which the actual distribution would change.

Even without a knowledge of the forces of change the result has value, because it tells us that even when the forces of change are systematically altering all the time, anything which is done to affect the properties of successive quasi-static equilibrium distributions in any particular fashion is likely eventually to alter the properties of the actual distribution in the same manner, but that there will be a lag of some years before these effects are produced in the actual distribution.

9. In Chapters 14, 15, 17 and 18, we discussed what would be the effects of various economic influences in imaginary worlds, where static or quasi-static equilibrium was established. In general, it was found to be true that the results which were obtained for the world of static equilibrium remained valid in the world of quasi-static equilibrium.

But still our results remained superficial, for they applied only to a world where the forces of change were steady or even constant. But our new discovery enables us to extend all these results to a world in which the forces of change are altering, provided that we remember that these influences will need time to work themselves into the actual distribution, and that their action will in the real world be repeatedly masked by the action of impulses of change.

All the influences whose effects we determined on the distributions in the imaginary worlds are likely to produce slowly the same sort of effects on the distributions of the real world: moreover, all sorts of other influences which our narrow experience precluded us from instancing could be analysed for their effects on the quasi-static equilibrium distributions, by the rules explained in the earlier chapters, and the effects which they would be likely to have on the actual distribution would be similar. If there be any importance in our discovery, it lies in this claim to a general method of investigating the effects on distribution of particular economic influences, rather than in the results which our fancy has selected for demonstration by this method.

10. One barrier between our method of analysis and the real world does still however remain. Unfortunately, in that real world the forces of change do not always alter smoothly and systematically. Nevertheless, over a long period of years it would probably be found that the motion of the forces of change consisted of random jerks to one side or another of a trend motion. It is then best to consider all forces of change, apart from those constituting the trend value of them, as impulses of change. For instance if the forces of change for some income-power range in some year

were $I_1 + i$, $I_2 + j$, $h + k$, where the trend values of these forces were I_1, I_2 and h, then it would be best to count only forces I_1, I_2 and h as forces of change, and to regard the extra forces contributing i, j, k, not as forces but as impulses of change.

Suppose, for example, that the trend values of the forces of change are (I_1, I_2, h) but that for some particular cause the actual values differ from these trend values: let the particular disturbing cause or causes produce an extra disturbance which has mean displacement i and variance of displacement j; then we know that the forces of change will be altered thereby from (I_1, I_2, h) to $(I_1 + i, I_2, +j, h)$ and we choose to count the extra forces not as forces of change at all, but as impulses of change. This after all is quite consistent with our definition of impulses of change as being causes of change which act for a short time only.

Since population usually changes fairly smoothly in any case, we are not likely to introduce much error by assuming that the value of h (proportionate rate of population growth for the members in the income-power group) is always equal to the trend value.*

11. If we adopt these conventions, so that the forces of change alter smoothly and all irregularties are represented by impulses of change, we may regard the actual distribution of income as striving towards the dynamic equilibrium distribution, knocked away first one way and then the other by the impulses of change.

We have discussed at some length the influences that determine the equilibrium distributions; to complete our study, we must now consider which are the most important influences determining the impulses of change, and what are their effects.

---

* This overlooks the possibility of disasters such as civil or international wars, flood and serious epidemics (1972).

20. Impulses of change

1. In this chapter we shall consider those economic events which do not happen smoothly in the ordinary course of change, but which take place suddenly, producing immediate effects on distribution, or altering the forces of change considerably for a short time, and then allowing them to return to their normal trend values. We have termed such disturbances impulses of change, to remind ourselves that their action is short-lived, although their immediate effects may be considerable, in redistributing income.

2. The pure example of the 'impulse of change' is a 'capital levy', which takes place without affecting people's expectation that there won't be a capital levy for a long time. This might be the case if a Conservative government suddenly decided to have a capital levy and to amend the constitution in such a way that there never could be one again. The effect of such a capital levy would be to remove qualifications for obtaining income from the rich and to hand them over to the poor; it will immediately cause a great change in the distribution of income. Yet, except in so far as it affects the forces of change, it will not alter the equilibrium distributions of income. Unless the forces of change are affected the levy will not alter permanently the form of the distribution of income; inequality will begin to develop again in the old mould, and will develop to that extent to which it had previously reached, or more precisely, to that level to which it would reach if there had been no capital levy.

The effects of a war may be to redistribute capital and monopoly advantages, but the form of the distribution of incomes will not be for very long affected, unless the war has altered also the forces of change as measured by I_1 and I_2 at each income-level.

166

Impulses of change

Another important impulse of change is a boom or a depression. In a boom, the real wage-rate tends to fall, whereas the rewards for possessing monopoly advantages rise, and with them the rewards for possessing productive equipment and land. The result must be a temporary increase in inequality, but it is not easy to predict the form that this increase would take. Perhaps we should expect a widening of the hump of the income-ratio-curve, but little modification in the sides. This would be the result that would follow if above £200 all incomes were benefited to the same proportional extent, but below that level they were benefited to a lesser extent.

Against this, it might be argued that the proportional increase of income caused by the boom would grow steadily greater, the higher the income considered, even above the level £200. In this case, in addition to the hump of the income-ratio-curve being widened, we should expect the slope to become less steep in the boom.

If this latter contention were correct, then when we plotted charts of the changes of the slope of the income-ratio-curve at various portions as time passed, as in Chart 17, p. 89, we should expect to find the curves rising and falling with prices. In order to decide more easily whether the curves do do this, they are charted again (Chart 30) with the trends removed [these curves have been brought up to 1966 using the surtax statistics given in later copies of the *Statistical Abstract* and the *Annual Abstract of Statistics* for the U.K.].

Comparing these curves with the curve of wholesale prices, it would be difficult to read into them any significant resemblance. The only verification is perhaps that the curves do seem to go down a bit for the great slump [1931–6], but this could also be accounted for by the heavier progressiveness of taxation and death-duties.

We may perhaps draw the following conclusion from this negative result. Although in a boom it seems reasonable to suppose that the rich as a whole gain more proportionately than the poor, and that in a slump they lose more proportionately of their income, yet it does not seem to be true that in a boom a very rich person gets a larger proportionate increase of income than a fairly rich person, or that in a slump he suffers a greater proportional decrease.

This result is contrary perhaps to what theoretical considerations would suggest, and it is indeed contrary to results which Sir Josiah Stamp has derived from exactly the same source as we have used, namely the super-tax statistics for this country since 1910.*

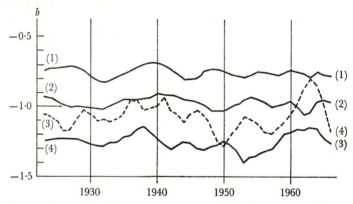

Chart 30   Trend-freed short-term movements of slopes of segments of income-ratio-curves for high incomes in U.K.

Stamp took the ratio of the income of the 10,000th person to that of the 25,000th person and showed that there were about 13 cases in 20 where a high proportion accompanied high prices or a low proportion accompanied low prices, whereas there were only 7 cases of the opposite relationship. He argued that this was significant. But if we take account of the fact that 3 of his 13 'successes' were due to the great increase of equality which has taken place since 1929, and which may be due to a cause other than the slump, and if we remove these three successes, we are left with 10 successes out of 17 years, and this is certainly not a significantly high proportion. I consider, therefore, that any significant relationship between trade cycle stages and the degree of inequality as between rich and very rich has yet to be

* See *Journal of the Royal Statistical Society*, Vol. 99, pp. 627–60.

established. The figures exist for many countries for clearing up this question, and the author hopes to proceed later to this piece of research.*

3. Since we have assumed that the forces of change alter smoothly we must include as impulses of change all economic events which cause a *sudden* alteration of the forces of change. Consider, for instance, a sudden increase in the rates of surtax: this will eventually produce a result in the *trend* value of the forces of change, and will set the income distribution moving to a new equilibrium; but immediately it will cause a small *impulse* of change, lasting until the forces of change (which we must assume *not* to change suddenly) have had time to alter. The effect of this impulse is simply to start the movement towards the new equilibrium directly the taxation occurs, instead of waiting for the trend value of the forces of change, the only value counted as forces proper, to have time to change, and start the dynamic-equilibrium distribution moving on ahead. This conclusion is not important, except in showing that our analysis does not lead to any ridiculous result in this case.

4. Since we have included so many economic disturbances under the heading 'impulses of change', it is evident that at any moment departure from the position of dynamic equilibrium may be quite considerable, owing to the disturbances caused by recent impulses of change.

The degree of disturbance from equilibrium at any moment may be considerable, but in the absence of further impulses of change we should expect this slowly to die down. If we were to draw a graph (for convenience on a logarithmic scale), showing the ratio of the actual amount to the equilibrium amount of income flowing to those in each income-power class, we should expect this curve to subside back towards the line $y = 1$ (the equilibrium position) in the absence of further impulses.

* This hope has not yet been satisfied [1972].

It is interesting however to realise that this return to equilibrium will be made at different rates at different income-levels. Although we might expect that at each income-level the proportion of actual aggregate income to its equilibrium amount will approach unity at the same rate or at the same proportionate rate, so that the graph described above would just subside smoothly into the equilibrium position, this would be a mistake. This is discussed in Appendix 3 in terms of w, the difference between b, the slope of the income-ratio-curve and b^* the equilibrium value of b. It is shown that the adjustment of the curve of $w = b - b^*$ will be a sort of stretching out to right and left combined with a straightening at all points, so that the obvious movements will be lateral and not a simple collapse towards the line $w = 0$.

The practical counterpart to this remark is that the effect of equalising measures may at first be to reduce in equal proportion the numbers in all rich income-classes, and so not affect the distribution of income *between* the rich.

5. The analysis in Appendix 3 also suggests that it may take a very long time for the effects of an impulse of change to die away, or for an income-distribution to adapt itself to a new equilibrium if the forces of change alter swiftly and greatly. The lag of the actual distribution behind even the dynamic equilibrium distribution may in such a case be very considerable. We must therefore regard the distribution of income at any moment as corresponding not to the equilibrium distribution of that moment, but to an average of the equilibrium distributions for some years, indeed some decades back.

This limits the practical application of the theory to measures which are intended to be permanent, and this limitation is particularly unfortunate at the present when events move so fast. Nevertheless, even politicians must consider the long-run effects of the policies which they advocate.

21. Interaction of cause and effect

1. In our analysis we have assumed that the forces of change will remain unaffected by any change in the distribution of income which they may cause.

This is not realistic, because in practice a change in the inequality of distribution will react in all kinds of ways on the economic influences acting to change incomes at various income levels: increased inequality is likely to increase the aggregate amount which people wish to save and this may affect the rate of fall of the rate of interest and through this the forces of change; increasing inequality may increase the demand for artistic goods and the relative value of qualifications mainly owned by the rich; increasing inequality may, by increasing the amount which people wish to save, cause chronic unemployment and the continued deterioration of qualifications (such as industrial plant) possessed by the rich.

2. We can adapt our analysis to this new complication, provided we know the manner in which the forces of change react to increased inequality.

Let us consider the 'rich', namely those with incomes of over £2,000. Suppose that the effect of a change in distribution, characterized by a uniform proportionate increase of b in the slope of the income-ratio-curve for the rich, is to increase I_1 by a proportion $f(b)$, where $f(b)$ is roughly the same for all rich income-levels. Then $f(0) = 0$ since no change has no effect, and we see that a positive df/db will mean that an increase of inequality alters the forces of change in favour of the rich.

Suppose that the distribution is initially in static equilibrium, but that the government now removes a tax from the rich people's incomes, and that this alters I_1 from I_1 to $I_1(1-e)$.

Then, apart from secondary effects, the negative slope of the equilibrium income-ratio-curve will be reduced from an initial value $-b$ to $-b(1-e)$: but this will have a secondary effect of further reducing $I_1(1-e)$ by a proportion

$$\left(1 - e\left(\frac{\mathrm{d}f}{\mathrm{d}b}\right)\right),$$

where $\mathrm{d}f/\mathrm{d}b$ is the derivative of $f(b)$. This will in turn produce a further effect on $-b$, and the final effect of all the series of reactions must be a reduction of $-b$ to

$$-b(1-(\mathrm{d}f/\mathrm{d}b)-e)/(1-(\mathrm{d}f/\mathrm{d}b)).$$

Hence the fact that $\mathrm{d}f/\mathrm{d}b$ differs from nought exaggerates the effect of any disturbing cause upon the slope of the income-ratio-curve by a proportion $1/(1-(\mathrm{d}f/\mathrm{d}b))$.

We may name $\mathrm{d}f/\mathrm{d}b$ the force-change elasticity.

3. If the force-change elasticity is greater than unity, any position of equilibrium is unstable, and the distribution will go on changing until the elasticity is no longer greater than one.

If the force-change elasticity, $\mathrm{d}f/\mathrm{d}b$, is negative (and it very well may be), then the effect of any change in economic influences upon the distribution will be damped down in ratio

$$1\left/\left(1 - \frac{\mathrm{d}f}{\mathrm{d}b}\right)\right..$$

4. The effect of taking this new factor into account should now be clear. In order to illustrate it, let us consider how the effect on taxation upon distribution of income among the well-to-do and rich will be modified by the consideration that increased equality, by reducing the amount which people wish to save, may reduce the trend level of unemployment, increase profits relative to wages and alter the forces of change in favour of the rich. It will be changed, let us suppose in such a way that 1% increase in the slope of the income-ratio-curve causes $\frac{1}{2}\%$ decrease of $-I_1$. Then

$df/db = -\frac{1}{2}$. Hence the change in slope of the income-ratio-curve will be damped down in ratio $\frac{2}{3}$. The following table illustrates the effect.

TABLE 32. *Effects of tax on b without damping and with damping*

income range	£300–£2,000	£2,000 and over
Slope of income-ratio-curve when there is no tax	−0·7	−0·9
Slope, when there is tax and no damping	−1·1	−2·5 (approx.)
Slope when there is tax and and damping	−1·0	−2·0 (approx.)

The effect on the proportionate reduction in the amount of income flowing to any particular income-class is to lower the proportionate reduction from any value $1-x$ to $1-x^{\frac{2}{3}}$. These changes are given in Table 33.

TABLE 33. *Reduction in income flow without damping and with damping*

Reduction in absence of damping (%)	10	20	30	40	50	60	90
Reduction when there is damping (%)	7	14	21	29	37	46	78

Hence, by comparing with Chart 22 *b*, it is easy to see how the effect of the income-tax there discussed will be modified if there is damping of this nature.

5. We may sum up the conclusions reached in this chapter by saying that the fact that changes in the distribution react on the forces which cause them does not invalidate our method of approach to the problem. This fact introduces a multiplier, which magnifies or damps the effect of an initial new measure, according as the changes in distribution reinforce or oppose the economic influences which cause them. Accordingly we may make allowance for the presence of this economic 'resonance', by exaggerating or diminishing

the effects which we should predict if resonance were absent, in accordance with our estimate of df/db, the elasticity of the forces to the changes they produce.

6. Where income-distribution is *mainly* determined by technical conditions, such as the industrial demand for workmen, the elasticity df/db is likely to be large and negative, because a shortage of workmen will set in action forces drawing incomes back towards the wage-level of workmen: hence the multiplier $1/(1 - (df/db))$ will be small, and the effect of any attempt, such as taxation or free education, to alter distribution among normal work people will be largely damped down by these other technical influences determining the distribution. For this reason, our theory is not very well suited for discussing distribution among wage-earners. In the case of wealthy people, mobility of qualifications is so much greater that df/db is not likely to be large and negative for any technical reasons: the chief reason why df/db may be negative for the rich is because increased inequality may cause hoarding, and hoarding may cause an increase in the trend level of unemployment, and a decline in the trend level of profits, and so diminish inequality. There is however no reason to suppose that df/db, if it is negative, will be very large, nor indeed is it certain that df/db is not positive, in which case, the effects of change would be magnified.

Suppose that this effect is such that a decrease of 10 % in the proportion of those with incomes over £2,000 who have incomes over £20,000 increases profits enough to decrease the average loss of income per annum by rich people at each income-level by 5 % (when income is measured in units chosen so as to maintain constant income per head for all income-receivers). This means that a proportionate increase of 4·3 % in $-b$ causes a proportionate decrease of 5 % in I_1. Hence $df/db = -1·16$.

We see that the effect of the death-duties will be damped down in ratio

$$\frac{1}{2·16} = 0·46.$$

22. Does the theory fit the facts?

1. Our theory is essentially a long-period theory, and accordingly it is extremely difficult to verify it or to refute it by appeal to the facts of the real world. For over a long period income-distribution is subject to so many influences which cannot be measured precisely, that the total effect of all of them on the distribution cannot be predicted. Our theory will predict the eventual effect of particular measures on the income-distribution, but in the real world the effects of particular measures cannot be isolated from those of others.

2. There are however two facts about distributions found in the real world which fit in very well with our theory. The first of these is that when plotted on an income-power scale, the frequency distribution of income (the income curve) always has a convenient fairly symmetrical form. This confirms our theory that the proportional effects of economic influences on the incomes of rich and poor are comparable, whereas their absolute effects are not.

The second fact that verifies our theory is that if we draw a frequency distribution of people among income-classes on ordinary scale, then over the range of income of well-to-do and rich people, we shall find in the case of most countries that the elasticity of the curve is constant. This is Pareto's law, and it may otherwise be expressed by saying that the income-ratio-curve and the people-ratio-curve will for most countries be practically straight over the well-to-do and rich income ranges. This was illustrated in Charts 15 and 16.

This phenomenon cannot be explained on any hypothesis that income or income-power is normally distributed. A normal distribution of income-power would give parabolas for the income-ratio-curve and the people-ratio-curve. Gibrat's hypothesis (see Chapter 9) will only give parabolas but will not account for the remarkable straightness of the curves from actual distributions shown in Charts 31 and A23, for example.

Our theory would interpret the straightness thus. The average proportional effect of economic influences on well-to-do and rich people at all their income-levels is roughly the same, and so is the degree to which they affect some people more than others at each of these income-levels.

Our theory leads us to expect that high taxation, by checking a larger proportion of people's saving the richer they were, would cause the income-ratio-curve to be slightly concave for the rich incomes. Heavy taxation should cause the slope of the curve for rich incomes to get steeper every

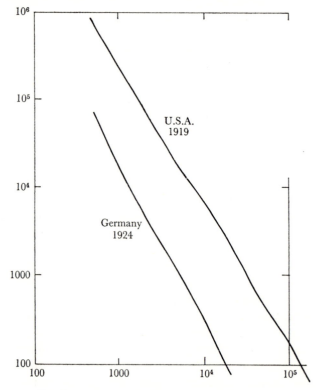

Chart 31   People-ratio-curves for Germany 1924 and U.S.A. 1919 (high incomes)

year. The latter phenomenon is found for British incomes since 1920, the only incomes which we have analysed. I have searched several countries for concavity: it is found to a marked degree in the British data as is shown by the fact that the four curves in Chart 17 are distinct, but it is not found to so marked a degree in other countries, except perhaps in India. In many countries, some convexity is found, especially among the incomes of the well-to-do (see Charts 15 and 16). The main impression which I have carried away

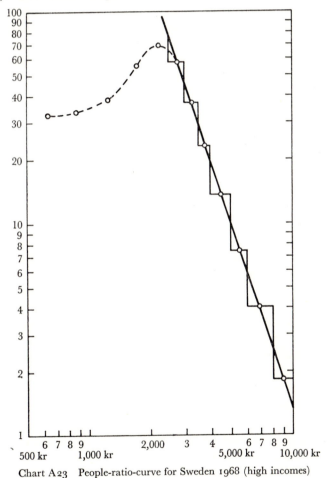

Chart A23   People-ratio-curve for Sweden 1968 (high incomes)

from a hobby of constructing some score of income-ratio-curves and even more people-ratio-curves, is one of amazement at their straightness, over the range of rich incomes. This is not properly brought out by charts 15–16 on pages 38–9, so I give above two people-ratio-curves, for the rich in Germany and the United States.†

I mistrust all tests of the significance of straightness by goodness-of-fit methods, and I hesitate to claim that this phenomenon verifies my contention that the forces of change acting on the incomes of fairly rich and of thoroughly rich and of very rich, are in many countries (not including the U.K.) very similar: yet this is my opinion, and I think also that my theory provides the explanation of the straightness of this portion of the ratio-curves. I am aware of the claim that all ratio curves have straight tails, but I consider it a false claim: most ratio curves are approximately parabolic, and they are no straighter in the tail than a parabola.

Our theory does not confirm Pareto's claim that the slopes of the tails of all income-ratio-curves should be the same for all countries at all times: nor do the facts. (See Charts 15 and 16.)

Pareto argues that all income-distributions were fore-ordained by laws of nature, and that taxes and duties were impotent against them.

Our theory suggests that taxes and inheritance duties may eventually have very large effects on distribution. In so far as redistribution sets in operation forces opposing itself, the effects of measures designed to redistribute income will of course be damped down. But it is also possible that forces will be set in motion to reinforce redistributive measures. Only where income distribution is determined rigidly by technical conditions of demand and supply will the damping of the effects of redistributive measures be complete. The downward slope of the curves shown at the end of Chapter 8 (and in the Appendix to Chapter 8) shows how inequality among the rich has been diminishing in the United Kingdom, and proves Pareto wrong.

† [Chart A 23 gives a later example: the people-ratio-curve for Sweden 1968 (high incomes)].

23. Conclusion to dissertation

1. We have constructed an analysis for examining the probable effects of measures designed to change the distribution of incomes. Whereas on the one hand it is argued that progressive taxes must dry up completely the incomes they suck from, and on the other that they are impotent because opportunities for getting rich will survive the taxes, we have shown that they will cause a definite amount of redistribution and then no more.

2. The information that would be required in order to use our apparatus efficiently is formidable, but not altogether unattainable. We require estimates for representative income-levels of the average increase of income per annum, and of the interquartile range of increase of income per annum, where account is taken of the difference in income between a man dying and of his heir. We must estimate also the average size of family at each income level and the rate of expansion of population and income per head.

To find the effect of any new measure we must know the average effect it will produce on incomes at each income-level: if changes in the distribution will cause further changes in the economic influences, then we must know the magnitude of this reaction: this is likely to damp down the effects of the new measure, but if the force-change elasticity is positive (i.e. if changes in distribution strengthen the forces producing them), the effect will be magnified and there may even be instability.

3. In general, however, we should expect the introduction of a new economic measure to have a definite effect on income distribution eventually, predictable from estimates of the sort indicated in the above paragraph. If the forces of change

were 'constant' or 'steady', this effect would appear as the difference between two eventual equilibrium distributions; if the forces of change were steadily altering, the eventual effect would appear in our analysis as the changing difference between two 'moving equilibrium' distributions. For to constant, steady or moving forces of change there correspond unique static, quasi-static or 'moving' equilibrium distributions, and we can find the change in these produced by the new measure.

In addition to forces of change there are always acting random impulses of change: but the effect of any measure must be assumed independent of these unpredictable events, whose effects on distribution die out in time.

4. The results of our analysis could never be verified, because they are results that take time to work themselves out, and during that time other influences would disturb the experiment. But certain facts in the real world fit in well with our theory: the first is that by plotting the distribution of income among income-power classes (income-power = logarithm of income) we obtain a more familiar type of curve than when we plot the distribution among income-classes. This verifies our underlying assumption that the proportional effects of economic influences upon the incomes of rich and poor are more alike than their absolute effects.

The second fact is that the tail of the income-ratio-curve is fairly straight for some countries and very straight for others, whereas we should ordinarily expect it to be a parabola, according to Gaussian law: this fact would be explained on our theory, if on the average over many years the forces acting to change the incomes of rich and very rich had been uniform in their average proportional effects, for incomes from £500 upwards. The third fact is that the slopes of different portions of the income-ratio-curve for the United Kingdom have since 1911 been moving fairly regularly and in the same way as each other: the effects of the Labour Government's legislation in 1929 and the slump are hard to disentangle, but they are in conformity with what our theory would lead us to expect.

5. We have made constant use of simplifying assumptions: these introduced a degree of roughness into our predictions that would be serious when we were considering the incomes of poor people, if the independent groups of causes of change of income were some of them large and abnormal in their effects upon income-power; we accordingly provided a method of making more exact predictions upon the basis of information about this abnormality.

Our analysis is not well fitted to discuss distribution of income among wage-earners, since this depends on the industrial demand and on trade union policy and politics, rather than on the type of forces which our analysis elaborates. In the earlier chapters we reformulated some of the familiar ideas about distribution, settling them in a form, claimed to be partly original, emphasizing one fact: that income is drawn in virtue of qualifications whose productivity to their owner bears no very close relation to their productivity to society, and whose possession is more often due to inheritance and influence than to industry or inborn ability. The relative value of qualifications possessed by rich and by poor will depend largely on conventions and political practice: these in turn will depend on distribution and the relative value of qualifications, and here again we have a regress whose effect is probably to make distribution more sensitive to initial changes.

This approach was left undeveloped, since it was necessarily political and speculative, and unsuited for quantitative or unbiassed discussion: the ideas thrown out may stimulate thought further along these lines.

6. For a similar reason we have avoided much discussion of welfare economics. This is not because welfare economics is outside economics, but because the meaning of welfare is hardly capable of exact treatment. Economics is an applied science, and (to the writer at least) its value as an academic exercise is small compared to its value as a set of tools for discovering what means will obtain the end wanted. This essay is intended to provide a new tool for this purpose, and as

such it is an essay on welfare economics, for welfare is nothing else than the thing wanted.

It is possible to argue at considerable length that welfare has or has not a subjective meaning, but that is entirely beside the point: utility or satisfaction need be discussed only if we want to increase them: in order to decide what we want to increase, it is not necessary to enter upon these abstract discussions. Either we do or we do not wish to take opportunities from the rich and give them to the poor; or to increase the opportunities of both: or vice versa, if we do wish to do this, then welfare is only what we wish for: if we are interested to apply our science it is welfare economics, and only otherwise is it pure economics. This is an exercise in welfare economics.*

* Although this is the end of the main text of the dissertation Appendices 1, 2, 3 and 4 are taken from it as well.

24. Income distribution re-visited after 35 years

1. On reading through the whole of this book after so long an interval the author was surprised to find with how little of it he now disagreed, and how many of the difficulties which he thought had only been brought to his attention later, had in fact been admitted and to some extent discussed in the original text. But, naturally, some weaknesses have become apparent in the proposed apparatus to which he was blind at the time when he first wrote about it, and possible improvements in it have been suggested by the events and writings of the intervening years.

To begin with the dissertation was exclusively concerned with the distribution of personal income *before* payment of tax, although for many questions the distribution of personal incomes *after* payment of taxes on income is of equal or greater interest. Secondly, although, when the book was written, the author was fairly well aware how very imperfect the published statistics of personal income distribution must be, this awareness has been increased in the intervening years, and especially by reading Professor Titmuss's book *Income Distribution and Social Change*.

These imperfections in the available statistics make it impossible to illustrate, verify or disprove with any precision the theories and predictions advanced in the book. Nevertheless the apparent changes in income-distribution since 1939, as illustrated in the new supplements to Chapters 3 and 8, have been so sweeping that it is difficult to believe that these appearances are entirely due to the kind of imperfections in the statistics to which Professor Titmuss has drawn attention.

2. Just how great the apparent levelling down of the highest incomes was in the United Kingdom during the periods of office of the coalition government (1940–5) and of the first two post-war Labour Governments (1945–51), is brought out in Tables A2 and A3 in the Appendix to Chapter 8 and in Chart 22: the same tables and chart show how little by comparison were the apparent changes during the following twelve years (1952–64) of Conservative Government and during the first three years (1964–67) of Labour Government after that. Even if the statistics give an exaggerated impression of the pace of levelling-down during 1939–51 it is difficult to believe that the contrast suggested between the courses of events in the various sub-periods is altogether misleading.

It is tempting to interpret the apparent changes since 1939 in the personal distribution of income in the United Kingdom as follows: the effect of measures taken during and shortly after the war was a rapid movement of the equilibrium distribution to one of far less inequality than before the war. During and for a few years after the period of rapidly moving equilibrium the actual distribution lagged behind the equilibrium, but steadily caught up on it. During the years since 1950 the movements in the equilibrium distribution have been far less and it has been approximately quasi-static, which means that it has mainly reflected the general increase in average money income per head and the small increase in the total number of income-receivers; following the last period, the movement of the actual distribution has conformed more and more closely with the state of quasi-static equilibrium distribution.

One would like to be able to check whether the actual changes agree with what theory would predict in the light of the various redistributive measures which were implemented during the years 1939–51. Quite apart from the imperfections of the statistics themselves, there are over-simplifications in the theoretical apparatus which would make this exercise almost impossible. It is to the removal of some of these over-simplifications that one would turn if one wished to develop the apparatus of analysis further: let us consider the more important of these over-simplifications.

3. The most sweeping over-simplification is the supposition that the prospects (the probability distribution) of proportional change in income at any one moment are then the same for all persons with the same income, and are independent both of the type of that income and of recent changes in that income.

In Chapter 7 it was pointed out that the theory was really only capable of discussing the distribution of income from a homogeneous source, and at the end of the important §7 of Chapter 4 it was indicated that the treatment of all sources of income as homogeneous in this way was far less defensible for low and moderate levels of income than for fairly high incomes.

The rigid assumption that prospects of proportional change are independent of recent changes in income rules out of consideration all kinds of serial correlation (i.e. continuous drift) in the change of individual incomes. In particular, it rules out the life cycle of income, namely the tendency of income to rise steadily during the early and middle years of a man's working life and to decline in his old age. The model can of course be modified so as to deal to some extent with this point, and the author indicated how this might be done in a theoretical article in the *Economic Journal* for June 1953, which is reproduced as an Appendix 6 to this book by kind permission of the editors of the *Economic Journal*. But this refinement of the model introduces so much complication in order to deal with this one point, that it is doubtful whether it is worth while, except if one has available statistics of personal income-distribution classified by the age of the income-receiver. The same article indicates how the overall income distribution may be analysed into sections relating to three or four main sources, but it evades the question of how to treat the incomes of persons obtaining substantial proportions of their total income from each of two or more of such sources.

The distribution of income between persons

Quite apart from the life-cycle phenomenon, one would from general experience expect that proportional changes in individual incomes would exhibit some degree of serial correlation from one year to the next. On the whole, at any given income-level, one would expect those who had been climbing faster up the scale for the last few years to climb faster than others in the next year. If such were to happen it would violate the assumption of independent prospects of proportional change.

Fortunately the theory still remains valid, when one drops the assumption that individual prospects of proportional change of income are independent of previous changes of income, provided that one retains the assumption that for the whole group of incomes at any given level the forces of change I_1 and I_2 are fixed, or are altering in a prescribed way which is independent of their earlier movement. This means that if one can estimate I_1 and I_2 at various income levels from the statistics of the change in individual incomes, one can estimate the corresponding equilibrium distribution, and if one can estimate also the modifications in I_1 and I_2 at various income-levels, which result from a particular measure, one can estimate also the modification which will result in the equilibrium distribution: and this still works although one drops the assumption that individual prospects of proportional change in income are independent of previous changes of income.

The reader may well feel that this sounds too good to be true, and there must be some snag. There is indeed a difficulty, namely this: in the case where the mechanism governing each individual's prospects of proportional change of income remains unchanged, but involves some serial correlation, one may not conclude from this that I_1 and I_2 at each income level will remain unaltered unless the distribution is already in equilibrium. In general, as the result of the serial correlation implied by the mechanism, I_1 and I_2 will at various levels be different from their eventual equilibrium values at those levels. Without an involved analysis of the whole mechanism it will not be possible to estimate what are these equilibrium values of I_1 and I_2, nor what is the corresponding equilibrium distribution of income.

The nature of the difficulty will perhaps become clearer if we consider the life-cycle of income. Prospects of proportional change of income depend, we may well suppose, not only on the level of one's income but also on age. Given these prospects at each age and income-level there will be a certain equilibrium age-and-income distribution. If this already ruled, the age-distribution being in equilibrium at each income-level, one could observe I_1 and I_2 at each income-level, and these being at their equilibrium values would enable one to calculate from them the equilibrium income distribution, even without using direct observations of it. But if one had not reached equilibrium, the age-distributions at various income levels would be likely to differ from the equilibrium age-distributions proper to those income-levels. Since at any income-level, prospects of proportional change of income depend on age, the values of I_1 and I_2 depend on age-distribution, so that a disequilibrium age-distribution will probably cause I_1 and I_2 to diverge from their equilibrium values. As a result, any attempt to estimate the equilibrium distribution of income from observed values of I_1 and I_2 based on historic changes of income is likely to result in inaccurate estimates, when age affects prospects of change of income: similar difficulties arise when for any reason prospects of change of income involve serial correlation.

It may be that the inaccuracy introduced in this manner is small compared with that present in any case, because of the unreliability of the statistics. One way to test this would be by computer simulation: one could set up a situation with well defined prospects of change of income depending on both age and income and then base crude estimates of the equilibrium distribution by using observations of I_1 and I_2 at various income levels and starting situations, and compare these crude estimates with the true equilibrium distribution.

4. The part of the dissertation which has dated the most is that which deals with different qualifications for receiving

income. The chapters concerning this were rather perfunctory, because of the author's anxiety to get to the point where he could lump all qualifications together as though they were homogeneous and deal with each man's income as a whole. The discussion of income from particular qualifications was based on the crudest marginalist assumptions, which almost no reputable economist would take seriously today. It was taken for granted early in Chapter 6 that 'accumulation is a force tending to lower the rate of interest by lowering the relative value of those qualifications which can be constructed'. To claim this in Cambridge, England today would be tantamount to suggesting that capital accumulation reduces the rate of profit, a lapse which would invite banishment to Cambridge, Massachusetts.

I would again draw the reader's attention to these chapters, since they contain the germ of an idea which may have more potentialities than were glimpsed at the time when the dissertation was written. The situation of the income-receivers was likened to that of a party of gamblers at cards (here again is an echo of Mr Keynes who likened the operations of the stock exchange to those of a casino). In the passage already quoted in the Appendix to Chapter 2, it was explained how the income of any player depends on the value of the hand of cards which he holds, and this hand depends on the deal, but also on the exchanges and on the shifts in the values of the individual cards in the various suits, which take place during the play of the game. The cards represent the players' qualifications for obtaining income and the implication of the analogy is that the players' own efforts and relative skills may have less to do with the distribution of scores (or incomes) than (i) the deal of the cards, and (ii) the operation of the rules of the game determining the values of the cards and the relative opportunities for altering the strength of one's hand as between those with strong hands (the rich) and those with weak hands (the poor). There are card-games and war-games on the market which illustrate this analogy: much of the fun of these games is that whereas for a time it appears that all players have roughly equal chances of prospering, the time usually comes when one or two players begin to get richer or more powerful than all the others, and after that, unless they have very bad luck, one or other of these rich or powerful players will be able to get richer and richer (or more and more powerful) and to ruin or annihilate all the other players. The rules of such games could of course have been framed so as to make it likely that all players could continue to do moderately well, but that would have been far less satisfactory in a game. Fortunately, the processes underlying the development of income-distribution do not lead to such ruthless inequality as these games exhibit, but the analogy remains instructive.

If today one were developing the theory of income-distribution in terms of the theory of distribution of the qualifications for obtaining income, one would concentrate the emphasis at rather different points. In the first place more emphasis should be laid on the qualifications for obtaining *earned* income and less on the possession of capital and land, important though these factors still are in the determination of the distribution of the very large incomes. In the second place, in discussing these qualifications for obtaining earned income, one would pay less attention to innate ability and more attention to other (almost) un-purchasable qualifications, such as race, sex and family background. In discussing the relative values of different kinds of qualifications, one would appeal far less to considerations of their marginal productivities and to the functioning of the market-price-mechanism, and far more to social norms and conventions, and to bargaining strength and readiness to struggle for economic 'rights' and to invest in propaganda and good public relations.

The fact is that, owing to the inflexibility of custom and social norms, the relative values of the various qualifications for obtaining earned incomes, unlike property values and share prices, do *not* respond readily to changes in conditions of supply and demand; moreover, the relative importance and relative values of qualifications that one inherits from one's parents, and of one's early environment, remain very high. Consequently, a theoretical model which stresses the elements of heredity and continuity in the development of the personal income distribution is, it may be hoped, well adapted for taking into account many of the more significant influences affecting income-distribution, and for discussing the effects of modifications to those influences.

It remains true that the degree of inequality of the personal income distribution is the outcome of a struggle between two sets of forces:

i forces causing inequality: (*a*) institutions and social norms, which give the wealthy and their heirs the monopoly of certain types of employment and of property, and (*b*) unsettled conditions which offer opportunities of large proportional gains and losses of income to many individuals.

ii forces limiting inequality: those such as progressive taxation and death duties and the social services, which provide better opportunities for some of the poor to become richer and which limit the tendency for the rich and their offspring to become richer still.

5. The task of 'determining the effects of particular economic influences upon the distribution of income between persons' is not completed when one has determined the effects upon the *equilibrium* distribution unless one has also indicated the speed and manner of the approach of the income-distribution towards that new equilibrium.

Thirty-five years ago, however, the greater part of economic theory was concerned with equilibrium positions of one sort or another, so that in a pioneer attempt to develop a new theory about income-distribution, it did not seem such a grave shortcoming merely to analyse equilibrium distributions and sketch in at the end a discussion of dynamic equilibria, that is of distributions changing smoothly under the influence of *smoothly* changing economic conditions. But no mere discussion of smoothly changing conditions could thrown much light on the short-run or even the medium-run effects of sudden but sizeable and permanent changes such as a considerable increase in the standard rate of income-tax.

It now appears that this shortcoming is particularly serious, since the indications are that the effects of such measures on the inequality of income distribution take decades to work themselves out at all fully; so that merely to state the very long-run effects on the equilibrium distribution is to give a very exaggerated impression of the short- and medium-run effects.

At the time when the dissertation was written and with the resources available, it would probably not have been practicable to obtain any simple answers to questions about the short- and medium-term effects of such sudden but permanent measures on income distribution, even if one knew their effect on the forces of change, I_1, I_2 etc., at all income levels. But now that high-speed computers are available, it should be reasonably simple to obtain such answers in any specific example, although by no means easy to provide approximate general formulae such as were proposed in Chapter 12 in the discussion of the very-long-run effects on the equilibrium distribution. What one would do would be to write down the estimated income-distribution at the date of the introduction of the new measure and trace and compare the developments in the distribution that would follow, (i) if the measure were introduced, and (ii) if the measure were not introduced, by applying the 'forces of change' I_1, I_2, etc., at each income-level at each date in the two sets of circumstances. To make the model convenient for computer simulation one would use it in the 'discrete' rather than the 'continuous' form, that is, one would consider the distribution of income as a distribution of persons between income-classes of equal proportionate extent, and consider the frequency distribution of the shifts of persons from each such income-class to other such classes, rather than as a continuous function relating to a continuous scale of income.

6. I have not undertaken so ambitious an exercise, but in order to gain some impression of the speed of approach to

long-run equilibrium from a position of disequilibrium I have simulated the following situation and the resultant changes in a set of calculations on a high-speed computer. I am indebted to Mr F. A. Cowell of Trinity College, Cambridge for carrying out the detail of the computer calculations.

TABLE 34. *Comparison of initial and equilibrium income-distributions in computer-simulation example*

range of incomes (£)	numbers of incomes in range	
	initial distribution	equilibrium distribution
less than 251·2	458,200[a]	78,125[a]
251·2–316·2	268,600	78,125
316·2–398·1	427,000	156,250
398·1–501·2	677,000	312,500
501·2–631·0	1,027,000	625,000
631·0–794·4	1,452,000	1,250,000
794·4–1000·0	1,830,000	2,500,000
1000–1259	1,830,000	2,500,000
1259–585	1,153,000	1,250,000
1585–995	457,000	625,000
1995–2512	204,000	312,500
2512–3162	97,350	156,250
3162–981	52,150	78,125
3981 and over	66,700[a]	78,125[a]
Total numbers	10,000,000	10,000,000

[a] For incomes below £251·2 the numbers in successive income classes of proportionate extent 1·259 are geometrical progressions of common ratios 0·63 and 0·50: for incomes over £3981, they are geometric progressions of common ratios 0·5613 and 0·5000.

Initially, a population of ten million income-receivers has an income-distribution of arithmetic mean £968 and of median £872, displaying a degree of inequality similar to that found in many of the countries considered above in the Appendix to Chapter 3. In particular, the Pareto-slope α for high incomes is $-2\cdot5$ so that the slope b of the income-ratio-curve, shown as the solid curve in Chart 32, p. 193, is $-1\cdot5$ for high incomes, which is a value similar to that found for the U.K. in 1967 (see chart A19) in the Appendix to Chapter 3). But the forces of change have recently shifted so that the equilibrium-income-distribution is more equal and richer than this initial distribution.

The equilibrium income-distribution has arithmetic mean £1,166 and median income £1,000 and in it the Pareto slope α for high income is $-3\cdot01$, so that the slope of the income-ratio-curve for high incomes is $-2\cdot01$, as is illustrated by the broken curve in Chart 32. The detailed figures for the initial distribution and the equilibrium distribution are shown in Table 34.

To represent the forces of change, the transition matrix for the 40 income-ranges was taken so that only its 9 leading

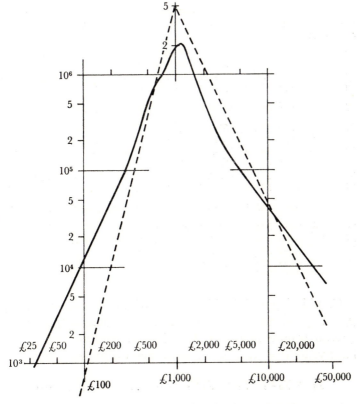

Chart 32   Initial and equilibrium income-ratio-curves

diagonals were non-zero and the entries in these 9 diagonals were those shown in Table 35.

This transition matrix was chosen so as to give roughly the same variance of change of income-power as that found in the transition matrix shown in Table 2 of Appendix 6, which matrix itself was estimated from the estimates shown in Table 1 of the same appendix, of movements of income in England and Wales between 1951 and 1952, and provided by the Oxford Institute of Statistics as a by-product of their survey of savings.

TABLE 35. *Transition matrix for computer-simulation exercise*

$s =$	−4	−3	−2	−1	0	1	2	3	4
$r = 10^6 p_{r,r+s}$									
0					812,508	157,426	27,697	2,296	73
1				157,426	525,354	261,754	50,875	4,445	146
2			13,849	130,877	536,943	262,829	50,911	4,445	146
3		574	12,719	131,414	536,962	262,829	50,911	4,445	146
4–16	*9*	*556*	*12,728*	*131,414*	*536,962*	*262,829*	*50,911*	*4,445*	*146*
17	9	556	12,728	131,414	536,962	262,829	50,984	4,445	73
18	9	556	12,728	131,414	536,998	265,051	50,984	2,223	37
19	9	556	12,746	132,526	562,491	265,051	25,492	1,111	18
20	18	1,111	25,492	265,051	562,491	132,526	12,746	556	9
21	37	2,223	50,984	265,051	536,998	131,414	12,728	556	9
22	73	4,445	50,984	262,829	536,962	131,414	12,728	556	9
23–35	*146*	*4,445*	*50,911*	*262,829*	*536,962*	*131,414*	*12,728*	*556*	*9*
36	146	4,445	50,911	262,829	536,962	131,414	12,719	574	
37	146	4,445	50,911	262,829	536,943	130,877	13,849		
38	146	4,445	50,875	271,754	525,354	157,426			
39	73	2,296	27,697	157,426	812,508				

Considering the initial income-distribution as a row-vector, $\mathbf{y}_0$, of 40 elements, and the transition matrix $\{\mathbf{p}_{r,s}\}$ as a 40×40 square matrix $\mathbf{P}$, the income-distributions $\mathbf{y}_t$ for later years ($t = 1, 2, 3, \ldots$) were then computed from

$$\mathbf{y}_1 = \mathbf{y}_0\mathbf{P}, \quad \mathbf{y}_2 = \mathbf{y}_1\mathbf{P}, \quad \ldots, \quad \mathbf{y}_t = \mathbf{y}_{t-1}\mathbf{P}, \quad \ldots .$$

The equilibrium distribution $\mathbf{y}^*$ was in fact selected before the matrix $\mathbf{P}$, which was chosen so as to be consistent with this $\mathbf{y}^*$, but $\mathbf{y}^*$ could be computed from $\mathbf{P}$ as the row-eigenvector of $\mathbf{P}$ corresponding to the eigenvalue unity, normalised so that the sum of its elements is 10^7, alternatively, the correctness of $\mathbf{y}^*$ can be confirmed by checking that $\mathbf{y}^* = \mathbf{y}^*\mathbf{P}$.

These income-distributions y_t during the approach towards equilibrium are tabulated in Table 36, which gives the distributions for the years $t = 0$, 10, 20, 30, 40, 50, 60 and 100 and in equilibrium; Table 37 gives the same distributions in cumulative form. It will be noticed how very slow is the approach to equilibrium in this simulation. In §8 below we shall suggest that this slowness may largely be due to the fact that our model ignores serial correlation in changes in income, but before trying to correct for this fault we may first regard the approach to equilibrium from another angle by considering the changes in the slope a of the people-ratio-curve at various income-levels. Table 38 gives the slope of the people-ratio-curve at various income-levels, initially and at $t = 1$, 3, 5, and 10: Table 39 gives the same slope at various income-levels at $t = 10$, 20, 50 and 100 and in equilibrium. We denote the gap $a - a^*$ between the actual and equilibrium values of a by w, and Chart 33, based on Table 38, shows how the gap w subsides in the short term: similarly Chart 34, based on Table 39, shows how the gap continues to subside in the longer term. Chart 35 is similar to Chart 17 in Chapter 8 and to Chart A22 in the appendix to that chapter: it shows the changes in a for four segments of the people-curve defined by rank of income.

7. It is interesting to interpret these charts in the light of the theoretical account, given in §3 of Appendix 4 of the dissertation, of the manner in which such a graph should move into the horizontal axis under the influence of constant forces of change. '...the motion of the curve $y = w(x)$ will consist at any point of two motions, (i) a motion to the left with velocity J_1 per annum, (ii) a motion upwards with

velocity $\frac{1}{2}J_2 w''(x)$ per annum. Since J_1 is usually positive for poor people and negative for rich people, the first motion will consist of a horizontal stretching outwards of the curve $y = w(x)$: the second motion will evidently flatten out all

TABLE 36. *Adjustment of numbers of incomes in various ranges of income*

range of incomes (£)	$t = 10$	20	30	40	50	60	100
			numbers of persons with incomes in range				
less than 251	322,700	232,000	173,710	137,710	115,440	101,610	81,950
251–501	945,900	757,800	665,290	617,640	587,810	571,580	550,570
501–1,000	4,394,100	4,381,750	4,377,050	4,373,450	4,383,940	4,374,820	4,374,950
1,000–995	3,849,860	4,097,480	4,219,560	4,284,700	4,312,270	4,342,470	4,370,160
1,995–3,981	425,771	467,609	497,809	516,633	528,149	535,215	545,015
3,981–5,012	29,074	31,287	33,575	35,376	36,639	37,485	38,785
5,012–6,310	14,964	15,523	16,482	17,377	18,064	18,551	19,348
6,310–7,943	7,942	7,840	8,157	8,557	8,907	9,174	9,647
7,943–10,000	4,298	4,041	4,084	4,236	4,399	4,537	4,807
10,000–12,590	2,378	2,128	2,074	2,112	2,180	2,245	2,395
12,590–15,850	1,324	1,142	1,072	1,065	1,085	1,114	1,192
15,850–19,950	740	623	563	544	545	555	593
19,950–25,120	415	344	302	281	276	278	295
25,120–31,620	234	191	163	148	141	139	147
31,620–39,810	131	107	89	79	74	71	73
39,810–50,120	74	60	50	42	38	37	37
50,120–63,000	43	34	28	23	20	19	18
63,000–79,430	24	19	15	13	11	10	9
79,403 and over	28	22	17	14	12	10	9

TABLE 37. *Medium- and long-run adjustment of numbers of incomes exceeding various levels*

| level of income £X | numbers of incomes exceeding the level (£X) | | | | | | | | |
| | initially | 10 years | 20 years | 30 years | 40 years | 50 years | 60 years | 100 years | in long-run equilibrium |
		after							
51	9,541,800	9,677,300	9,768,000	9,826,290	9,862,290	9,884,560	9,898,390	9,918,050	9,921,875
501	8,169,200	8,731,400	9,010,200	9,161,090	9,244,650	9,296,750	9,326,730	9,367,480	9,375,000
1,000	3,860,200	4,377,300	4,628,450	4,784,040	4,871,200	4,921,810	4,951,910	4,992,530	5,000,000
1,995	420,200	487,440	530,970	564,480	586,500	600,540	609,440	622,370	625,000
3,981	66,700	61,669	63,361	66,671	69,867	72,391	74,225	77,355	78,125
5,012	37,430	32,595	32,074	33,096	34,491	35,752	36,740	38,570	39,062
6,310	21,000	17,631	16,551	16,614	17,114	17,688	18,189	19,222	19,531
7,943	11,780	9,689	8,711	8,457	8,557	8,781	9,015	9,575	9,766
10,000	6,610	5,391	4,670	4,373	4,321	4,382	4,478	4,768	4,883
12,590	3,710	3,013	2,542	2,299	2,209	2,202	2,233	2,373	2,441
15,850	2,080	1,689	1,400	1,227	1,144	1,117	1,119	1,181	1,221
19,950	1,170	949	777	664	600	572	564	588	610
25,120	660	534	433	362	319	296	286	293	305
31,620	370	300	242	199	171	155	147	146	153
39,810	210	169	135	110	92	81	76	73	76
50,120	120	95	75	60	50	43	39	36	38
63,100	70	52	41	32	27	23	20	18	19
79,430	40	28	22	17	14	12	10	9	10

waves and humps in the curve $y = w(x)$. We see then that the manner in which the curve subsides into a horizontal straight line is by being stretched out sideways and by having all its waves and humps ironed out.'

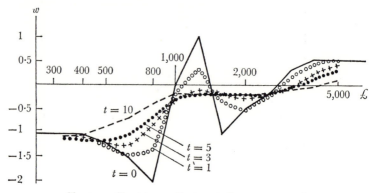

Chart 33 Short-term adjustment of gap, $w = a - a^*$

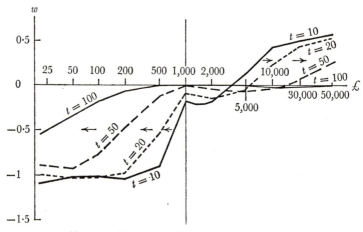

Chart 34 Long-term adjustment of gap, $w = a - a^*$

The short-term adjustments shown in Chart 33 clearly illustrate the second of these motions, namely a flattening out of waves and humps in the curve, and this part of the motion is largely completed by the end of the first ten years: the longer-term adjustments illustrated in Chart 34 clearly

Income distribution revisited after 35 years

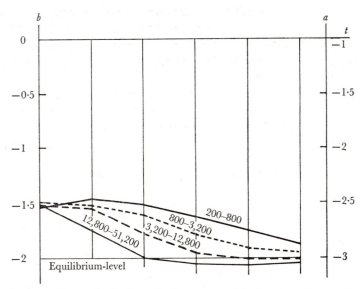

Chart 35   Changes in the slopes, *b*, of 4 segments of the income-ratio-curve for high incomes

TABLE 38. *Slope a of the people-ratio-curve at* $t = 0, 1, 3, 5$ *and 10*

income level (£)	$t = 0$	1	3 slope *a*	5	10	equilibrium slope *a***
316	2·01	2·00	1·96	1·93	1·96	3·01
398	2·00	1·95	1·88	1·88	1·99	3·01
501	1·81	1·77	1·78	1·86	2·11	3·01
631	1·50	1·53	1·78	2·00	2·32	3·01
794	1·00	1·65	2·14	2·34	2·59	3·01
1,000	0·00	−0·20	−0·27	−0·25	−0·17	0·00
1,259	−2·01	−2·66	−3·11	−3·20	−3·20	−3·01
1,585	−4·02	−3·36	−3·16	−3·19	−3·21	−3·01
1,995	−3·50	−3·52	−3·29	−3·21	−3·20	−3·01
2,512	−3·21	−3·26	−3·25	−3·20	−3·17	−3·01
3,162	−2·71	−2·86	−3·03	−3·08	−3·11	−3·01
3,981	−2·51	−2·59	−2·76	−2·88	−3·01	−3·01
5,012	−2·51	−2·51	−2·60	−2·70	−2·88	−3·01

The distribution of income between persons

illustrate the first of the two motions, namely a movement to the left of that part of the curve for which a^* is positive, the part relating to incomes under £1,000, and a movement to the right of that part of the curve for which a^* is negative, the part relating to incomes above £1,000. The theoretical velocities along the income-power scale are given by the values of $-J_1$ over the two ranges (below and above the income-level £1,000): these values, reckoning logarithms to the base 10, are 0·022 per annum to the left and to the right

TABLE 39. *Slope a of the people-ratio-curve at t = 10, 20, 50 and 100*

income level (£)	$t = 10$	20	50	100	equilibrium slope a^*
		slope a			
50	2·00	1·99	2·08	2·67	3·01
63	2·00	1·99	2·12	2·73	3·01
79	2·00	2·00	2·17	2·79	3·01
100	2·00	1·99	2·24	2·84	3·01
126	2·00	2·00	2·33	2·89	3·01
159	1·99	2·00	2·43	2·92	3·01
200	1·97	2·03	2·54	2·95	3·01
251	1·96	2·08	2·65	2·97	3·01
316	1·96	2·17	2·75	2·98	3·01
398	1·99	2·31	2·83	2·99	3·01
501	2·11	2·48	2·89	3·00	3·01
630	2·32	2·65	2·94	3·00	3·01
794	2·59	2·81	2·97	3·01	3·01
1,000	−0·17	−0·08	−0·02	−0·00	0·00
1,259	−3·20	−3·12	−3·03	−3·01	−3·01
1,585	−3·21	−3·14	−3·04	−3·01	−3·01
1,995	−3·20	−3·15	−3·05	−3·01	−3·01
2,512	−3·17	−3·15	−3·05	−3·02	−3·01
3,162	−3·11	−3·14	−3·06	−3·02	−3·01
3,981	−3·01	−3·10	−3·07	−3·02	−3·01
5,012	−2·88	−3·04	−3·07	−3·02	−3·01
6,300	−2·76	−2·97	−3·07	−3·02	−3·01
7,943	−2·65	−2·88	−3·06	−3·02	−3·01
10,000	−2·58	−2·79	−3·05	−3·03	−3·01
12,590	−2·54	−2·70	−3·03	−3·03	−3.01
15,850	−2·52	−2·63	−2·99	−3·03	−3·01
19,950	−2·51	−2·58	−2·95	−3·03	−3·01
25,120	−2·50	−2·54	−2·90	−3·03	−3·01
31,620	−2·49	−2·52	−2·85	−3·03	−3·01
39,810	−2·47	−2·50	−2·80	−3·03	−3·01
50,120	−2·44	−2·49	−2·75	−3·03	−3·01

respectively: thus it should take about ($1 \div 0 \cdot 022 =$) 45 years to travel the horizontal distance from £1,000 to £10,000. The actual movements shown for the curve show such horizontal motion roughly, but not exactly: one reason that it is not shown exactly is that at the same time some vertical motion of the curve was still taking place due to the curvature still remaining in it, and another reason is that the theoretical account given in Appendix 4 to the dissertation was based on various approximations and simplifying assumptions which are not fully satisfied in our numerical example.

8. Returning now to the question of the slowness of the approach to equilibrium, it seems likely that this may be largely due to the fact already hinted at in §6 above that we assumed that change of income in any year from a given level was independent of the change in that income over the previous year. To test this view, one may consider what would happen to the changes of income-power over a period of a number of years, if in any one year the 'forces' of change were kept the same, but if the shift of an individual's income-power, $\Delta_t z$, were influenced by the shift of his income-power $\Delta_{t-1} z$ in the previous year according to the rule

$$\Delta_t z = \rho \Delta_{t-1} z + u_t,$$

where u_t is a random variate with mean and variance dependent on the level of income. So far we have been considering the case where $\rho = 0$, and the equilibrium analysis, in terms of the forces of change of income-power over one year, remains just the same even when ρ is positive: but the speed of approach to this equilibrium distribution will be affected by the size of ρ, which is the measure of serial correlation between income-power changes at successive dates. Let us consider some given initial income-power level and denote by $M_1'(t)$ and $M_2(t)$ the mean and variance of the change from that level of income-power over the whole of the next t years. Then on the assumption that we can ignore the changes of these measures with income-power in the neighbourhood of our given income-power, we know that the equilibrium slope of the income-ratio-curve is given by $b = 2M_1'(t)/M_2(t)$ in the case where $\rho = 0$. In this case, $M_1'(t)/M_1'(1) = M_2(t)/M_2(1) = t$, but when ρ is positive, these relations no longer hold for values of t greater than unity. It turns out that instead

$$M_1'(2)/M_1'(1) = M_2(2)/M_2(1) = 2(1+\rho),$$
$$M_1'(3)/M_1'(L) = M_2(3)/M_2(1) = 3+4\rho+2\rho^2,$$
$$M_1'(4)/M_1'(1) = M_2(4)/M_2(1) = 4+6\rho+4\rho^2+2\rho^3,$$

etc.

For example, when $\rho = 0.8$,

$$M_1'(5)/M_1'(1) = M_2(5)/M_2(1) = 5+8\rho+6\rho^2+4\rho^3+2\rho^4$$
$$= 18.1072$$

indicating that owing to the high value of ρ, both parameters M_1' and M_2 relating to only a 5-years interval are as large and indeed larger than, in the case of zero ρ, they would be for an 18-year interval, with the same values $M_1'(1)$ and $M_2(1)$ after only one year.

This has the result that with $\rho = 0.8$, if the degree of adjustment towards equilibrium during the first year were just the same as in the case $\rho = 0$, yet (with $\rho = 0.8$) it would only need another four years to achieve the further adjustment which, with $\rho = 0$, would need more than another 17 years.

The general formula for finding the relation between N_0 and N_ρ, the numbers of years needed to achieve the same degree of adjustment towards equilibrium with $\rho = 0$ and with ρ taking any other value, is

$$N_0 = \{(1+\rho)/(1-\rho)\} N_\rho - \{2\rho(1-\rho^{N_\rho})/(1-\rho)^2\}, \quad \text{(A)}$$

whence also

$$N_\rho = \{(1-\rho)/(1+\rho)\} N_0 + \{2\rho(1-\rho^{N_\rho})/(1-\rho^2)\}. \quad \text{(B)}$$

Chart 36 provides graphs for reading off the values of N_ρ up to 10 years for given values of N_0 for $\rho = 0.2, 0.4, 0.6$

and 0·8; for larger values of N_0, provided ρ does not exceed 0·8, quite accurate values of N_ρ can be obtained in terms of N_0 and ρ, by ignoring the term involving ρ^{N_0} and using the approximate formula

$$N_\rho = (1-\rho)/(1+\rho)\ N_0 + 2\rho/(1-\rho^2),$$

where the values of $(1-\rho)/(1+\rho)$ and of $2\rho/(1-\rho^2)$ may be read from Table 40.

TABLE 40. *Values of $(1-\rho)/(1+\rho)$ and of $2\rho/(1-\rho^2)$*

ρ	0·1	0·2	0·3	0·4	0·5	0·6	0·7	0·8
$(1-\rho)/(1+\rho)$	0·818	0·667	0·538	0·429	0·333	0·250	0·176	0·111
$2\rho/(1-\rho^2)$	0·202	0·415	0·659	0·952	1·333	1·875	2·745	4·444

For example, with $N_0 = 62$ and $\rho = 0·8$, we find

$$N_\rho = (0·111 \times 62) + 4·444 = 11·326,$$

whereas the correct value is $N_\rho = 10·95$. The error of about 0·38 is due to ignoring the term ' $-2\rho^{N_\rho+1}/(1-\rho^2)$ '.

In the light of these formulae, we are now enabled to make a rough allowance for the effect of any serial correlation in changes of income-power on the adjustment process

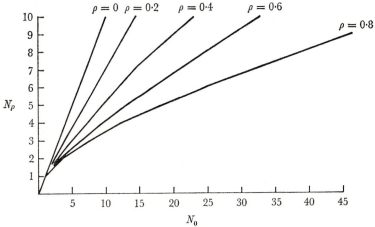

Chart 36 N_ρ plotted against N_0 for selected values of ρ

in our model. Suppose, for example, that the serial correlation is given by $\rho = 0.6$, between one year and the next, then to reach the degree of adjustment indicated in Table 36 and Chart 34 as obtained in 20 years, when $\rho = 0$, we can read off from Chart 36 that we should need only about seven years; whereas to reach the stage of adjustment shown in Table 36 as achieved in 60 years, we should need about $60(1-\rho)/(1+\rho) + 2\rho/(1-\rho^2)$ years, with $\rho = 0.6$, and with the aid of Table 40, we see that this works out at about 17 years only.

These corrections are of course only very rough ones, since the formula for the effect of ρ is based on the simplifying assumption that the initial distribution is not far from equilibrium; whereas in our computer-simulation example, the initial degree of disequilibrium is fairly large. Nevertheless the corrections probably do indicate the rough extent of the speeding-up of adjustment afforded by serial correlation if ρ is indeed correctly estimated.

At present it is not very profitable to speculate about what is the true value of ρ, beyond guessing that it probably lies within the range from 0.2 to 0.8. However, the task of estimating ρ from data about changes in individual incomes should prove no more formidable than those which have in any case to be faced in estimating the transition matrix of changes from one year to the next. It would for example be sufficient, in order to estimate ρ at each income-level, to be provided with both the transition matrix over an interval of one year and the transition matrix over an interval of two years. It may not therefore be particularly optimistic to suppose that at current rates of advance in empirical research, reasonable estimates of ρ will become available within the next few years, or at any rate within very few decades.

9. Another area in which further research may be fruitful is in considering the links between the incomes of parents and those of their children. There are two points to be here considered: (i) the manner in which the average and vari-

ance of the distribution of the ratio of the son's to the father's income vary according to the father's income, and (ii) the inaccuracies which are introduced into the equilibrium theory by the fact that the jump in income-power (or proportional jump in income) when passing from the father's to the son's income is by no means 'small' in most cases. The first point is one whose consideration calls for empirical study, and the subject is complicated by the widespread practice among the wealthy of arranging to pass some of their wealth to their sons whilst they (the parents) are still living. The second point is one which is difficult to handle by pure mathematical theory, but which should be easy to cover in a year-by-year computer simulation of the changing of the income-distribution.

10. All economic theories contain certain simplifying assumptions which render them unrealistic, and the usefulness of an economic theory depends not so much on how realistic it is as on the nature of its lack of realism: the most useful economic theories are those whose departure from realism is in directions which do not much matter for discussing those particular questions to which the theory is to be applied.

Very often, the simplifying assumptions take the form that certain parameters or certain relations between variables are assumed to be exogeneous, or given by conditions determined outside of the model, so that the effects of economic measures can be traced without the complication of any indirect effects through changes in these parameters and variables, in virtue of their supposed immutability and exogenous determination. It is such simplifying assumptions of the exogeneous determination of parameter values and of relations between variables that most frequently prove the Achilles heel of an economic theory, since the neglect of possible indirect effects of economic measures through changes in the supposedly exogenous variables may not in applications to real life be prudent, whatever may be assumed in the theoretical model. This is a particularly dangerous source of unrealistic conclusions in theoretical discussions of the effects of economic measures on income-distribution. How often, for example, one hears discussions about the effects of this and that on income distribution based on the assumption that the proportions saved out of profits and out of wages are two specified numbers, without any mention of the possibility that this and that may have the effect of altering either of these proportions.

11. The theory of income distribution which was presented in the dissertation is vulnerable to the same kind of criticism, in that when it discusses the effects of particular economic measures on the income-distribution it does so by examining the *direct* effects of them on the forces of change $(I_1, I_2,$ etc.$)$ and the influences of the direct effects on I_1, I_2, etc. on the equilibrium distribution of income. Except in Chapter 21 and the appendices, nothing is said about possible indirect effects on the forces of change through shifts in other economic variables, and in particular through changes in the income-distribution itself.

It is true that in Chapter 21 a perfunctory attempt is made to allow for this last kind of indirect effect, but it is really only applicable to cases where the effects of income distribution on the forces of change at a particular level all happen to operate through changes in the slope of the people-ratio- (or income-ratio) curve at that particular income level. This is a very special case, although quite useful for illustrative purposes. But the need to study and take account of the feed-back from changes in income distribution to the transition matrix which generates further changes in the income distribution is a much wider and deeper need than is covered by the discussion of the special case offered in Chapter 21.

12. The fact is that the effects of economic measures on income distribution are subject to certain constraints, which may to a considerable extent modify the conclusions which analysis along the simple lines indicated in the earlier chapters may suggest.

One such constraint is that any set of changes in prospects

of change of income at individual levels which a set of measures is supposed to imply must be consistent with the possible changes in the total income of the community. It may be true that there are wide limits within which the total income may change, granted that prices are flexible, but this is not a very safe let-out unless one can explain just how the measures under discussion are likely to affect in the necessary manner the levels of prices.

A second and even more significant restraint is that imposed by the accounting identity crudely described by the mnemonic 'savings equals investment'. Any changes caused by economic measures on personal income distribution will be accompanied by changes in the disposition and capacity of personal income receivers both individually and in total to save: unless they are balanced by compensating changes in the accumulation of real assets or in government expenditure or revenue or in savings by companies, there will be resulting disturbances to other balancing items such as the external balance-of-payments, and these in turn are likely to cause repercussions on the forces of change of income on top of the effects of the initial economic measures.

To illustrate this point we may consider the argument that the effect of lowering the rate of tax on high incomes would eventually be to increase the inequality of even *pre-tax* income, because the lowering of tax would enable the rich to save more and thus accumulate more wealth faster and increase their incomes at a more rapid proportionate rate compared with the poor than otherwise. It might be objected that aggregate savings must equal aggregate investment, which is however autonomously determined, and that any tendency for incomes to become less equally distributed would be thwarted by a tendency for 'ex ante' savings to exceed 'ex ante' investment, which would result in a buyers' market and a consequent fall in profit margins, which would shift the forces of change of income against the rich again sufficiently so as to offset the immediate effects of the change in tax towards increasing inequality. The objection may be a weak one, but it cannot be dismissed without careful examination of all the indirect effects of the original measure, and the logical point is perfectly sound that, in so far as a change in the distribution of income will cause changes in ex-ante savings, one can only properly investigate the effects of any measure on income-distribution if one also takes account of the feed-back effects via the change in ex-ante savings on inflationary or deflationary tendencies and hence on income-distribution at a later date.

The influences of such a 'savings equals investment' restraint is of course particularly important when one is considering the effect on personal income-distribution of measures to stimulate economic activity. One method in which the extra savings required for a higher rate of investment may be provided is by causing a redistribution of income from persons with a low marginal propensity to save to others with a higher marginal propensity to save. Since Keynes drew attention to this in his pamphlet on 'how to pay for the war', other economists, such as Professor N. Kaldor, have argued that demand inflation due to increased home investment (or government expenditure out of borrowing) will cause such a transfer; to the extent that this is true, any theory of income-distribution which completely ignores such inflationary of deflationary effects on the forces of change of income is likely to be highly misleading. These admissions do not however mean that the apparatus deployed in this dissertation has to be abandoned: it means that to study such effects, full account must be taken of how these effects work out in terms of the prospects of change of income at each income-level and at each date.

To understand fully the results for personal income distribution of any economic measure, such as one designed to stimulate home investment, one needs in fact to trace its effects, both direct and indirect, period by period, on the prospects of change of income at each level, and not merely its immediate direct effects on the 'forces of change' and on the corresponding equilibrium. Obviously such a complete step-by-step analysis would be an almost impossibly complicated procedure, but this is neither surprising nor a damaging criticism of the proposed method of approach. The reason is simply that the question of what the effects of the measure on personal income-distribution would be does concern us and does impose an almost impossibly complex process: any *realistic* answer to the question *must* therefore consider an apparently impossible tangle of repercussions. This is why *realistic* answers about the ultimate effects of economic policies are scarcely ever attainable nor would be identifiable as realistic even if they were: the best that can be expected are answers to questions about the effects of measures relating to theoretical model economies which resemble real economies in certain important respects only: having constructed these theoretical model economies, the study of the nature of the effects of particular economic measures on these theoretical economies may well draw attention to a part of the probable effects of such measures in the real world which might otherwise have been overlooked.

13. This may seem a very meagre accomplishment for so much effort, but it may also be very much better than nothing. If one does wish to gain any insight into the effects of particular measures on the frequency distribution of personal incomes, it is difficult to see how else this can be done than by studying the actual events which have followed similar measures, if they have already been implemented somewhere, or if they have not, by simulating their repercussions in a theoretical model. The theoretical model which has been proposed in this dissertation may be capable of further development for use in some such simulation studies.

APPENDIX: PROOF OF THE FORMULA
GIVING N_ρ IN TERMS OF N_0 AND ρ

Denote by x_0 the shift in income-power during the year *before* the base-date $t = 0$, and by $x_1, x_2, ..., x_t, ...$ the shifts in income-power during the 1st, 2nd, ..., t'th, ... years after the base-date. We suppose that

$$x_t = \rho x_{t-1} + u_t \quad \text{for} \quad t = 0, 1, 2, ..., \tag{1}$$

and that for persons with income-power at the given level X at the base-date, the u_t are independent normal variates of mean $\bar{u}$ and variance σ_u^2. From (1) we derive

$$x_t = \rho^{t-1} x_1 + \rho^{t-2} u_2 + \rho^{t-3} u_3 + ... + \rho u_{t-1} + u_t. \tag{2}$$

Denoting var (x_1), $E(x_t)$ and cov (x_s, x_t) by σ_x^2, $\bar{x}_t$ and c_{st}, we then have

$$\bar{x}_t = \rho^{t-1}\bar{x}_1 + (1 - \rho^{t-1})(1 - \rho)^{-1}\bar{u} \quad \text{if} \quad \rho \neq 0 \quad \text{and} \quad t \geqslant 1, \tag{3}$$

$$c_{ss} = \rho^{2(s-1)}\sigma_x^2 + (1 - \rho^{2(s-1)})(1 - \rho^2)^{-1}\sigma_u^2 \quad \text{if} \quad \rho \neq 0 \quad \text{and} \quad s \geqslant 1 \tag{4}$$

$$c_{st} = \rho^{t-s} c_{ss} \quad\quad\quad \text{if} \quad t \geqslant s \geqslant 1. \tag{5}$$

Now let $y_t = x_1 + x_2 + ... + x_t$, the total shift in income-power during the first t years following the base-date, then the expected value and variance of y_t are, by (3)

$$\bar{y}_t = \bar{x}_1 + \bar{x}_2 + ... + \bar{x}_t = (1 - \rho^t)(1 - \rho)^{-1}\bar{x}_1 + \{t(1 - \rho)^{-1} - (1 - \rho^t)(1 - \rho)^{-2}\}\bar{u}, \tag{6}$$

and by (4), (5),

$$\text{var}(y_t) = \sum_{s=1}^{t}\left\{c_{ss} + 2\sum_{r=s+1}^{t} c_{rs}\right\} = \sum_{r=1}^{t} c_{ss}\left\{1 + 2\sum_{1}^{t-s}\rho^r\right\}$$

$$= (1 - \rho)^{-1}\sum_{s=1}^{t} c_{ss}\{1 + \rho - 2\rho^{t+1-s}\},$$

$$\therefore \ \mathrm{var} \ (y)_t = (\mathrm{I}-\rho)^{-1}\{\sigma_x^2 - (\mathrm{I}-\rho^2)^{-1}\sigma_u^2\} \sum_{s=1}^{t} (\mathrm{I}+\rho-2\rho^{t+1-s})$$

$$\times \rho^{2(s-1)} + (\mathrm{I}-\rho^2)^{-1}(\mathrm{I}-\rho)^{-1}\sigma_u^2 \sum_{s=1}^{t} \{\mathrm{I}+\rho-2\rho^{t+1-s}\}$$

$$= (\mathrm{I}-\rho)^{-2}\{\sigma_x^2 - (\mathrm{I}-\rho^2)^{-1}\sigma_u^2\}(\mathrm{I}-\rho^t)^2$$

$$+ (\mathrm{I}-\rho^2)^{-1}(\mathrm{I}-\rho)^{-2}\sigma_u^2\{(\mathrm{I}-\rho^2)\,t - 2\rho(\mathrm{I}-\rho^t)\}$$

so that

$$\mathrm{var} \ (y_t) = (\mathrm{I}-\rho^t)^2(\mathrm{I}-\rho^2)^{-1}\sigma_x^2 + \{(\mathrm{I}-\rho^2)\,t - 2\rho(\mathrm{I}-\rho^t)$$
$$- (\mathrm{I}-\rho^t)^2\}(\mathrm{I}-\rho^2)^{-1}(\mathrm{I}-\rho)^{-2}\sigma_u^2. \quad (7)$$

Equations (6) and (7) will yield formulae for $\bar{y}_t/\bar{y}_1$ and var $(y_t)/$var (y_1), provided we can obtain estimates of $\bar{u}/\bar{x}_1$ and of σ_u^2/σ_x^2. To obtain these estimates we consider the special case where the initial distribution of x_1 was normal and where at the base-date, for income-power near X, the distribution of income was in equilibrium and the slope of the income-ratio-curve was constant at the value a. Then writing $f(x)$ for

$$\frac{\mathrm{I}}{\sqrt{(2\pi)}\,\sigma_x}, \ \mathrm{e}^{-(x-\bar{x}_1)^2/2\sigma_x^2}$$

we know that

$$\int_{-\infty}^{\infty} f(x)\,\mathrm{e}^{-ax}\,\mathrm{d}x = \mathrm{I},$$

$$\int_{-\infty}^{\infty} xf(x)\,\mathrm{e}^{-ax}\,\mathrm{d}x = \bar{x}_0,$$

and

$$\int_{-\infty}^{\infty} x^2 f(x)\,\mathrm{e}^{-ax}\,\mathrm{d}x = \bar{x}_0^2 + \sigma_0^2.$$

From these equations it follows that

$$a = -2\bar{x}_1/\sigma_x^2, \quad \bar{x}_0 = -\bar{x}_1 \quad \text{and} \quad \sigma_0^2 = \sigma_1^2.$$

We know from (1) that

$$\bar{x}_1 = \rho\bar{x}_0 + \bar{u} \quad \text{and that} \quad \sigma_1^2 = \rho^2\sigma_0 + \sigma_u^2$$

and hence we obtain

$$\bar{u} = (\mathrm{I}+\rho)\,\bar{x} \quad \text{and} \quad \sigma_u^2 = (\mathrm{I}-\rho^2)\,\sigma_x^2. \quad (8)$$

Substituting from (8) into (6) we obtain, since $y_1 = x_1$,

$$\bar{y}_t/\bar{y}_1 = (\mathrm{I}-\rho^t)(\mathrm{I}-\rho)^{-1} + (\mathrm{I}+\rho)$$
$$\times \{t(\mathrm{I}-\rho)^{-1} - (\mathrm{I}-\rho^t)(\mathrm{I}-\rho)^{-2}\}$$

The distribution of income between persons

and after simplification,

$$\bar{y}_t/\bar{y}_1 = \{(1-\rho^2)\,t - 2\rho(1-\rho^t)\}\,(1-\rho)^{-2}. \qquad (9)$$

Substituting from (8) into (7), we obtain

$$\text{var}\,(y_t)/\text{var}\,(y_1) = (1-\rho^t)^2\,(1-\rho)^{-2} + \{(1-\rho^2)\,t - 2\rho(1-\rho^t)$$
$$- (1-\rho^t)^2\}\,(1-\rho)^{-2}$$
$$= \{(1-\rho^2)\,t - 2\rho(1-\rho^t)\}\,(1-\rho)^{-2}. \qquad (10)$$

In the notation of §8 of Chapter 24, and writing N_0 for t, equations (9) and (10) become

$$M_1'(N_0)/M_1'(1) = M_2(N_0)/M_2(1)$$
$$= \{(1+\rho)/(1-\rho)\}\,N_0 - 2\rho(1-\rho^{N_0})/(1-\rho)^2, \qquad (11)$$

whence we obtain the formula A in the same §8 of Chapter 24.

These estimates were obtained from the estimates (8), which were based on the assumption that the system was already in equilibrium, but we may use them as being approximately correct if the system is close to equilibrium.

Appendix 1: The construction of people-curves and income-curves

1. The form in which statistics of income-distribution are usually found is in a table of the type illustrated below.

Sometimes the second or third column is not available. I have devised various methods for fitting income-curves and people-curves to such data. A thorough account would be tedious: I give a summary of seven methods.

TABLE 41. *Income in Sweden 1930*

income class in Kroner	number of persons having income	total income (,00 Kroner)
Under 1,000	1,072,953	5,878,849
1,000–2,000	785,616	10,732,244
2,000–3,000	385,930	9,264,270
3,000–4,000	184,273	6,218,446
4,000–5,000	74,336	3,260,427
5,000–6,000	34,770	2,022,225
6,000–8,000	35,837	2,439,385

2. (1) The easiest way is to construct histograms like those in Charts 1 and 2 of Chapter 3, p. 25 and to pass a curve through the tops in such a way that the area under the curve between the ordinates bounding any of the six rectangles is equal to the area of the rectangle.

Suppose $y = f(x)$, $y = g(x)$ to be the people-curve and income-curve thus found. Then we can plot the curves $y = 10^{-x}g(x)$ and $y = 10^{x}f(x)$ to give us a second pair of estimates of the people-curve and the income-curve.

(2) Another method is to construct step-curves on the ratio-scale, like those in Charts 5 and 6 in Chapter 3 §9, and to pass smooth curves through their mid-points. Let these curves then be plotted again on the ordinary scale to give us another pair of estimates for the income-curve and the people-curve: if these are $y = F(x)$ and $y = G(x)$, we may then plot $y = 10^{-x} G(x)$ and $y = 10^{x}F(x)$ to obtain a further pair of estimates.

The advantage of interpolating for the ratio curves, instead of for the original curves, is that the ratio curves seem usually to be fairly straight over a large part of their length.

(3) By plotting on logarithmic probability paper (log-scale one way and probability scale the other way) income along the logarithmic scale, and the percentage of people with income greater than that along the other axis, and pricking through the points obtained on to an ordinary scale, we usually obtain a curve to which a cubic of the type $By + Cy^3 = x - A$ gives a good fit, where changes in x correspond to changes in income, and the origin is taken on the 50 % line. This curve can be pricked back in as many points as we wish on to the logarithmic probability paper, to give us very detailed information. From this new curve and from the corresponding curve for income instead of people, we can construct a very detailed table of the type illustrated in §1. From this we can proceed by any of the methods explained in sections 2 and 3.

(4) Where the data refer to large incomes only, we can obtain a table relating the logarithm of income to the logarithms of (*a*) the number of people with income greater than that, and (*b*) their income.

We can now interpolate between any two points by passing a cubic through them and the two points on either side. We can then obtain the people curve and the income curve, by using a table of anti-logarithms.

(5) Let $10^{F(x)}$ be the number of people with income greater than 10^x. Then if $U = \log_e 10$

$$y = F(x) + \log_{10} U + \log_{10} F'(x)$$

is the people-ratio-curve.

We can find a series of values for $F(x)$ and deduce values for $F'(x)$ by interpolation by divided differences.

Since $F'(x)$ is usually very constant over wide ranges of income, this gives us a close estimate. Hence we obtain a set of points on the people-ratio-curve, and can find the corresponding points on the people-curve. We can treat the data about income in the same way, to obtain the income-curve.

(6) A very quick method is to work out on a slide rule

the number of people per £ of income interval and plot this against the central income of the class on a double logarithmic scale: this will give, roughly, the people-ratio-curve displaced vertically through $\log_{10}\{\log_e 10\}$. By a single setting of the slide rule, we can then read off from a smooth curve through the points as many points as we wish of the people-curve. This method is inaccurate if the classes are very wide.

(7) By observing several income-ratio-curves I have been led to the conclusion that in general they possess the following characteristics:

i Their tails are fairly straight but their slopes are different for different countries.

ii They are fairly symmetrical.

iii The shape of their hump varies considerably.

The curve can then vary in four ways:

i, ii The co-ordinates of the mode.

iii The degree to which it is humped.

iv The slope of the sides.

The equation

$$y = \frac{A}{\cosh(Bx-C)-D} = \phi(Bx-C)$$

gives an income-curve possessing the above properties. $-B$ will be the slope of the Pareto tail: D may vary from -1 to $+1$ and measures the humpiness. It can then be shown that

$$\int_x^\infty \phi(u)\,du \Big/ \int_{-\infty}^\infty \phi(u)\,du = (1/\theta)\tan^{-1}\frac{\sin\theta}{D+x},$$

where $D = \cos\theta$.

Obtain points of $y = \ln F(x)$ where $F(x)$ is the number with income-power greater than x; estimate the slope of the tail of the curve to find B. Now plot $y = \ln F(x/B)$.

By having a piece of tracing paper on which are plotted curves

$$y = (1/\theta)\tan^{-1}\frac{\sin\theta}{\cos\theta+x}+k,$$

215

where $\cos \theta = D$, when k is so chosen as to make the tails of all the curves have the same asymptote, it is easy to slide the tracing paper over our curve $y = \ln F(x/B)$ and find which value of D provides a curve on the tracing paper which fits on the curve of our data. By placing the curves so as to fit, we obtain the values of C/B and of A. This enables us to plot the income-curve

$$y = A/(\cosh (Bx - C) - D).$$

This sounds long-winded, but the fitting consists of 5 easy processes:

i forming the cumulative table,

ii plotting a few points of this on logarithmic paper in order to estimate the slope B, of the asymptote,

iii plotting the whole cumulative curve on logarithmic paper but now taking B as unit of x,

iv fitting the tracing paper to the given curve and reading off A, C and D,

v plotting the income-curve.

3. I prefer any of these seven methods to that of fitting by moments.

Appendix 2: Equilibrium under given forces of change

Let us suppose that there are K income-power classes numbered from 1 up to K. Initially, let there be x income-receivers, of which $x_0(1)$, $x_0(2)$, ..., $x_0(K)$ reside in the income-power classes 1, 2, ..., K. Then

$$x = \sum_{r=1}^{K} x_0(r). \tag{1}$$

Now suppose that, for all r, s in the range 1, 2, ..., K, a proportion $p(r, s)$ of the income-receivers in the class r are transferred into the class s during the year. Let us assume that every $p(r, s)$ is positive, and that for each r

$$\sum_{s=1}^{K} p(r,s) = 1 \tag{2}$$

so that no income-receivers die and no new ones occur. Then after one year there will be $x_1(1), x_1(2), ..., x_1(K)$ income-receivers in the various classes, where

$$x_1(s) = \sum_{r=1}^{K} p(r,s)\, x_0(r) \quad (r = 1, 2, ..., K, \ s = 1, 2, ..., K).$$

Now suppose that during the second year the same forces of change act again, so that a proportion $p(r, s)$ of the income-receivers in the class r are transferred to the class s. Then after the two years there will be $x_2(1), x_2(2), ..., x_2(K)$ people in the classes, 1, 2, ..., K, where

$$x_2(s) = \sum_{r=1}^{K} p(r,s)\, x_1(r) \quad (r = 1, 2, ..., K, \ s = 1, 2, ..., K).$$

Similarly, if the same forces act again and again in the same manner once every year, we know that, if after t years there are $x_t(1), x_t(2), ..., x_t(K)$ income-receivers in the classes $1, 2, ..., K$, then

$$x_t(s) = \sum_{r=1}^{K} p(r,s)\, x_{t-1}(r) \quad (r = 1, 2, ..., K, \ s = 1, 2, ..., K).$$

If we let X_t denote the set $x_t(1) \ldots x_t(K)$, and if we let P denote the operator $\sum\limits_{r=1}^{K} p(r,s)$, then we may abbreviate this equation to

$$X_t = PX_{t-1}. \tag{3}$$

If we now denote by $P^2, P^3, \ldots, P^m, \ldots$ the operations $P.P, P.P.P, \ldots, P$ m times, $\ldots$ consisting of the operation P repeated 2, 3, $\ldots, m, \ldots$ times, in the usual notation adopted with operators, we obtain by repeated application of equation (3)

$$X_t = P^t X_0 \quad \text{and} \quad X_{m+t} = P^t X_m. \tag{4}$$

The operator P^t can be expanded to the form

$$P^t \equiv \sum_{r=1}^{K} p^t(r,s), \tag{5}$$

where $p^t(t,s)$ is not negative for any pair (r,s).

Now let us make the assumption that for every pair (r,s) of values in the range 1, 2, $\ldots, K$ whose difference does not exceed unity, $p(r,s)$ is positive and not zero. This assumption means that each year in each income-power class, some proportion at least remain in that income-power class and some proportion move into each of the adjacent classes.

It follows from our assumption that for every pair of values r, s in the range, 1, 2, $\ldots, K$, whose difference does not exceed 2, $p^2(r,s)$ is positive and not zero. Similarly it follows that for every pair (r,s) in the range whose difference does not exceed t, $p^t(r,s)$ is positive and not zero. In particular it follows that every $p^K(r,s)$ is positive and not zero: hence we can find a small number e such that for every pair r, s,

$$p^K(r,s) > e > 0. \tag{6}$$

We may now prove that on the basis of our assumptions, every $x_t(s) \to x(s)$, a definite limit, as $t \to$ infinity. We may take as our data the properties which we have already assumed or proved, and we shall prove our theorem by first proving a set of lemmas.

Appendix 2

$x_0(1), x_0(2), ..., x_0(K)$ are an arbitrary set of positive numbers denoted collectively by X_0,

$$\sum_{r=1}^{K} x_0(r) = x. \tag{1}$$

$\{p(r, s)\}$, $r = 1, 2, ..., K$, $s = 1, 2, ..., K$, is a matrix and no $p(r, s)$ in it is negative.

For every r,

$$\sum_{s=1}^{K} p(r, s) = 1. \tag{2}$$

$x_t(1), x_t(2), ..., x_t(K)$, $t = 1, 2, 3, ...$, are sets denoted by X_t and defined from X_0 by the equations

$$X_t = PX_{t-1}, \tag{3}$$

where P denotes the operator $\sum_{r=1}^{K} p(r, s)$. P^t denotes the operator 'P repeated t times' so that, by (3),

$$X_t = P^t X_0 \quad \text{and} \quad X_{m+t} = P^t X_m. \tag{4}$$

P^t can be expanded in the form

$$P^t \equiv \sum_{r=1}^{K} p^t(r, s), \tag{5}$$

$$p^K(r, s) > e > 0 \quad \text{for all } (r, s) \text{ in the range.} \tag{6}$$

THEOREM I

$\lim_{t \to \infty} X_t$ exists.

Outline of Proof

We shall prove the theorem by establishing in turn the following lemmas:

Lemma 1

Where $y_m(1), y_m(2), ..., y_m(K)$ are a set, Y_m, of positive and negative numbers whose sum is zero, and where $:Y_m:$ denotes the sum $\sum\limits_{r=1}^{K} |y_m(r)|$,

$$:Y_{m+1}: \leqslant :Y_m: \quad \text{if} \quad Y_{m+1} \equiv PY_m.$$

Lemma 2

If $Y_{m+K} = P^K Y_m$, there exists a $d > 0$, such that

$$:Y_{m+K}: \leqslant (\mathrm{I} - d):Y_m:.$$

Lemma 3

If $Y_{m+t} = P^t Y_m$,

$$:Y_t: \to \mathrm{o} \quad \text{as} \quad t \to \infty \quad \text{and}$$

Lemma 4

$$\operatorname*{Lim}_{T \to \infty} \sum_{t=0}^{T} Y_{m+t} \text{ exists.}$$

Proof of Lemma 1

$$:Y_{m+1}: = \sum_{s=1}^{K} |y_{m+1}(s)| \leqslant \sum_{s=1}^{K} \sum_{r=1}^{K} p(r,s) |y_m(r)|$$

$$= \sum_{r=1}^{K} \sum_{s=1}^{K} p(r,s) |y_m(r)|.$$

Hence, by datum (2)

$$:Y_{m+1}: \leqslant \sum_{r=1}^{K} |y_m(r)| = :Y_m:$$

which establishes the lemma.

Proof of Lemma 2

$$:Y_{m+K}: = \sum_{s=1}^{K} |y_{m+K}(s)| = \sum_{s=1}^{K} \left| \sum_{r=1}^{K} p^K(r,s) y_m(r) \right|$$

$$= \sum_{s=1}^{K} \left| \sum_{r=1}^{K} \{p^K(r,s) - e\} y_m(r) \right| \leqslant \sum_{s=1}^{K} \sum_{r=1}^{K} \{p^K(r,s) - e\}$$

$$\times |y_m(r)| \quad \text{by datum (6)}$$

$$= \sum_{r=1}^{K} \sum_{s=1}^{K} \{p^K(r,s) - e\} |y_m(r)| = (\mathrm{I} - Ke) \sum_{r=1}^{K} |y_m(r)|$$

$$\text{by datum (2).}$$

Hence $:Y_{m+K}: \leqslant (\mathrm{I} - Ke):Y_m:$ which establishes Lemma 2.

Proof of Lemma 3

From Lemmas 1 and 2 it follows that

$$:Y_{m+t}: \leqslant (1 - Ke)^{\frac{t}{k}-1}:Y_m:$$

and since Ke is positive and less than unity, this proves Lemma 3.

Proof of Lemma 4

The series $\sum\limits_{t=0}^{\infty} (1 - Ke)^{\frac{t}{k}-1}$ is a convergent g.p. Hence, since

$$:Y_{m+t}: \leqslant (1 - Ke)^{\frac{t}{k}-1}$$

$$\sum_{t=0}^{\infty} :Y_{m+t}: \quad \text{is convergent;}$$

hence each series

$$\sum_{t=0}^{\infty} y_{m+t}(r) \quad \text{is convergent.}$$

Hence $\lim\limits_{T\to\infty} \sum\limits_{t=0}^{T} Y_{m+t}$ exists, and the lemma is established.

Proof of the Theorem

With the aid of Lemma 4 we may now prove the theorem that $\mathop{\mathrm{Lim}}\limits_{T\to\infty} X_T$ exists.

In the notation of page 218, let Z_0 be the set

$$z_0(1), z_0(2), ..., z_0(K),$$

where for each r $(r = 1, 2, ..., K)$

$$z_0(r) = x_1(r) - x_0(r)$$

and let Z_t be the set $P^t Z_0$ so that for each t,

$$Z_t \equiv X_{t+1} - X_t.$$

Then,

$$\sum_{r=1}^{K} z_0(r) = 0,$$

so that we may apply Lemma 4 to prove that

$$\text{Lim} \sum_{t=0}^{T} Z_t \quad \text{exists;}$$

hence

$$\text{Lim} \sum_{t=0}^{T-1} (X_{t+1} - X_t) \quad \text{exists}$$

and hence

$$\text{Lim}_{T \to \infty} X_T \quad \text{exists.}$$

This completes the proof of Theorem 1.

The interpretation of Theorem 1 is that under constant forces of change, where no income-receiver dies and no new income-receiver arrives, if for each income-power class in each year some proportion remain in it and some pass into each of the two adjacent classes then if the number of classes is finite, the distribution will tend to a 'limiting' distribution under the action of the constant forces: it will then be in equilibrium.

Adopting the same notation as before, and denoting

$$\lim_{T \to \infty} X_T \quad \text{by} \quad X,$$

we may proceed to prove a second theorem.

THEOREM 2

Given P and x, X is independent of X_0.

Proof

If Theorem 2 is not true we must be able to choose two sets X_0 and X_0' such that

$$\sum_{r=1}^{K} x_0(r) = x = \sum_{r=1}^{K} x_0'(r)$$

but

$$\text{Lim}_{T \to \infty} P^T X_0 \neq \text{Lim}_{T \to \infty} P^T X_0'.$$

Now let Z_0 be the set $X_0' - X_0$ and let Z_T be the set $P^T Z_0$, which must equal $P^T X_0' - P^T X_0$. Then we must have

$$\sum_{r=1}^{K} Z_0(r) = 0 \quad \text{and yet} \quad \text{Lim}_{T \to \infty} Z_T \neq 0.$$

This contradicts Lemma 3 to Theorem 1, which we would believe true: hence the supposition that Theorem 2 is not true leads us to the conclusion that Lemma 3 to Theorem 1 is not true, although we have proved it true. It follows that Theorem 2 is true. This completes the proof.

Theorem 2 establishes the fact that any two initial distributions amongst communities of x people each, will, under the action of constant forces of change, tend to the same equilibrium distribution, provided that in every year in each income-power class some people maintain income-power unchanged, some gain a little and some lose a little.

We may now go on to consider what will happen when population is changing. We may first of all consider the case where the forces of change acting on any income-power class remain the same, but it is no longer true that each man has exactly one heir when he dies. The data remain the same as those for Theorem 1, except that now we are no longer given

that for each r, $\sum\limits_{s=1}^{K} p'(r,s) = 1$. We shall prove that under

these circumstances the distribution will settle down to quasi-equilibrium, where the only change is a constant geometric rate of growth of population, the same for each income-power class.

We set out the data formally below.

DATA

$x_0'(1), x_0'(2), ..., x_0'(K)$ are an arbitrary set of positive numbers denoted collectively by X_0'.

$$\sum_{r=1}^{K} x_0'(r) = x'. \tag{1}$$

$\{p'(r,s)\}$ $(r = 1, 2, ..., K, s = 1, 2, ..., K)$, is a matrix and no $p'(r,s)$ is negative.

$x_t'(1), x_t'(2), ..., x_t'(K)$ $(t = 1, 2, 3, ...)$ are sets denoted by X_t' and defined from X_0' by the equations

$$X_t' = P'X_{t-1}' \tag{2}$$

where P' denotes the operator $\sum\limits_{r=1}^{K} p'(r,s)$.

P'^t denotes the operator 'P' repeated t times' so that by (2)

$$X'_t = P'^t X'_0 \quad \text{and} \quad X'_{t+g} = P'^t X'_g \tag{3}$$

P'^t can be expanded in the form

$$P'^t \equiv \sum_{r=1}^{K} p'^t(r,s), \tag{4}$$

$$p'(r,s) > 0 \quad \text{for any pair, } r, s, \text{ such that } |r-s| < 2 \tag{5}$$

and hence

$$p'^K(r,s) > e > 0 \quad \text{for some } e \text{ and all } (r,s) \text{ in the range.} \tag{6}$$

THEOREM 3

For some real positive m, there exists $\lim\limits_{T\to\infty} m^{-T} X'_T$ (not $\equiv 0$) depending on x' and P' but not on X'_0.

Proof

Let $m_1, m_2, ..., m_K$ and m be $(K+1)$ numbers satisfying the $\overline{K+1}$ equations

$$\sum_{s=1}^{K} m_s p'(r,s) = m.m_r \quad \text{for each } r \quad (r = 1, 2, ..., K), \tag{1}$$

$$\sum_{s=1}^{K} m_s = K. \tag{2}$$

Let

$$p(r,s) = \frac{m_s}{m.m_r} p'(r,s) \quad \text{for each } (r,s)$$

and let

$$x_t(r) = \frac{m_r x'_t(r)}{m^t} \quad \text{for each } r \text{ and each } t.$$

Let P denote the operator $\sum\limits_{r=1}^{K} p(r,s)$ and let X_t denote each set $x_t(1), x_t(2), ..., x_t(K)$. Then we know that for each t

$$X'_t = P' X'_{t-1},$$

$$\therefore \quad \frac{m^t}{m_s} x_t(s) = \sum_{r=1}^{K} p'(r,s) \frac{m^{t-1}}{m_r} x_t(r).$$

$$\therefore \quad (m/m_s) x_t(s) = \sum_{r=1}^{K} (m/m_s) x_{t-1}(r) p(r,s).$$

$$\therefore \quad x_t(s) = \sum_{r=1}^{K} p(r,s) x_{t-1}(r).$$

$$\therefore \quad X_t = PX_{t-1}.$$

Moreover,

$$\sum_{s=1}^{K} p(r,s) = \sum_{s=1}^{K} (m_s/m.m_r) p'(r,s) = 1$$

for each r, by equation (1).

$\therefore$ by Theorem 1, $\lim\limits_{T \to \infty} X_T$ exists.

$\therefore$ $\lim\limits_{T \to \infty} x_T(r)$ exists and is not identical with 0.

$\therefore$ $\lim\limits_{T \to \infty} (m_r x'_T(r)/m^T)$ exists and is not identical with 0.

$\therefore$ $\lim\limits_{T \to \infty} (x'_T(r)/m^T)$ exists and is not identical with 0.

$\therefore$ $\lim\limits_{T \to \infty} (X'_T/m^T)$ exists and is not identical with 0.

Since $x'_T(r)$ is real and not negative for all T and for each r, it follows that m is real and positive. This completes the proof of Theorem 3.

We may now consider the case where income-power per head is steadily increasing.

DATA

$\{p''_0(r,s)\}$ is a matrix of which no element $p''_0(r,s)$ is negative, and in which

$$p''_0(r,s) > 0 \quad \text{when} \quad |r-s| < 2 \quad (r \text{ and } s = 1, 2, ..., K).$$

P''_T denotes the operator

$$\sum_{r=bT+1}^{bT+k} p''_0(r-bT, s-bT),$$

where b is a positive integer.

X_T'' denotes the set

$$x_T''(bT+1), \quad x_T''(bT+2), \quad ..., \quad x_T''(bT+K),$$

where

$$x_{T+1}''(s) = \sum_{r=bT+1}^{bT+K} p_0''(r-bT, s-bT+1)\, x_T''(r),$$

so that $X_{T+1}'' = P_T'' X_T''$ for each value of T.

If X_T' denotes the set

$$x_T'(1), \quad x_T'(2), \quad ..., \quad x_T'(K),$$

where $x_T'(r) = x_T''(r+bT)$ for each r and T, then

THEOREM 4

For some real positive m, there exists a unique $\underset{T\to\infty}{\text{Lim}}\ (m^{-T}X_T')$ (not all zero) depending only on $x_0'' = \sum_{r=1}^{K} x_0''(r)$, and on P_0'' but not otherwise on X_0''.

Proof of Theorem 4

It follows from the data that for all T, $P_0'' X_{T-1}' = X_T'$: hence Theorem 4 follows at once from Theorem 3.

Theorem 4 establishes the fact that if population and income per head are increasing, but the forces of change remain the same, apart from moving up the income scale in step with the increase in income per head, then the income-distribution must settle down to a unique quasi-static equilibrium distribution, independent of the initial income-distribution.

We shall now prove a fifth theorem relating to altering forces of change. We shall now have to assume again that population is constant and that each income-receiver has only one heir. Under these conditions we shall prove that any two initial distributions among the same numbers of income-receivers must eventually become (asymptotically) the same distribution, and that this is a limiting distribution.

Appendix 2

DATA

$x_0(1), x_0(2), ..., x_0(K)$ are an arbitrary set of positive numbers denoted collectively by X_0

$$\sum_{r=1}^{K} x_0(r) = x, \tag{1}$$

$p_t(r, s)$ $(r = 1, 2, ..., K, \quad s = 1, 2, ..., K, \quad t = 1, 2, 3, ...)$ are matrices and no $p_t(r, s)$ is negative. For every r and t

$$\sum_{s=1}^{K} p_t(r, s) = 1. \tag{2}$$

$x_t(1), x_t(2), ..., x_t(K)$ $(t = 1, 2, ...)$ are sets denoted by X_t and defined from X_0 by the equations

$$X_t = P_{t-1} X_{t-1}, \tag{3}$$

where P_{t-1} denotes the operator $\sum\limits_{r=1}^{K} p_{t-1}(r, s)$ and $P_T^{T'}$ denotes the operator

$$P_{T'}, P_{T'-1}, P_{T'-2}, ..., P_{T+1}, P_T$$

so that by (3)

$$X_t = P_0^{t-1} X_0 \quad \text{and} \quad X_{m+t} = P_m^{m+t-1} X_m. \tag{4}$$

P_m^t can be expanded in the form

$$P_m^t = \sum_{r=1}^{K} p_m^t(r, s), \tag{5}$$

$$p_t(r, s) > 0 \quad \text{for} \quad |r - s| \leqslant 1, \tag{6}$$

hence $p_t^{t+K-1}(r-s) > e > 0$ for all r, s and all t less than some very large G, and we can go on to prove, exactly as in Theorem 2, that

THEOREM 5

Given two different X_0, namely X_0' and X_0'', then

$$\lim_{t \to \infty} (X_t' - X_t'') = 0.$$

Theorem 5 establishes the fact that even when the forces of change are altering, yet two initial different distributions must become more and more alike. This is only true necessarily if fertility in all income-groups is the same. Theorem 5 only establishes its truth when population is not changing, and when income-per-head is not indefinitely increasing. It is however easy to see that we can extend the theorem in the same way to the cases where income-per-head increases indefinitely, and population changes uniformly at all income-levels, in the same way as before.

It should be noticed, however, that we cannot extend the theorem to the case where fertility in different income-groups is different. This is because in that case we cannot show that two initial distributions could not become *less* and *less* like each other, because a malevolent providence (or some other influence) chose to breed children in just those income-ranges where the difference between the two populations was already the most different.

The author does not consider that this limitation is of any serious significance to the general result that there is usually a unique equilibrium distribution in the dynamic, as well as in the static and quasi-static fields.

Appendix 3: The condition for equilibrium under constant or steady forces of change

1. In the later chapters of the book, we have made frequent use of the formula

$$b = \frac{2I_1}{I_2}$$

to give us the approximate slope of the income-ratio-curve in equilibrium. I_1 was defined as the average proportional increase of income during one year for people in a given income-class at the beginning of the year, and I_2 was defined as the variance (the mean square deviation from the mean) of this proportional change for these people. I_1 and I_2 were measured in thousandths, but this did not affect the ratio $2I_1/I_2$, and for the purposes of this appendix we shall measure I_1 and I_2 in ordinary units and not in thousandths. The formula for b gave us the approximate slope of the income-ratio-curve for each income-level, and the slopes at different income-levels might be different.

2. We did however suggest one assumption that we must make, if our formula was not to give false results: namely, that for neighbouring income-classes, I_1 and I_2 and certain other parameters J_3, J_4, ..., describing the action of economic influences on incomes, must be roughly similar for neighbouring income-levels; we also suggested that if the causes of change could be divided up into only a few independent groups, and the distribution of effects due to one of these groups was highly abnormal, then the value given for b by our formula might be seriously wrong, especially if that value did not lie between nought and one.

3. In this appendix, we shall further explain the meaning of these assumptions and the reasons for them; we shall also establish the approximate truth of the formula in question which gives the value of b the slope of the income-ratio-curve in equilibrium. This will be a *mathematical* appendix.

The distribution of income between persons

4. The parameters $I_1, I_2, J_3, J_4, \ldots$ were chosen as the most convenient measures of the properties of the frequency distribution $p(x, y)$, giving the distribution after one year among income-classes e^{x+y} of *people* whose incomes at the beginning of the year were e^x. This section will be devoted to an elucidation of this point.

Let $p(x, y)\,dy$ be the proportion of those people who at the beginning of any year had income e^x,* who after one year had income lying between e^{x+y} and e^{x+y+dy}, dy being very small, i.e. whose incomes had increased in proportions between e^y and e^{y+dy}. Then, assuming immortality of income receivers we know that for all x, $\int_{-\infty}^{\infty} p(x, y)\,dy = 1$. Following the usual practice of statisticians, we may now define the semi-invariants $J_1, J_2, J_3, \ldots$ of the distribution $p(x,y)$, for any given x, by the equation (A)

$$F(k) = \ln \int_{-\infty}^{\infty} p(x, y)\,e^{ky}\,dy = J_1 k + (J_2 k^2/2!) + (J_3 k^3/3!) + \ldots$$

so that each J_r $(r = 1, 2, 3, \ldots)$ will be a function of x alone. Then, for any given x, the parameters $J_1, J_2, J_3, \ldots$ are known to describe completely the function $p(x, y)$. Hence, our condition of constancy of forces of change ($I_1, I_2, J_3, \ldots$ remaining constant) will imply that $p(x, y)$ remains constant if it implies that J_1 and J_2 remain constant.

5. Let us now express our parameters I_1 and I_2 in terms of the J_r's. Since I_1 is the average proportional increase of income, we have at once $1 + I_1 = \int_{-\infty}^{\infty} p(x, y)\,e^y\,dy$; hence,

$$\ln(1 + I_1) = F(1). \tag{1}$$

Similarly, I_2 is given by

$$(1 + I_1)^2 + I_2 = \int_{-\infty}^{\infty} p(x, y)\,e^{2y}\,dy,$$

so that

$$\ln\{(1 + I_1)^2 + I_2\} = F(2). \tag{2}$$

* The discussion here is in terms of powers of e and of logarithms to the base e instead of powers of 10 and logarithms to the base 10: this introduces no significant modification [1972].

Hence, if we know $I_1, I_2, J_3, J_4, \ldots$, equations (1) and (2) reduce to the form

$$A = J_1 + \tfrac{1}{2}J_2 + B, \quad C = 2J_1 + 2J_2 + D$$

where A, B, C, D are all known. Hence, if $I_1, I_2, J_3, J_4, \ldots$ all remain constant, then also J_1 and J_2 must remain constant. It follows that when our condition that $I_1, I_2, J_3, J_4, \ldots$ should remain constant is satisfied, then *every* J_r and hence also every $p(x, y)$ for all x, y must be constant also through time.

6. Let us now consider the conditions for equilibrium of the income-distribution, when the forces of change $I_1, I_2, J_3, \ldots$ and hence the functions $p(x, y)$ remain constant.

Suppose that at the beginning of the year the number of people with income between e^x and e^{x+dx}, dx being small, is given by $e^{f(x)}dx$. Then the condition for equilibrium is that $f(x)$ should remain constant for all x. Remembering the definition of the functions $p(x, y)$, we may express this condition for equilibrium in the form

$$e^{f(x)} = \int_{-\infty}^{\infty} p(x-y, y)\, e^{f(x-y)}\, dy$$

or

$$1 = \int_{-\infty}^{\infty} p(x-y, y)\, e^{f(x-y)-f(x)}\, dy.$$

7. In order to reduce this condition to the required form, we should have to assume three distinct things, none of which is strictly true:

i That we could neglect $J_3, J_4, \ldots$.

ii That we could neglect the differences between $p(x, y)$ and $p(x-y, y)$.

iii That we could neglect $f''(x)$ and higher derivatives.

8. J_3 and J_4, etc. will only be zero if each $p(x, y)$ is a normal distribution in y, and there is no reason to expect that this will be the case, unless changes are due to a large number of groups

of causes each of which is independent of the others for its proportional effects upon incomes. If the number of groups is fairly large, then we may expect J_3, J_4 ... to be small. The reasons for this are common knowledge.

9. This assumption is reasonable, because we may assume that where x and z differ by little, the forces acting to change incomes of e^x and e^z will be similar, and hence $p(x, y)$ and $p(z, y)$ will be roughly the same. Where y is small then $p(x, y)$ and $p(x - y, y)$ will differ by little. On the other hand, where y is not small, both $p(x, y)$ and $p(x - y, y)$ will be small, and hence again they will be roughly the same.

10. The assumption that $f''(x, y)$ etc. can be neglected amounts to the assumption that the people-ratio-curve is fairly straight: this is usually found to be the case for high incomes but not for low incomes.

11. In order to prove the formula, we will make all three assumptions, and then we will remove them one by one and see the adjustments that are thereby introduced into the formula.

Our equilibrium condition was

$$\int_{-\infty}^{\infty} p(x - y, y)\, e^{f(x - y) - f(x)}\, dy = 1.$$

Neglecting $f''(x)$ and the difference between $p(x - y, y)$ and $p(x, y)$ we may write this

$$\int_{-\infty}^{\infty} p(x, y)\, e^{-yf'(x)}\, dy = 1$$

so that by definition of $F(k)$ (equation A, p. 230)

$$F(-f'(x)) = 0;$$

writing a for $f'(x)$, we discover,

$$J_1 a - \tfrac{1}{2}J_2 a^2 + \tfrac{1}{3}J_3 a^3 \ldots = 0$$

as our equilibrium condition.

Appendix 3

For reasons explained in the footnote,* $a = 0$ is not a satisfactory solution except when $J_1 = 0$: hence our condition becomes $a = 2J_1/J_2$ if we neglect J_3, J_4, etc.

By equation (1) and (2), if we neglect $J_3, J_4, \ldots$,

$$\ln (1 + I_1) = J_1 + \tfrac{1}{2} J_2,$$
$$\ln \{(1 + I_1)^2 + I_2\} = 2J_1 + 2J_2,$$

and we have just shown that $a = 2J_1/J_2$. Hence,

$$a + 1 = (2J_1 + J_2)/J_2 = 2 \ln (1 + I_1) \Big/ \ln \left\{1 + \frac{I_2}{(1 + I_1)^2}\right\}:$$

hence, neglecting I_1^2 and I_2^2,

$$a + 1 = 2I_1/I_2$$

is the equilibrium condition.

Now, b, the slope of the income-ratio-curve, is

$$\frac{d}{dx} \ln (e^x e^{f(x)})$$

and this is equal to $1 + df/dx$, namely to $(1 + a)$; hence the equilibrium condition may be written $b = 2I_1/I_2$.

12. Now let us relax our simplifying assumptions. First, take into account the fact that J_3, J_4, etc., need not be zero. Then we may still prove as before that in equilibrium $F(-a) = 0$, and in general

$$F(1) = \ln (1 + I_1) \text{ and } F_2(2) = \ln \{(1 + I_1)^2 + I_2\}.$$

If we draw the graph of $y = F(x)$, we know the points corresponding to $x = 0$, 1, and 2; they are $(0, 0)$, $(1, \ln (1 + I_1))$, $(2, \ln \{(1 + I_1)^2 + I_2\})$, or, in the notation of Chapter 12, §12;

---

* We may also write the condition that the number of people with income *greater* than x remains the same

$$\int_{-\infty}^{\infty} e^{f(x-y)} \int_{y}^{\infty} p(x, z) \, dz \, dy = \int_{x}^{\infty} e^{f(u)} \, du$$

or

$$\int_{-\infty}^{\infty} p(x, y) \int_{0}^{y} e^{f(x-z)-f(x)} \, dz \, dy = 0$$

which can*not* be satisfied by $f'(x) = 0$, since $\int_{-\infty}^{\infty} p(x, y) \int_{0}^{y} e^0 \, dz \, dy \neq 1$.

The distribution of income between persons

$(0, 0)$, $(1, \ln H_1 - \ln I)$, $(2, \ln H_2 - 2 \ln I)$; where H_r is the average of the r'th power of income, one year later, and I is what it had been. By assuming J_3, J_4, etc. to be zero, we assumed this curve to be a parabola, and hence that the curve of $y = F(x)/x$ was a straight line.

When we drop this last assumption, we must plot more points $\left(r, \dfrac{1}{r} \ln H_r \right)$ as well as those for $r = 1$ and 2, in order to get a good estimate of the root in x (other than zero) of $F(x) = 0$, by finding the intercept with $y = \ln I$ of the curve through the points $\left(r, \dfrac{1}{r} \ln H_r \right)$.

Let X be this root, then we know that $a = -X$ and hence that $b = 1 - X$.* The error introduced by assuming J_3 etc. to be zero, so that the curve of $y = F(x)/x$ was assumed linear, will obviously be small when the root X lies between the two known points of the curve; this will be the case when X lies between 1 and 2, and b lies between 0 and -1; fortunately, this is usually found to be the case of distribution among well-to-do and rich people. (Since the Second World War, b has for many countries lain between -1 and -2.)

13. Now let us restore our assumption that we neglect J_3, etc. but no longer assume that d^2f/dx^2 is very small. What effect will this have on our estimate of a? Writing f' and f'' for df/dx and d^2f/dx^2, the taking account of f'' makes our equilibrium condition become:

$$\int_{-\infty}^{\infty} e^{-yf' + \frac{1}{2}y^2 f''} p(x, y) \, dy = 1$$

if we still neglect any difference between $p(x-y, y)$ and $p(x, y)$.

Writing m'_r for $\displaystyle\int_{-\infty}^{\infty} y^r p(x, y) \, dy$, the condition becomes

$$\ln \left(1 - f'm'_1 + \tfrac{1}{2}(f'^2 + f'') m'_2 - \tfrac{1}{6}(f'^3 + 3f'f'') m'_3, \dots \right) = 0.$$

---

* It should be pointed out here that this leads to the result asserted in Chapter 12 §12: for the curve through the points

$\left(r - 1, \dfrac{1}{r} \ln H_r \right)$ will contain the point $(X - 1, 0)$ where $X - 1 = -b$.

234

Hence

$$\ln\left(1 - f'm_1' + \tfrac{1}{2}f'^2m_2' - \tfrac{1}{6}f'^3m_3', \ldots\right) = \ln\left(1 - \tfrac{1}{2}f''m' + \tfrac{1}{2}f'f''m_3' \ldots\right)$$

and neglecting $f'f''m_3'$ and higher order terms,

$$\ln\left(1 - f'm_1' + \tfrac{1}{2}f'^2m_2' - \tfrac{1}{6}f'^3m_3', \ldots\right) = -\tfrac{1}{2}f''m_2'.$$

Hence, in place of the equation $J_1 a - \tfrac{1}{2}J_2 a^2 = 0$, we now have the equation

$$J_1 a - \tfrac{1}{2}J_2 a^2 = (J_2 + J_1^2)f'' \quad \text{(since } m_2' = J_2 + J_1^2\text{)}.$$

Hence, if f'' is fairly small its effect is to change a from $2J_1/J_2$ to $(2J_1/J_2) - (2f''/a)$ neglecting J_1^2.

We have seen above that $1 + (2J_1/J_2) = 2I_1/I_2$ and that $b = 1 + a$, hence the effect of taking account of f'' is to change b from $2I_1/I_2$ to $(2I_1/I_2) - 2f''/(b-1)$.

Hence when the curve is concave ($f'' < 0$), the slope a of the people-ratio-curve will be thereby steepened a little over what was indicated by the formula $a + 1 = b = (2I_1/I_2)$.

14. Now let us consider the effect on a and b, the slopes of the people-ratio-curve and the income-ratio-curve, when we take account of the possible difference between $p(x-y, y)$ and $p(x, y)$. Suppose for instance that J_1 and J_2, the first two semi-variants of $p(x, y)$, vary with x. Denoting by $J_1(x+z)$ the value of J_1 at income level e^{x+z}, and denoting $J_1(x)$ by J_1, suppose that $J_1(x+z) = J + qzJ_1$ and in similar notation suppose that $J_2(x+z) = J_2 + rzJ_2$, q and r being so small that we may neglect $O(q^2)$ and $O(r^2)$.

Consider the situation when $p(x+z, y+tz) = p(x, y)$; then evidently

$$J_1(x+z) = J_1 + tz \quad \text{and} \quad J_2(x+z) = J_2,$$

so that

$$q = t/J_1 \quad \text{and} \quad r = 0.$$

The equilibrium condition then becomes

$$\int_{-\infty}^{\infty} e^{-(1+t)f'(x)y}\, p(x, y)\, dy = 1 - t,$$

that is, neglecting terms in t^2,

$$\ln\int_{-\infty}^{\infty} e^{-(1+t)f'(x)y}\, p(x, y)\, dy = -t;$$

hence

$$f'(x) = -2(1-t) J_1/J_2 + (J_2/2J_1) t \quad \text{approximately.}$$

We see that the effect of variation of this type in J_1 only is to alter a from a to $a - t(a + 1/a)$ or since $q = t/J_1$, from a to $a - qJ_1(a + 1/a)$.

Similarly by considering the situation where

$$p(x+z, y+syz) \, d(y+syz) = p(x, y) \, dy$$

in which evidently

$$J_1(x+z) = (1+sz) J_1, \quad J_2(x+z) = (1+2sz) J_2$$

so that

$$q = s; \quad r = 2s,$$

we can show that a is changed from a to $a + s$.

Hence if in general we have any two values for q and r, and these are to change a from a to

$$a - qQ - rR$$

we can find Q and R from our two special cases, which tell us that

$$Q = J_1\left(a + \frac{1}{a}\right), \quad Q + 2R = -1,$$

hence

$$R = -\tfrac{1}{2} - \tfrac{1}{2}J_1\left(a + \frac{1}{a}\right).$$

15. We have thus seen that our formulae for the slopes of the ratio curves become inexact when we take into account the abnormalities of the functions $p(x, y)$, the curvature of the curves themselves and the gradual change of the economic influences at work as we pass along the income scale. But we have seen that the error will be small provided that these disturbances are small.

When we come to consider the effect of the introduction of new causes, these errors partly cancel out, because we are interested in the differences between the distributions before and after the change, and the errors before and after the change may be expected to be roughly the same.

Appendix 4: Motion towards equilibrium

1. Let $e^{f(x)}\,dx$ be the actual number and $e^{g(x)}\,dx$ be the equilibrium number of people with incomes lying between e^x and e^{x+dx}, and let $w(x) = f(x) - g(x)$. Then $y = f(x)$ and $y = g(x)$ are the people-ratio-curves in practice and under the conditions for equilibrium. $y = w(x)$ will be a curve showing the difference between the actual people-ratio-curve and the equilibrium curve. If there was equilibrium in practice, the curve $y = w(x)$ would lie along the x-axis.

2. When the actual distribution is moving towards equilibrium, the curve $y = w(x)$ will move towards the x-axis, and its motion in that direction will give us the best simple account of the manner in which the actual distribution approaches the equilibrium. Accordingly let us analyse how the function $w(x)$ will change in disequilibrium.

3. Consider the case of constant forces of change, where the function $g(x)$ remains the same. Consider the changes in $f(x)$ and $w(x)$ during one year. Let $p(x, y)\,dy$ be the proportion of people with income e^x whose incomes change in proportion between e^y and e^{y+dy} during one year. Then if during one year $f(x)$ and $w(x)$ become $f(x) + \dot{f}(x)$ and $w(x) + \dot{w}(x)$,

$$\dot{w}(x) = \dot{f}(x)$$

since $g(x)$ remains the same, and

$$e^{\dot{f}(x)} = \int_{-\infty}^{\infty} e^{f(x-y)-f(x)} p(x, y)\,dy$$

where we neglect the difference between $p(x-y, y)$ and $p(x, y)$.

$$1 = \int_{-\infty}^{\infty} e^{g(x-y)-g(x)} p(x, y)\,dy,$$

hence, ignoring terms of order y^3,

$$e^{\dot{f}(x)} - 1 = \int_{-\infty}^{\infty} \left(e^{f'y+\frac{1}{2}f''y^2} - e^{g'y+g''y^2}\right) p(x, y)\,dy.$$

237

Denoting $\displaystyle\int_{-\infty}^{\infty} y^r p(x,y)\,\mathrm{d}y$ by m'_r,

$$e^{f(x)} - 1 = -w'm'_1 + \tfrac{1}{2}w''m'_2 + g'w'm'_2 + \tfrac{1}{2}w'^2 m'_2,$$

where w' and w'' denote the first two derivatives of $w(x)$. Now, $J_1 = m'_1$ and $J_2 = m'_2 - m'^2_1$, so that, ignoring higher powers of f,

$$\dot{f}(x) + \tfrac{1}{2}(\dot{f}(x))^2 = -w'm'_1 + \tfrac{1}{2}w''m'_2 + g'w'm'_2 + \tfrac{1}{2}w'^2 m'_2,$$

$$\dot{f}(x) = -w'J_1 + \tfrac{1}{2}w''(J_2 + J^2_1) + g'w'(J_2 + J^2_1) + \tfrac{1}{2}w'^2(J_2 + J^2_1)$$
$$- (\tfrac{1}{2}(\dot{f}(x))^2,$$

so that, neglecting J^2_1, J^2_2 and $\dot{f}^2$, and w'^2,

$$\dot{f}(x) = \dot{w}(x) = -w'J_1 + \tfrac{1}{2}w''J_2 + g'w'J_2.$$

But $g'(x) = 2J_1/J_2$, hence, finally,

$$\dot{w}(x) = J_1 w'(x) + \tfrac{1}{2}J_2 w''(x).$$

This equation tells us that the motion of the curve $y = w(x)$ will consist at any point of two motions,

i a motion to the left with velocity J_1 per annum,

ii a motion upwards with velocity $\tfrac{1}{2}J_2 w''(x)$ per annum.

Since J_1 is usually positive for poor people and negative for rich people, the first motion will consist of a horizontal stretching outwards of the curve $y = w(x)$; the second motion will evidently flatten out all waves and humps in the curve $y = w(x)$. We see then that the manner in which the curve subsides into a horizontal straight line is by being stretched out sideways and by having all its waves and humps ironed out.

Appendix 5: Numerical examples

1. Many of the results obtained in Appendix 3 can be well illustrated in terms of the computer-simulation example of Chapter 24, §6.

Denoting by $\mathbf{P}$ the transition-matrix summarized in Table 35, the exact long-run-equilibrium distribution of income $\mathbf{y}^*$ must satisfy $\mathbf{y}^* = \mathbf{y}^*\mathbf{P}$ and can be computed as 'the row-eigenvector of $\mathbf{P}$ corresponding to the eigenvalue unity, normalised so that the sum of its elements is 10^7. The vector $\mathbf{y}^*$ in fact contains the elements

$$y_r \quad (r = 0, 1, 2, ..., 39)$$

given by

$y_0 = y_{39} = 2^{-20}10^7$, $y_r = y_{39-r} = 2^{r-21}10^7$ for $(r = 1, 2, ..., 19)$. y_0 denotes the number of persons with income-power less than $1\cdot1$, i.e. with income less than $£10^{1\cdot1} = £12.59\text{p}$; y_r denotes the number of persons with income-power between $1 + (r/10)$ and $1 + (r+1)/10$, i.e. with income between

$$£10^{1+r/10} \quad \text{and} \quad £10^{1+(r+1)/10} \quad \text{for} \quad (r = 1, 2, ..., 38);$$

and y_{39} denotes the number with income over $£10^{4\cdot9}$, i.e. with income over $£79,433$. Denoting $1\cdot05 + (r/10)$ by s, the corresponding people-ratio-curve will have the equation

$$z_s = 7 - (21 - r)\log_{10}2 \quad \text{for} \quad (r = 1, 2, ..., 19)$$

and the equation

$$z_s = 7 - (r - 18)\log_{10}2 \quad \text{for} \quad (r = 20, 21, ..., 38)$$

and the gradient of this equilibrium people-ratio-curve will be

$\Delta z_s/\Delta s = 10\log_{10}2 = 3\cdot0103$ for incomes of less than $£1,000$,

$\Delta z_s/\Delta s = 0$ for incomes of $£1,000$,

$\Delta z_s/\Delta s = -10\log_{10}2 = -3\cdot0103$ for incomes of more than $£1,000$.

239

Denoting by a this gradient of the equilibrium people-ratio-curve, the gradient of the corresponding equilibrium income-ratio-curve is $b = a+1$. Thus for incomes under £1,000, $a = 3.01$ and $b = 4.01$; for incomes over £1,000, $a = -3.01$ and $b = -2.01$, and for incomes of £1,000, $a = 0$ and $b = 1$.

2. Knowing the true values of b, the slope of the equilibrium income-ratio-curve, we can now test the performance of the various approximate formulae for b and for a provided in Chapter 12 of the dissertation and in the Appendices 3 and 4.

For those parts of the income-power range for which the elements $p(i,j)$ of the transition matrix $\mathbf{P}$ are constant for fixed $j-i$, when i varies, the simple approximation $b = 2I_1/I_2$ may be tried, where I_1 and I_2 are the mean and variance of proportionate increase of income and are given by

$$I_1 = \sum_{j=-4}^{4} 10^{j/10} p(i,i+j) - 1,$$

$$I_2 = \sum_{j=-4}^{4} 10^{j/5} p(i,i+j) - (1+I_1)^2;$$

for $i = 4, 5, \ldots, 16$ and $j = i-4, i-3, \ldots, i+4$, we see from Table 35 that

$$10^6 p(i,j) = (9;\ 556;\ 12{,}728;\ 131{,}414;\ 536{,}926;\ 262{,}829;$$
$$50{,}911;\ 4{,}445;\ 146)$$

whereas for $i = 23, 24, \ldots, 35$ and $j = i-4, i-3, \ldots, i+4$,

$$10^6 p(i,j) = (146;\ 4{,}445,\ 50{,}911;\ 262{,}829;\ 536{,}962;\ 131{,}414;$$
$$12{,}728;\ 556;\ 9).$$

Hence, for $i = 4, 5, \ldots, 16$, we obtain from the above equations for I_1 and I_2

$$I_1 = 0.07045, \quad I_2 = 0.04232$$

and by the approximate formula for b,

$$b = 2I_1/I_2 = 3.329,$$

whereas for $i = 23, 24, \ldots, 35$ we similarly obtain

$$I_1 = -0.03311, \quad I_2 = 0.03201 \quad \text{and} \quad b = -2I_1/I_2 = -2.069.$$

Seeing that the true values of b are 4.01 for the lower range of incomes and -2.01 for the higher range of income, the performance of the approximate formula $b = 2I_1/I_2$ is rather poor for the lower range (3.329 differs considerably from 4.01), but quite reasonable for the high range (-2.069 does not greatly differ from -2.01).

3. There are several reasons why the formula $b = 2I_1/I_2$ is inexact. The first reason, that $p(i, i+j)$ may change as i changes, does not apply in the particular set of calculations we have just made, since we chose our values of i to ensure that $p(i, i+j)$ did not so change. However, a second reason is that the equation $b = 2I_1/I_2$ is only a first approximation to the more exact formula $b = (\log I_1')/(\tfrac{1}{2} \log I_2' - \log I_1')$ where I_1' and I_2' are the first two moments.

$$I_1' = \sum_{j=-4}^{4} 10^{j/10} p(i, i+j) = 1 + I_1,$$

$$I_2' = \sum_{j=-4}^{4} 10^{j/5} p(i, i+j) = I_2 + (1 + I_1)^2.$$

Applying this more exact formula, we should obtain for $i = 4, 5, \ldots, 16$, $I_1' = 1.07045$, $I_2' = 1.18814$ whence

$$b = (\log I_1')/(\tfrac{1}{2} \log I_2' - \log I_1') = 3.758$$

and for $i = 2, 24, \ldots, 35$, $I_1' = 0.96689$, $I_2' = 0.96723$, whence

$$b = (\log I_1')/(\tfrac{1}{2} \log I_2' - \log I_1') = -1.969.$$

In the case both of the low-incomes range and of the high-incomes range the error of estimate has been roughly halved, and the estimate $b = -1.979$ for the high-income range is now close to the true value $b = -2.01$.

4. To obtain more accurate estimates of b, one may draw a graph of $y = (\log H_{N+1})/(N+1)$, where H_N is the average of the N'th power of incomes at the end of one year which were of

amount I at the beginning of the year. It was explained in
§12 of Chapter 12 and in Appendix 3 that the point $(-b, \log I)$
will lie almost exactly on this curve.

If we now extend our notation for I_1' and I_2' so that in general
I_r' denotes the r'th moment, given in our example by

$$I_r' = 10^{r/10}p(i, i+j),$$

of the proportion which income, initially at level I, bears to
that level I one year later, then $I_r' = H_r/I^r$, so that

$$(\log H_{N+1})/(N+1) = (\log I_{N+1}')/(N+1) - \log I.$$

It follows that since the point $(-b, \log I)$ lies on the curve
$y = (\log H_{N+1})/(N+1)$ the point $(-b, 0)$ lies on the curve
$y = (\log I_{N+1}')/(N+1)$, so that the value of $-b$ may be found
as the non-zero co-ordinate of the point of intersection of the
curve with the horizontal axis.

Table 42 gives for the two ranges of values of r the values of
$(\log I_n')/n$, for integer values of n near zero.

TABLE 42. *Values of* $(\log I_n'/n)$

| values of r ... ... | 4 to 16 | 23 to 35 |
values of n	\multicolumn{2}{c}{values of log (I_n'/n)}
−3	0·000075	·
−2	0·00724	−0·03743
−1	0·01462	−0·02956
0	0·02200	−0·02200
1	0·02957	−0·01462
2	0·03743	−0·00724
3		−0·000075

Plotting these values we obtain the two curves shown in Chart
37. We find that they cut the horizontal axis at $+3\cdot01$ and
$-3\cdot01$. Remembering that n corresponds to $N+1$ in the formula, we obtain the two values of $-b$ as $-4\cdot01$ and $2\cdot01$.
To the two places of decimals, these estimates are exactly
right.

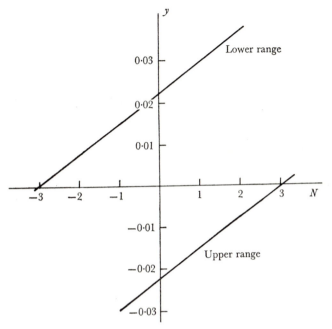

Chart 37   Graphs of $y = (1/n) \log I'_n$

5. In this particular example, where the income-distribution is classified into intervals of equal proportionate extent, it would have been simpler to have used the approximate formula for a, the slope of the people-ratio-curve, namely,

$$a = 2m'_1 (\log_{10} e)/m_2,$$

where m'_1 and m_2 are the arithmetic mean and variance of the shift in income-power from a given initial level, and which in this example are given by

$$m'_1 = (1/10) \sum_{j=-4}^{4} jp(i, i+j) - 1,$$

$$m_2 = (1/100) \sum_{j=-4}^{4} j^2 p(i, i+j) - (1 + m'_1)^2.$$

We should have found for the income-power in the ranges for $r = 4$ to 16

$$m_1' = 0.022000, \quad m_2 = 0.006479, \quad a = 0.86859m_1'/m_2 = 2.95,$$

$$b = a + 1 = 3.95$$

and for income-power in the ranges for $r = 23$ to 35

$$m_1' = -0.022000, \quad m_2 = 0.06479, \quad a = -2.95$$

and $$b = a + 1 = -1.95.$$

The result for the higher income-range is no less accurate than that found from the rough formula $b = 2I_1/I_2 = -2.07$; but for the lower income-range the accuracy of the estimate 3.95 is far higher both than that obtained by the rough formula $b = 2I_1/I_2 = 3.33$ and than that obtained by the improved formula $b = \log I_1'/(\frac{1}{2}\log I_2' - \log I_1') = 3.76$, since the true value is 4.01.

Appendix 6: A model of income distribution[1]

SUMMARY

In the models discussed in this paper the distribution of incomes between an enumerable infinity of income ranges is assumed to develop by means of a stochastic process. In most models the stochastic matrix is assumed to remain constant through time. Under these circumstances, and provided certain other conditions are satisfied, the distribution will tend towards a unique equilibrium distribution dependent upon the stochastic matrix but not on the initial distribution. It is found that under fairly general conditions, provided the prospects of change of income as described by the matrix are in a certain sense independent of income for incomes above some limit, then the Pareto curve of the equilibrium distribution will be asymptotic to a straight line. This result is preserved even when some of the effects of age on income are allowed for, and also when allowance is made for the effect of an occupational stratification of the population. Some consideration is also given to the fact that changes in the income distribution may cause the stochastic matrix itself to change. Some discussion is also given of cases where the Pareto curve of the equilibrium distribution is not asymptotic to a straight line.

I. INTRODUCTION

In a recent article[2] instructions were given for graduating the distribution of personal incomes before tax by means of the distribution function

$$F(t) = \frac{N}{\theta} \tan^{-1} \frac{\sin \theta}{\cos \theta + (t/t_0)^\alpha}, \qquad (1\cdot1)$$

where $F(t)$ is the number of incomes exceeding t, and N, α, t_0

---

[1] Reprinted from the *Economic Journal*, June 1953.

[2] D. G. Champernowne 'The Graduation of Income Distribution', *Econometrica*, October, 1952.

and θ are fitted parameters. For high incomes this formula closely approximates the form

$$F(t) = Ct^{-\alpha} \qquad (1 \cdot 2)$$

with
$$C = \frac{N\pi}{180} t_0^\alpha \sin \theta$$

which is the form predicted by Pareto's law.

It has been frequently claimed that actual distributions do approximate closely to this form for high income levels, and it is the purpose of this note to seek theoretical reasons for this. I am indebted to Mr M. Crum of New College, Oxford, for critical advice and enabling me to correct several inaccuracies. Needless to say, he is in no degree responsible for any misstatements which may remain.

2. THE DEVELOPMENT OF INCOME DISTRIBUTION REGARDED AS A STOCHASTIC PROCESS

The forces determining the distribution of incomes in any community are so varied and complex, and interact and fluctuate so continuously, that any theoretical model must either be unrealistically simplified or hopelessly complicated. We shall choose the former alternative but then give indications that the introduction of some of the more obvious complications of the real world does not seem to disturb the general trend of our conclusions.

The ideas underlying our theoretical model have been briefly indicated in an earlier publication,* but a more complete statement may be conveniently put forward at the present time, since recent developments in the theory of stochastic processes involving infinite matrices have enabled more rigorous and neater formulation to be made than was previously found possible.

We shall suppose that the income scale is divided into an enumerable infinity of income ranges, which, for reasons to be later explained, we shall assume to have uniform proportionate extent. For example, we might consider the ranges of

* 'Notes on Income distribution', *Econometrica*, 1937. Report of Econometric Conference at New College Oxford in 1936.

income per annum to be £50–£100, £100–£200, £200–£400, £400–£800, ... although a finer graduation would be more interesting. We shall regard the development through time of the distribution of incomes between these ranges as being a stochastic process, so that the income of any individual in one year may depend on what it was in the previous year and on a chance process. In reality new income receivers appear every year and old ones pass away, but an obvious and fruitful simplifying assumption to make is that to every 'dying' income receiver there corresponds an heir to his income in the following year, and vice versa. This assumption will imply that the number of incomes is constant through time and that the incomes live on individually, although their recipients are transitory. Not very much difficulty would be involved in allowing more or less than one heir to each dying person, but on the whole the loss of simplicity would be likely to outweigh the advantages due to the gain in verisimilitude.

Under such assumptions any historical development of the distribution of incomes could be summarily described in terms of the following vectors and matrices, $X_r(0)$, telling us the number $X_r(0)$ of the income receivers in each range $R_r, r = 1, 2, ...$ in the initial year Y_0 and a series of matrices $p'_{rs}(t)$ telling us in each year Y_t, the proportions of the occupants of R_r who are shifted to range R_s in the following year Y_{t+1}. With these definitions the income distributions $x_r(t)$ in the successive years will be generated according to

$$X_s(t+1) = \sum_{r=0}^{\infty} X_r(t) \, p'_{rs}(t). \qquad (2\cdot1)$$

If we suppose, as is convenient, that the income ranges are paraded in order of size (there being a lowest income range R_0), then there will be some advantage in defining a new set of matrices

$$p_{ru}(t) = p'_{r,r+u}(t) \qquad (2\cdot2)$$

and rewriting $(2\cdot1)$ in the form

$$X_s(t+1) = \sum_{u=-\infty}^{s} X_{s-u}(t) \, p_{s-u,u}(t) \qquad (2\cdot3)$$

$p_{ru}(t)$ then tells us the proportion in Y_t of the occupants in R_r who shift up by various numbers u of ranges.

The advantage arises from the fact that in the real world the sizes of such shifts from year to year are mostly fairly limited, so that each $p_{ru}(t)$, regarded as a frequency distribution in u, is likely to be centred round $u = 0$.

In order to make simple models, we should like to be able to assume that the $p_{ru}(t)$ regarded as a frequency distribution in u differed very little in form for variations over a wide range of values of r and t.

When we consider the practical counterpart to this suggestion we see that it means that the prospects of shifts upwards and downwards along the ladder of income ranges differ little as between the occupants of different income ranges, and differ little from year to year.

This obviously cannot apply to all income ranges. For example, a rich man's income must be allowed some risk through death or misadventure of being degraded to a lower range in the following year; but the incomes in the lowest range cannot by definition be allowed this possibility. Again the *absolute* changes in income are liable to be much higher for incomes of £1,000,000 than for incomes of £100, so that the ranges must have a greater absolute width for high than for low incomes if our simplification is to have any plausibility. The obvious choice of ranges is that indicated above whereby each range has equal proportionate extent, for then any universal effects, such as prices and interest movements, which are likely to alter income prospects for widely different ranges R_r and R_q in approximately the same manner proportionately, will affect the various functions $p_{ru}(t)$ and $p_{qu}(t)$ in roughly the same fashion.

Our other assumption that the functions $p'_{r,r+u}(t) = p_{ru}(t)$ remain constant as t changes through time, takes us far from reality: but an essential preliminary to the study (not here attempted) of the dynamic equilibrium with moving $p'_{rs}(t)$ is to examine the static equilibrium generated by a fixed set of functions $p'_{rs}(t)$.

For it is known that under very general conditions the repeated application of the same set of income changes represented by an irreducible matrix $p'_{rs}(t)$ will make *any* initial income distribution eventually approach a unique equilibrium distribution which is determined by the matrix $p'_{rs}(t)$ alone. Considerable interest may therefore be found in the question of the type of income distribution which will correspond to the repeated operation of the changes represented by any realistic form of the matrix $p'_{rs}(t)$.

It would be a great advantage in constructing models of income distribution if we had empirical evidence about the matrices $p'_{rs}(t)$ describing actual movements of income in modern communities. Some such evidence could presumably be compiled from the records of the income-tax authorities, but this information has not been tapped for such a purpose. The only figures available to the writer have been kindly supplied by the Institute of Statistics at Oxford and are a by-product of their survey of savings. Unfortunately these figures are regarded as unreliable by the authors of the survey, and they can therefore merely be given in illustration of the discussion which is to follow.

Table I gives a summary of the estimates provided by the

TABLE I

Gross income 1951, £:	0–199	200–399	400–599	600–999	1,000 and over
1952 income as percentage of 1951 income	Proportion of cases per hundred.				
150 and over . .	7·53	2·62	0·99	0·70	0·36
125 to 149. . .	4·65	5·47	1·90	3·87	0·89
115 to 124. . .	4·68	6·50	6·68	5·64	6·57
105 to 114. . .	24·53	20·69	23·36	23·87	20·35
101 to 104. . .	7·67	16·16	18·13	14·40	7·00
100 exactly . .	46·51	36·53	30·33	29·57	43·55
96 to 99 . . .	0·27	0·96	2·36	2·61	1·10
86 to 95 . . .	1·47	4·93	6·69	4·12	5·61
76 to 85 . . .	0·74	2·23	5·69	6·93	6·52
51 to 75 . . .	1·95	2·41	2·81	7·06	7·32
50 and under . .	—	1·35	1·06	1·21	0·72
Not available . .	—	0·14	—	—	—
All ratios . . .	100·00	100·00	100·00	100·00	100·00

Institute of Statistics. With comparatively little manipulation, these figures can be used to provide an estimate of the elements in the matrix $p'_{rs}(t)$ for low values of s and t. Taking for R_0 the range £89–£111, and in general for R_r the range £$10^{1.95+r/10}$ to £$10^{2.05+r/10}$, the resulting estimates for $p'_{rs}(t)$ for $r = 0$–11, $s = 0$–14 are shown in Table II.

This table shows some degree of regularity in the figures in each diagonal, with a tendency for the lowest incomes to shift upwards by rather more ranges on the average than the high incomes. The reader may find it useful to refer back to it later when considering some of the simplifying assumptions which we will use in constructing our models.

It is unfortunate, however, that the figures tell us virtually nothing about the changes among the incomes of the rich: it is with these that our basic postulate will be mainly concerned.

3. A SIMPLE MODEL GENERATING AN EXACT PARETO DISTRIBUTION

As an expository device it will be convenient at this stage to consider what will result from very simple assumptions indeed about the matrix $p'_{rs}(t)$ and the corresponding distributions $p_{ru}(t) = p'_{r,r+u}(t)$. Although the assumptions of this section do not approach reality at all, the results they lead to will resemble reality in one respect, and this will assist an understanding of one possible explanation of this aspect of actual distributions.

Let us assume, then, that for every value of t and r, and for some fixed integer n

$$p'_{r,r+u}(t) = p_{r,u}(t) = 0 \quad \text{if} \quad u > 1 \quad \text{or} \quad u < -n. \quad (3.1)$$

This means that no income moves up by more than one income range in a year, or down by more than n income ranges in a year,

$$p'_{r,r+u}(t) = p_{r,u}(t) = p_u > 0 \quad (3.2)$$

if

$$-n \leqslant u \leqslant 1 \quad \text{and} \quad u > -r.$$

We may refer to this equation (3.2), and to later modifications of it, as our *basic postulate*. It here means that the prospects of shifts upwards and downwards along the ladder of income

250

TABLE II. Estimates of some elements in the matrix p'_{rs} for England and Wales 1951–2

Income range (£)	r =	\(s=\) 0	1	2	3	4	5	6	7	8	9	10	11	12	13	14
								p'_{rs}								
89–111	0	n.a.	n.a.	n.a.	n.S.	n.a.	—	—	—	—	—	—	—	—	—	—
112–141	1	0·020	0·672	0·202	0·083	0·023	—	—	—	—	—	—	—	—	—	—
142–177	2	0·015	0·020	0·674	0·204	0·068	0·019	—	—	—	—	—	—	—	—	—
177–221	3	0·007	0·014	0·030	0·676	0·205	0·053	0·015	—	—	—	—	—	—	—	—
222–281	4	—	0·012	0·015	0·040	0·672	0·207	0·043	0·011	—	—	—	—	—	—	—
282–354	5	—	—	0·016	0·017	0·052	0·666	0·209	0·033	0·007	—	—	—	—	—	—
355–445	6	—	—	—	0·015	0·018	0·075	0·666	0·200	0·023	0·004	—	—	—	—	—
446–562	7	—	—	—	—	0·013	0·020	0·096	0·658	0·198	0·013	0·002	—	—	—	—
563–707	8	—	—	—	—	—	0·016	0·035	0·100	0·632	0·200	0·015	0·022	—	—	—
708–892	9	—	—	—	—	—	—	0·018	0·049	0·104	0·607	0·205	0·015	0·002	—	—
893–1,119	10	—	—	—	—	—	—	—	0·017	0·050	0·106	0·625	0·190	0·010	0·002	—
1,120–1,409	11	—	—	—	—	—	—	—	—	0·015	0·051	0·108	0·646	0·178	0·005	0·001

ranges are distributed in a manner independent of present income, apart from the limitations imposed by the impossibility of descending below the bottom rung of the ladder. This is the postulate which we shall retain in some modified form in nearly all our models, and which always leads to an income distribution which obeys Pareto's law at least asymptotically for high incomes.

We also need to assume that for each value of r and t

$$\sum_{s=0}^{\infty} p'_{rs}(t) = \sum_{u=-r}^{\infty} p_{ru}(t) = 1 \qquad (3\cdot3)$$

which by $(3\cdot2)$ also implies

$$\sum_{u=-n}^{1} p_u = 1. \qquad (3\cdot3a)$$

This assumption $(3\cdot3)$ expresses the fiction that all incomes preserve their identity throughout time in the manner described in Section 2 above.

One other assumption must be introduced in order to ensure that the process is not dissipative, i.e., that the incomes do not go on increasing indefinitely without settling down to an equilibrium distribution. Let us denote

$$g(z) \equiv \sum_{u=-n}^{1} p_u z^{1-u} - z \qquad (3\cdot4)$$

then our stability assumption is that

$$g'(1) \equiv - \sum_{u=-n}^{1} u p_u \quad \text{is positive.} \qquad (3\cdot5)$$

This means that for all incomes, initially in any one of the ranges $R_n, R_{n+1}, R_{n+2}, \ldots$, the average number of ranges shifted during the next year is negative.

This completes the list of assumptions for our first model and when $n = 5$ they give rise to a matrix of Diagram 1.

Now we may determine the equilibrium distribution corresponding to any matrix $p'_{r,r+u}(t) = p_{r,u}(t)$ conforming to our assumed rules. Owing to the uniqueness theorem mentioned above in Section 2, it will be sufficient to find any distribution

$s=$	0	1	2	3	4	5	6	7	8 ....
$r=$				$p'_{rs}(t)$					
0	$1-p_1$	p_1	0	0	0	0	0	0	0 ....
1	$1-p_0-p_1$	p_0	p_1	0	0	0	0	0	0 ....
2	$p_{-5}+p_{-4}+p_{-3}+p_{-2}$	p_{-1}	p_0	p_1	0	0	0	0	0 ....
3	$p_{-5}+p_{-4}+p_{-3}$	p_{-2}	p_{-1}	p_0	p_1	0	0	0	0 ....
4	$p_{-5}+p_{-4}$	p_{-3}	p_{-2}	p_{-1}	p_0	p_1	0	0	0 ....
5	p_{-5}	p_{-4}	p_{-3}	p_{-2}	p_{-1}	p_0	p_1	0	0 ....
6	0	p_{-5}	p_{-4}	p_{-3}	p_{-2}	p_{-1}	p_0	p_1	0 ....
7	0	0	p_{-5}	p_{-4}	p_{-3}	p_{-2}	p_{-1}	p_0	p_1 ....
8	0	0	0	p_{-5}	p_{-4}	p_{-3}	p_{-2}	p_{-1}	p_0 ....

DIAGRAM I

which remains exactly unchanged under the action of the matrix $p'_{rs}(t)$ for one year. For this distribution when found must (apart from an arbitrary multiplying constant) be the unique distribution which will be approached by all distributions under the repeated action of the matrix multiplier $p'_{rs}(t)$ year after year.

Our assumptions (3·1) to (3·5) have deliberately been chosen so as to make the solution obvious. Indeed, if X_s is the desired equilibrium distribution, we need by (2·3), (3·1) and (3·2)

$$X_s = \sum_{-n}^{1} p_u X_{s-u} \quad \text{for all } s > 0 \qquad (3\cdot6)$$

and

$$X_0 = \sum_{-n}^{0} q_u X_{-u} \quad \text{where} \quad q_u = \sum_{v=-n}^{u} p_r. \qquad (3\cdot7)$$

We need only satisfy (3·6), since (3·6), (3·1), (3·2) and (3·3) ensure the satisfaction of (3·7) as well.

Now an obvious solution of (3·6) is

$$X_s = b^s \qquad (3\cdot8)$$

where b is the real positive root other than unity of the equation

$$g(z) = \sum_{u=-n}^{1} p_u z^{1-u} - z = 0 \qquad (3\cdot9)$$

where $g(z)$ was already defined in (3·4) above.

The distribution of income between persons

Descartes' rule of signs establishes the fact that $(3\cdot9)$ has no more than two real positive roots: since unity is one root, and $g(0) = p_0 > 0$, and $g'(1) > 0$ by $(3\cdot5)$, the other real positive root must satisfy

$$0 < b < 1. \tag{3·10}$$

Hence the solution $(3\cdot8)$ implies a total number of incomes given by

$$N' = \frac{1}{1-b} \tag{3·11}$$

and, to arrange for any other total number N, we need merely modify $(3\cdot8)$ to the form

$$X_s = N(1-b)\,b^s. \tag{3·8\,a}$$

Now suppose that the proportionate extent of each income range is 10^h, and that the lowest income is $y_{\min.}$: then X_s is the number of incomes in the range R_s whose lower bound is given by

$$y_s = 10^{sh}y_{\min.} \quad \text{whence} \quad \log_{10} y_s = sh + \log_{10} y_{\min.} \tag{3·12}$$

By summing a geometrical progression, using $(3\cdot8a)$, we now find that in the equilibrium distribution the number of incomes exceeding y_s is given by

$$F(y_s) = Nb^s \quad \text{whence} \quad \log_{10} F(y_s) = \log_{10} N + s\log_{10} b. \tag{3·13}$$

Now put

$$a = \log_{10} b^{-1/h} \quad \text{and} \quad \gamma = \log_{10} N + \alpha \log_{10} y_{\min.} \tag{3·14}$$

Then it follows from $(3\cdot12)$ and $(3\cdot13)$ that

$$\log_{10} F(y_s) = \gamma - \alpha \log_{10} y_s. \tag{3·15}$$

This means that for $y = y_0, y_1, y_2, \ldots$, the logarithm of the number of incomes exceeding y is a linear function of y. This states Pareto's law in its exact form.

Thus if all ranges are of equal proportionate extent, our simplifying assumptions ensure that any initial distribution of income will in the course of time approach the exact Pareto distribution given by $(3\cdot14)$, $(3\cdot15)$.

The very simple model discussed in this section brings out clearly the tendency for Pareto's law to be obeyed in a community where, above a certain minimum income, the prospects of various amounts of percentage change of income are independent of the initial income.

Most of the remainder of the article will be spent in generalising this very simple model so that it is less unrealistic.

In actual income distributions, Pareto's law is not even approximately obeyed for low incomes: if logarithm of income is measured along the horizontal axis, the frequency distributions found in practice are not J-shaped like that obtained in our model, but single humped and moderately symmetrical. The first modification which we make to our model is to remove the assumption that there is a lowest income range R_0 and to set up conditions which lead to a two-tailed distribution, one for the poor and one for the rich.

In these simple models, Pareto's law is obeyed exactly, not merely asymptotically. We next introduce two generalisations which limit observance of the law to the occupants of high income groups and render it no longer exact but asymptotic. These generalisations consist in:

i allowing incomes to shift upwards by more than one range in a year;

ii limiting our basic assumption (3·2) that the prospects of various amounts of percentage change of income are independent of initial income to apply to higher incomes only.

These two generalisations bring our model much closer to the conditions indicated by Table II above.

In real life a man's age has a great influence on his prospects of increasing his income. Our next generalisation takes this into account. We now allow a man's prospects of change of income to depend on his age. Finally, we use the same technical device to allow a man's occupation to influence his prospects of change of income.

Despite these generalisations of the model, it is still found that the Pareto curve must be asymptotic to a straight line. Is it then possible that the approximate linearity over high income ranges of the Pareto curves found for many modern communities is due to the approximate fulfiment in the real world of our basic assumption? This question is briefly discussed in the final sections of the paper.

4. A MODEL GENERATING A TWO-TAILED INCOME DISTRIBUTION OBEYING PARETO'S LAW

The simple model described in the last section generated a distribution with only one Pareto tail. The essential modifications required to introduce a two-tailed distribution are the following:

i We drop the assumption that there is a lowest income-range R_0, and adopt an infinite sequence of income ranges R_r, of equal proportionate extent, allowing r to run from minus infinity to plus infinity.

ii We adopt assumptions about that part of the matrix $p'_{rs}(t)$ for which r is negative analogous to those adopted about that part for which r is positive.

iii We allow for some movement of incomes to and fro between ranges R_r for which r is positive and those for which r is negative.

In particular, we assume as in (3·1)

$$p'_{r,r+u}(t) = p_{ru}(t) = 0 \quad \text{when} \quad r \geqslant 0 \quad \text{and} \quad u \geqslant 1 \quad \text{or} \quad u < -n \tag{4·1}$$

and we retain our basic postulate (3·2)

$$p'_{r,r+u}(t) = p_{ru}(t) = p_u > 0 \quad \text{if} \quad -n \leqslant u \leqslant 1 \quad \text{and} \quad u > -r. \tag{4·2}$$

We further assume that

$$\text{when} \quad r \geqslant 0 \quad \text{and} \quad u < -r, \quad \text{and when} \quad r < 0 \tag{4·3}$$
$$\text{and} \quad u > r, \quad u < -1 \quad \text{or} \quad u > v,$$
$$p'_{r,r+u}(t) = p_{ru}(t) = 0.$$

We now introduce a positive integer r and non-negative constants $\pi_{-1}\pi_0\pi_1...\pi_v$ and satisfying

$$\lambda = 0 \; \pi_{-1} > 0 \, \pi_0 > 0 \, \pi_1 > 0 \, \pi_v > 0 \; \sum_{s=1}^{v} \pi_s = 1 \; \sum_{u=1}^{v} u\pi_u > 1 \tag{4·4}$$
$$1 - \lambda - \pi_{-1} > 0 \quad 1 - \lambda - p_1 > 0$$

and put

$$p_{ru}(t) = \pi_u \quad \text{when} \quad r < 0 \quad \text{and} \quad u < -t-1 \quad (4\cdot5)$$
$$\text{and} \quad -1 \leqslant u \leqslant v$$
$$p_{0,-1}(t) = p_{-1,2}(t) = \lambda \quad p_{00}(t) = 1 - \lambda - p_1 > 0$$
$$p_{-10}(t) = 1 - \lambda - \pi_{-1} > 0$$

and assume as before that for all r

$$\sum_{u=-\infty}^{\infty} p_{ru}(t) = 1 \quad \text{and} \quad p'_{r,r+u}(t) = p_{ru}(t). \quad (4\cdot6)$$

These assumptions can best be understood by considering their effects when n and v take particular values. Thus when $n = 3$ and $v = 2$, they give rise to a matrix for $p'_{rs}(t)$ whose centre is of the following form:

$s =$	-4	-3	-2	-1	0	1	2	3	4	5
$r =$										
-5	π_1	π_2	0	0	0	0	0	0	0	0
-4	π_0	π_1	π_2	0	0	0	0	0	0	0
-3	π_{-1}	π_0	π_1	π_2	0	0	0	0	0	0
-2	0	π_{-1}	π_0	$1-\pi_0-\pi_{-1}$	0	0	0	0	0	0
-1	0	0	π_{-1}	$1-\lambda-\pi_{-1}$	λ	0	0	0	0	0
0	0	0	0	λ	$1-\lambda-p_1$	p_1	0	0	0	0
1	0	0	0	0	$1-p_0-p_1$	p_0	p_1	0	0	0
2	0	0	0	0	$p_{-3}+p_{-2}$	p_{-1}	p_0	p_1	0	0
3	0	0	0	0	p_{-3}	p_{-2}	p_{-1}	p_0	p_1	0
4	0	0	0	0	0	p_{-3}	p_{-2}	p_{-1}	p_0	p_1
5	0	0	0	0	0	0	p_{-2}	p_{-1}	p_0	
6	0	0	0	0	0	0	p_{-3}	p_{-2}	p_{-1}	

DIAGRAM 2

We retain our assumption $(3\cdot5)$ that

$$g'(1) = -\sum_{u=-n}^{1} u p_u \text{ is positive} \quad (4\cdot7)$$

and introduce the analogous assumption that

$$\gamma'(1) = -\sum_{v=-1}^{m} v \pi_v \text{ is negative} \quad (4\cdot8)$$

where

$$\gamma(z) \equiv \sum_{v=-1}^{1} \pi_v z^{1-v} - z. \quad (4\cdot9)$$

257

Then, by an argument analogous to that of Section 3, the equation

$$\gamma(z) = 0 \tag{4.10}$$

must have a single real root β satisfying

$$\beta > 1 \tag{4.11}$$

It may be easily verified that the distribution

$$X_s = Ab^s \quad \text{when} \quad s \geqslant 0$$
$$X_s = A\beta^{s+1} \quad \text{when} \quad s < 0 \tag{4.12}$$

satisfies the equilibrium condition

$$X_s = \sum_{r=-\infty}^{\infty} p'_{rs}(t)\, X_r. \tag{4.13}$$

Hence for some value of A, this must be the equilibrium distribution towards which any actual distribution must tend under the repeated action of the multiplying matrix $p'_{rs}(t)$ determined by the various assumptions of this model.

To secure any total number of incomes, N say, we need only put

$$A = \frac{(1-b)\,(\beta-1)\,N}{2\beta - b\beta - 1}. \tag{4.14}$$

In this solution there are two Pareto tails, one relating to high incomes and one to low incomes. The distribution is kept stable by the two conditions (4.7), (4.8), which ensure that for large incomes the expected change u is negative and for small incomes it is positive. This pair of conditions is needed to offset the continual dispersal of incomes due to the variance of the frequency distributions in u, p_u and π_u.

This example has been hand-picked so as to yield a crystal-clear solution, but one essential feature of this solution, namely the conformity to Pareto's law of the distribution, will be found to be approximately preserved through a series of modifications and relaxations of our simplifying assumptions. The basic postulate which leads to the approximate obedience of this law was retained in assumption (4.2), which determines that the functions of type $p_{ru}(t)$ should be the same for all values of r relating to high income ranges.

Appendix 6

One minor generalisation which can be made to the above example without essentially altering the form of the solution is to enlarge the channels of communication between income ranges with $r \geqslant 0$ and those with $r < 0$, hitherto limited to the flow of a proportion λ from each of R_{-1} and R_0. We may adjust the values of $p'_{r,-1}(t)$ and $p'_{r0}(t)$ in such a manner as to allow the flow of incomes from each of $R_0 R_1 \ldots R_{n-1}$ to R_{-1} and from each of $R_{-1} R_{-2} \ldots R_{-r}$ to R_0 without altering the solution further than to the form

$$x_s = B'b^s \quad \text{when} \quad s \geqslant 0$$
$$x_{-s} = B\beta^{s-1} \quad \text{when} \quad s < 0$$

where the ratio between B' and B will now depend on the value of $p'_{r,-1}(t)$ and $p'_{r0}(t)$, and need no longer be unity.

5. A MORE GENERAL MODEL GENERATING A DISTRIBUTION ASYMPTOTIC TO A PARETO DISTRIBUTION

One of the most restrictive assumptions in the example we have discussed was that

$$p_{ru}(t) = 0 \quad \text{when} \quad u > 1 \quad \text{and} \quad r \geqslant 0$$

The abandonment of this assumption destroys the complete simplicity of the solution.

In order to concentrate attention on the new generalisation, let us first restore the assumption that R_0 is the minimum income range so that we shall only have to consider one tail of the distribution. Then let us replace the assumption (3·1) by

$$p_{ru}(t) = 0 \quad \text{if} \quad u > m \text{ a given positive integer or } u < -n \quad (5\cdot1)$$

and modify (3.2) to the form

$$p_{ru}(t) = p_u \quad \text{(defined for} \quad u = -n, 1-n, \ldots, m) \quad (5\cdot2)$$

if $u+r \geqslant m$ where $\displaystyle\sum_{u=-n}^{m} p_u = 1$ and no p_u is negative.

We may retain assumptions (3·3), (3·4) and (3·5) (extending the summation in (3·4) and (3·5) from $-n$ to m).

9-2

The assumptions made so far have defined $p'_{rs}(t)$ for $s \geqslant m$ and

determined $\sum_{s=0}^{m-1} p'_{rs}(t)$ for each $r = 0, 1, \ldots, n$ and $\sum_{s=r-n}^{m-1} p'_{rs}(t)$

for each $r = n+1, \ldots, n+m-1$. But the individual values $p'_{rs}(t)$ for $r = 0, 1, \ldots, n+m-2$ and $r-n \leqslant s < m$ are, subject to these linear restraints, still at our disposal. We shall make no further assumption about these individual values, except that none are negative and that when $|r-s| \leqslant 1$, $p'_{rs}(t)$ is positive.

The effect of these assumptions in the case $n = 2$, $m = 3$ is to give the matrix $p'_{rs}(t)$ the following form:

$p'_{00}(t)$	$p'_{01}(t)$	$p'_{02}(t)$	p_1	0	0	0	$0 \ldots$
$p'_{10}(t)$	$p'_{11}(t)$	$p'_{12}(t)$	p_2	p_3	0	0	$0 \ldots$
$p'_{20}(t)$	$p'_{21}(t)$	$p'_{22}(t)$	p_1	p_2	p_3	0	$0 \ldots$
0	$p'_{31}(t)$	$p'_{32}(t)$	p_0	p_1	p_2	p_3	$0 \ldots$
0	0	p_{-2}	p_{-1}	p_0	p_2	p_2	$p_3 \ldots$
0	0	0	p_{-2}	p_{-1}	p_0	p_1	$p_2 \ldots$
0	0	0	0	p_{-2}	p_{-1}	p_0	$p_1 \ldots$
0	0	0	0	0	p_{-2}	p_{-1}	$p_0 \ldots$
$\cdot$	$\cdot$	$\cdot$	$\cdot$	$\cdot$	$\cdot$	$\cdot$	$\ldots$
$\cdot$	$\cdot$	$\cdot$	$\cdot$	$\cdot$	$\cdot$		$\ldots$

DIAGRAM 3

subject to the conditions:

i that the sum of the elements in each row is unity;

ii that the elements in the three central diagonals are all positive, and no elements are negative.

In the general case where m is some positive integer, the equation

$$g(z) = \sum_{u=-n}^{m} p_u z^{m-u} - z^m = 0 \tag{5.3}$$

will still have just one positive root b_1 less than unity, provided we retain our assumption (3.5) in the form

$$g'(1) = -\sum_{u=-n}^{m} u p_u > 0. \tag{5.4}$$

Appendix 6

This assumption ensures, by a theorem due to Mr F. G. Foster,* that the matrix $p'_{rs}(t)$ is 'non-dissipative', and hence that a unique finite non-zero equilibrium distribution will be approached in the limit under the repeated application of the changes embodied in this matrix.

Let the $m+n$ roots of (5·3) be $b_1 b_2 ... b_{m+n}$; and let

$$x_s(s = 0, 1, 2, ...)$$

denote the equilibrium distribution, which must satisfy the equilibrium equations

$$\left. \begin{array}{l} x_s = \sum_{r=0}^{\infty} p'_{rs}(t) x_r \quad s = 0, 1, 2... \\[2mm] \sum_{s=0}^{\infty} x_s = N. \end{array} \right\} \tag{5·5}$$

This set of equations may be subdivided into

$$x_s = \sum_{r=0}^{\infty} p'_{rs}(t) x_r \quad s = 0, 1, 2, ..., m-1 \tag{5·6}$$

$$x_s = \sum_{u=-n}^{m} p_u x_{s-u} \quad s = m, m+1, m+2... \tag{5·7}$$

$$\sum_{s=0}^{\infty} x_s = N. \tag{5·8}$$

The solution is known, because of Foster's theorem, to exist: hence there exist coefficients $B_1 ... B_{m+n}$ such that

$$x_s = \sum_{k=1}^{m+n} B_k b_k^s \quad s = 0, 1, 2 ... m+n-1. \tag{5·9}$$

It will then follow from (5·3) and (5·7) that

$$x_s = \sum_{k=1}^{m-n} B_k b_k^s \quad s = m+n, m+n+1, ... \tag{5·10}$$

Amongst those roots whose coefficients in (5·10) are not zero there will be one (at least) whose modulus is not exceeded by that of any other. Let its modulus be b: then for large s, (5·10) will reduce to the form

$$x_s = b^s \left\{ B'_1 + B'_2(-1)^s + \sum_{k=0}^{k} B'_k \cos (s\theta_k + \phi_k) + o(1) \right\}. \tag{5·11}$$

* Foster, 'Some Problems in the Mathematical Theory of Probability', unpublished D.Ph. thesis Bodley's Library, Oxford.

The distribution of income between persons

Since no x_s can be negative

$$B_1' > 0 \qquad (5\cdot12)$$

and b itself must be one root of $(5\cdot3)$. But since all the co-efficients of non-zero powers of z in the expansion of $z^{-m}g(z)$ are positive, there can then be no other root of modulus b than b itself. Hence $(5\cdot11)$ may be reduced to

$$x_s = b^s\{B_1' + o(1)\} \qquad (5\cdot13)$$

It follows from $(5\cdot8)$, $(5\cdot12)$ and $(5\cdot13)$ that $|b| < 1$ and hence

$$x_s = b_1^s\{B_1 + o(1)\} \qquad (5\cdot14)$$

where b_1 is the real root lying between o and 1. $(5\cdot14)$ expresses the fact that the Pareto curve for the equilibrium distribution is asymptotic to a straight line.

It is always possible to find the coefficients B_k in the exact solution $(5\cdot9)$, $(5\cdot10)$ by finding b_1 and the roots $b_2...b_m$ of modulus less than b_1 and fitting B_1 to B_k so as to satisfy $(5\cdot6)$.

It is perhaps of some interest to state that by a suitable choice of the elements $p'_{rs}(t)$ in the top left-hand corner of the matrix illustrated in Diagram 3, which were left with arbitrary values, it is always possible to arrange that all the terms except the first vanish in the expansion for x_s so that in this case Pareto's law is exactly obeyed throughout the whole income scale as in the example of Section 3. A variety of such suitable choices is available, but the result has so little practical relevance that it may be left to the curious reader to verify it if he so wishes.

It is now convenient to relax our assumption $(5\cdot2)$ so that the distribution $p_{ru}(t)$ need only conform to the standard form p_u for high incomes. We replace $(5\cdot2)$ by

$$p_{ru}(t) = p_u \quad \text{defined for} \quad u = -n, 1-n, ..., m$$
$$\text{if} \quad u+r \geqslant m+w \qquad (5\cdot15)$$

where w is a non-negative integer

$$\sum_{u=-n}^{m} p_u = 1 \quad \text{and no } p_u \text{ is negative.}$$

The $p_{ru}(t)$ thus freed from the restriction $(5\cdot3)$ are those for which $m-r \leqslant u \leqslant m+w-r$ and $-n \leqslant u \leqslant m$, and these may be left free, apart from the usual requirements that no $p_{ru}(t)$ is negative, all $p_{r1}(t)$, $p_{r0}(t)$ and $p_{r-1}(t)$ are positive and the survival assumption (5·2).

In the case $n = 1$, $m = 2$, $w = 2$, the effect of these assumptions on the appearance of the matrix $p'_{rs}(t)$ is shown below.

$r =$	0	1	2	3	3	4	5
$s =$							
0	$p'_{00}(t)$	$p'_{01}(t)$	$p'_{02}(t)$	0	0	0	0
1	$p'_{10}(t)$	$p'_{11}(t)$	$p'_{12}(t)$	$p'_{13}(t)$	0	0	0
2	0	$p'_{21}(t)$	$p'_{22}(t)$	$p'_{23}(t)$	p_2	0	0
3	0	0	$p'_{32}(t)$	$p'_{33}(t)$	p_1	p_2	0
4	0	0	0	$p'_{43}(t)$	p_0	p_1	p_2
5	0	0	0	0	p_{-1}	p_0	p_1
6	0	0	0	0	0	p_{-1}	p_0

DIAGRAM 4

The reader may compare this diagram with the figures of Table II.

The effect of the change in our model on the solution is in principle not very great. As before, we find $b_1 \ldots b_m$ those m roots of (5·3) which have modulus less than unity and we try solutions of the form (5·9) for $x_w x_{w+1} \cdots$.

But we can no longer expect $x_0 x_1 \ldots x_{w-1}$ to conform to the rule (5·9), and we need w more equations to determine these w further unknowns. These equations are provided by extending the equations (5·6) to cover $s = 0, 1, \ldots, m+w-1$.

Subject to these modifications, the solution is exactly the same as before, and again the Pareto curve for high incomes must be asymptotic to a straight line.

The extension of these results to the case where there are two tails in a generalized form of the example discussed in Section 4 above involves no difficulty in principle.

6. A MODEL MAKING ALLOWANCE FOR SOME EFFECTS OF AGE- AND OCCUPATION-STRUCTURE

An obvious objection to a theory based on the constancy over time of the movement matrices $p_{rs}(t)$ is the fact that age and death play such an important part in determining the changes in an income. In this section we shall modify our assumptions so as to go some way towards meeting this difficulty.

Our method will be to suppose that our population is divided between C 'colonies', and that income-receivers can migrate from one colony to another, the prospects of change of income varying from colony to colony. When we wish to discuss the effect of age on income distribution, the 'colonies' will represent age-groups: if the width of the age-groups exceeds one 'year', then an income attached to one individual may either remain in that age-group or pass on to the next age-group above, or if the individual dies, pass with an appropriate reduction in size to the age-group containing the heir.

But the method could be used also to study the effects on income distribution of the tendency for families to remain in the same occupation: for this purpose we would make the 'colonies' represent occupations. As in occupations, the income prospects in some colonies would be better than in others: most incomes would remain in one colony, but there would again be some movements between colonies.

We shall find that provided within each colony the $p_{ru}(t)$ functions have a form independent of the income range, for all large incomes the asymptotic approach of the Pareto curve to a straight line will be preserved under these far more general assumptions.

We now set down formally the notation for our model modified to include colonies.

Let
$$_{cd}p'_{rs}(t) = {}_{cd}p_{rs-r}(t)$$

denote the proportion of the incomes in range R_r in colony c in year t which move into range R_s in colony d in year $t+1$.

If $_c x_r(t)$ denotes the number of incomes in range R_r in colony c in year t, then by definition

$$_d x_s(t+1) = \sum_{c=1}^{C} \sum_{r=0}^{\infty} {}_{cd}p'_{rs}(t) \, _c x_s(t) \qquad (6\cdot1)$$

and if an equilibrium distribution $_dx_s$ exists it must satisfy the condition

$$_dx_s = \sum_{c=1}^{C} \sum_{r=0}^{\infty} {}_{cd}p'_{rs}(t) \, {}_cx_r \qquad (6\cdot2)$$

for every $d = 1, 2, \ldots C$ and $s = 0, 1, 2, \ldots$.

The assumptions for our model can now be set down in a form closely analogous to those of the simpler model of Section 5, We assume

$$_{cd}p_{rs}(t) = {}_{cd}p'_{r,r+s}(t) = 0 \qquad (6\cdot3)$$

when $\qquad s > m_d \quad$ or $\quad s < -n_d$

where m_d and n_d are positive integers $d = 1, 2, \ldots, C$

$$_{cd}p_{ru}(t) = {}_{cd}p'_{r,r+u}(t) = {}_{cd}p_u \geqslant 0 \qquad (6\cdot4)$$

if $\qquad s = r+u \geqslant m_d + w_d$

and $\qquad m_d \geqslant u \geqslant -n_d$

where the w_d are non-negative integers for $d = 1, 2, \ldots, C$, and the $_{cd}p_u$ are constants satisfying for each $c = 1, 2, \ldots C$, the survival condition

$$\sum_{d=1}^{c} \sum_{u=-n_d}^{m_d} {}_{cd}p_u = 1. \qquad (6\cdot5)$$

It is convenient at this stage to introduce the notion of the accessibility of one income range R_s in one colony C_d from the income range R_r in colony C_c.

Range R_s in C_d will be called accessible in one step from range R_r in C_c if $_{cd}p'_{rs}(t)$ is positive: it will be called accessible in two steps from R_r in C_c if it is accessible in one step from any range in any colony which itself is accessible from R_r in C_c in one step. In general, the definition may be extended one by one to any larger number of steps, by always defining R_s in C_d to be accessible in n steps from R_r in C_c, if it is accessible in one step from any range in any colony, which itself is accessible from R_r in C_c in $(n-1)$ steps.

Finally, R_s in C_d will be termed accessible from R_r in C_c if for any n it is thus accessible in n steps.

We now make the further assumption

Each range in any colony is accessible from
each range in every colony. $\qquad (6\cdot6)$

The purpose of this assumption is to ensure that the equilibrium income distribution is unique.

The survival postulate now takes the form

$$\sum_{d=1}^{c} \sum_{u=-n_d}^{m_d} {}_{cd}p_{ru}(t) = 1 \tag{6.7}$$

and we require one further postulate in order to rule out solutions involving periodic fluctuations from one distribution to another. This postulate may take the form that

> There is some pair of ranges R_s in C_d and R_r in C_c and some integer n such that R_s in C_d is accessible from R_r in C_c both in n steps and in $(n+1)$ steps. (6.8)

The effect of these assumptions on the matrices ${}_{cd}p'_{rs}(t)$ may be illustrated by a numerical example with $C = 3$. In this example, the three colonies represent the young, middle-age and old-age groups 20–35, 35–50 and 50–65 years, and the unit of time during which the matrix ${}_{cd}p'_{rs}(t)$ operates once is taken as fifteen calendar years. It is supposed that all the young survive to middle-age, but half the middle-aged die and their incomes pass with suitable reduction to young heirs in the next period, while the other half reappear as the old in the next period, then to die and transmit their incomes to the young in the following period.

We arrange

$$m_1 = 0 \quad m_2 = 1 \quad m_3 = 1 \quad C = 3$$
$$w_1 = 1 \quad w_2 = 0 \quad w_3 = 0$$

and choose the following nine matrices ${}_{cd}p'_{rs}(t)$ for $c = 1, 2, 3$ and $d = 1, 2, 3$.

We put identically equal to zero those five of the matrices for which either $c = d$ or $c = 1$ and $d = 3$, or $c = 3$ and $d = 2$. The other four matrices we chose are as shown in Diagram 5.

It may be noted that R_0 in C_1 is accessible from R_0 in C_2 both in one step and in two steps. Thus the matrices satisfy the postulate (6.8).

In any generalized model of this type we shall have C sets

$_{12}p'_{rs}(t) =$	0·1	0·9	0	0	etc.
	0	0·1	0·9	0	etc.
	0	0	0·1	0·9	etc.
	0	0	0	0·1	etc.
			etc.		

$_{23}p'_{rs}(t) =$	0·1	0·4	0	0	etc.
	0	0·1	0·4	0	etc.
	0	0	0·1	0·4	etc.
	0	0	0	0·1	etc.
			etc.		

$_{21}p'_{rs} =$	0·5	0	0	0	etc.
	0·4	0·1	0	0·	etc.
	0·2	0·2	0·1	0	etc.
	0	0·2	0·2	0·1	etc.
	0	0	0·2	0·2	etc.
			etc.		

$_{31}p'_{rs} =$	1	0	0	0	0	etc.
	0·9	0·1	0	0	0	etc.
	0·8	0·1	0·1	0	0	etc.
	0·5	0·3	0·1	0·1	0	etc.
	0	0·5	0·3	0·1	0·1	etc.
	0	0	0·5	0·3	0·1	etc.
			etc.			

DIAGRAM 5

of equilibrium equations to be satisfied by the equilibrium distributions $_dx_s$, namely

$$_dx_s = \sum_{c=1}^{c} \sum_{r=0}^{\infty} {}_{cd}p'_{rs}(t)\, {}_cx_r \quad d = 1, 2, \dots C. \qquad (6\cdot9)$$

For $s > m_d + w_d$, these conditions become

$$_dx_s = \sum_{c=1}^{c} \sum_{u=-n_d}^{m_d} {}_{cd}p_u\, {}_dx_{s-u} \quad d = 1, 2, \dots C. \qquad (6\cdot10)$$

We are thus led to investigate the C simultaneous equations

$$A_d = \sum_{c=1}^{c} \sum_{u=-n_e}^{m_d} {}_{cd}p_u A_c z^{-u} \quad d = 1, 2, \dots C \qquad (6\cdot11)$$

which we may write again as

$$\sum_{c=1}^{c} P_{cd}(z)\, A_c = 0 \quad d = 1, 2, \dots C \qquad (6\cdot12)$$

where

$$P_{cd}(z) = \left\{ \sum_{u=-n_d}^{m_d} {}_{cd}p_u z^{-u} - 1 \right\} \quad \text{if} \quad c = d$$

$$= \sum_{n=-n_d}^{m_d} {}_{cd}p_u z^{-u} \quad \text{if} \quad C \neq d. \qquad (6\cdot13)$$

Elimination of the coefficients A_c leads to

$$\text{Det.}\,|P_{cd}(z)| = G(z), \quad \text{say} = 0. \qquad (6\cdot14)$$

This function $G(z)$ can be expressed in the form

$$G(z) = \sum_{u=-n}^{m} p_u z^{-u} \quad m = \sum_{c=1}^{C} m_c \quad n = \sum_{c=1}^{c} n_c \qquad (6\cdot15)$$

The distribution of income between persons

and plays a similar role in the theory to the function $g(z)$ in earlier sections. In particular, if we postulate

$$G'(1) = -\sum_{u=-n}^{m} u p_u > 0 \qquad (6 \cdot 16)$$

it can be proved by an application of Foster's theorem that the process is non-dissipative and that a unique equilibrium distribution exists.

We can again prove by the methods of Section 5 that for large s, where x_s is the equilibrium distribution

$$x_s = b_1^s \{B_1 + o(1)\} \qquad (6 \cdot 17)$$

where b_1 is a real positive root of $(6 \cdot 14)$.

Thus again the Pareto curve is asymptotic to a straight line in the region of high incomes.

The procedure for finding an exact solution is the following. First find b_1 the largest real positive root and $b_2 \dots b_m$ the roots of lesser modulus. Let B_{ce} denote the co-factor of $P_{c1}(b_e)$ in the determinant $G(z)$. Then

$$\sum_{c=1}^{c} B_{ce} P_{c1}(b_e) = G(b_e) = 0 \quad e = 1, 2, \dots m. \qquad (6 \cdot 18)$$

and $(6 \cdot 12)$ will clearly be satisfied, provided

$$A_c = \sum_{e=1}^{m} B_{ce} \lambda_e, \quad \text{where } \lambda_e \text{ are any numbers.} \qquad (6 \cdot 19)$$

We have still to determine not only the m values λ_e but also those values $_d x_s$ for which $s < w_d$: the number of these is given by

$$w = \sum_{d=1}^{c} w_d. \qquad (6 \cdot 20)$$

We have thus $(w+m)$ unknowns to find. To discover them we have the $w+m$ equations determining the equilibrium of those $_c x_s$ for which $s < m_c + w_c$: namely $(6 \cdot 2)$ for these values of c and s. These equations are not linearly independent, and only determine the ratios between the $w+m$ unknowns. Apart from a scale factor, this is sufficient to determine all the $_c x_s$, and the scale factor can then be found if we know the original total population.

Appendix 6

It can be proved exactly as before that the distribution

$$x_s = \sum_{c=1}^{C} {}_c x_s \tag{6.21}$$

so determined is the unique equilibrium distribution and that the term involving b_1^s will dominate the whole value of x_s for sufficiently large s. Thus the Pareto curve for sufficiently large incomes will preserve its property of being asymptotic to a straight line, despite the greater generalisation introduced in this model.

As in simpler models, we could remove the restriction that there is a minimum income range R_0 and elaborate the model so as to secure an equilibrium distribution with two Pareto tails, one for the poor and one for the rich. The exposition is tedious, and since our conclusions would not be substantially affected, this refinement is eschewed.

7. NUMERICAL EXAMPLE INVOLVING THE EFFECT OF AGE STRUCTURE ON INCOME DISTRIBUTION

The general method of solution indicated in the last section can be made much clearer by applying it to the numerical example described above in Diagram 4.

In this example, $C = 3$, $m = 2$, and the determinant of $P_{cd}(z)$ is

$$G(z) = \begin{vmatrix} -1 & 0.9z^{-1}+0.1 & 0 \\ 0.1+0.2z+0.2z^2 & -1 & 0.4z^{-1}+0.1 \\ 0.1+0.1z+0.3z^2 \\ +0.5z^3 & 0 & -1 \end{vmatrix} \tag{7.1}$$

$$= 0.36z^{-2}+0.139z^{-1}-0.688+0.420z+0.088z^2 \\ +0.005z^3.$$

By differentiation

$$G'(1) = 0.4 > 0 \tag{7.2}$$

so that, since $m = 2$, the equation $G(z) = 0$ must have just two roots of modulus less than unity. These may be found by Horner's method

$$\text{as} \quad b_1 = 0.4563136 \quad b_2 = -0.1453788. \tag{7.3}$$

269

The distribution of income between persons

The six co-factors B_{ce} of $p_{c1}(b_e)$ in the determinants $D(b_e)$ are

$$B_{1e} = 1 \quad B_{2e} = 0 \cdot 9b_e^{-1} + 0 \cdot 1$$
$$B_{3e} = (0 \cdot 9b_e^{-1} + 0 \cdot 1)(0 \cdot 4b_e^{-1} + 0 \cdot 1) \; e = 1, 2 \qquad (7 \cdot 4)$$

and their numerical values are

$$B_{11} = 1 \quad B_{21} = 2 \cdot 072\,327 \quad B_{31} = 2 \cdot 023\,814$$
$$B_{12} = 1 \quad B_{22} = -6 \cdot 090\,724 \quad B_{33} = -6 \cdot 310\,8. \qquad (7 \cdot 5)$$

We now put

$$
\begin{array}{ll}
{}_1x_s = \lambda_1 b_1^s + \lambda_2 b_2^s & \text{for} \quad s = 1, 2, 3 \ldots \\
{}_2x_s = \lambda_1 B_{21} b_1^s + \lambda_2 B_{22} b_2^s & \text{for} \quad s = 0, 1, 2 \ldots \\
{}_3x_s = \lambda_1 B_{31} b_1^s + \lambda_2 B_{32} b_2^s & \text{for} \quad s = 0, 1, 2 \ldots
\end{array}
\right\} \qquad (7 \cdot 6)
$$

and we still have to determine λ_1, λ_2 and ${}_1x_0$.

We have available for this purpose the three equations

$$
\begin{aligned}
{}_1x_0 &= 0 \cdot 5\,{}_2x_0 + 0 \cdot 4\,{}_2x_1 + 0 \cdot 2\,{}_2x_2 + 3\,{}_0x_0 + 0 \cdot 9\,{}_3x_1 \\
&\qquad\qquad + 0 \cdot 8\,{}_3x_2 + 0 \cdot 5\,{}_3x_3 \\
{}_2x_0 &= 0 \cdot 1\,{}_1x_0 \\
{}_3x_0 &= 0 \cdot 1\,{}_2x_0
\end{aligned}
\right\} \qquad (7 \cdot 7)
$$

Fortunately, any two equations contain all the fresh information provided by the three, and we accordingly take the two simple ones and rewrite them as

$$
\begin{aligned}
\lambda_1 B_{21} + \lambda_2 B_{22} &= 0 \cdot 1\,{}_1x_0 \\
\lambda_1 B_{31} + \lambda_2 B_{32} &= 0 \cdot 1\,(\lambda_1 B_{21} + \lambda_{22} B_{22}).
\end{aligned}
\right\} \qquad (7 \cdot 8)
$$

If we leave aside the scale factor we may arbitrarily put $\lambda_1 = 10{,}000$ and, substituting our numerical values for $B_{21}\,B_{22}\,B_{31}$ and B_{32}, we then find from the second equation that

$$\lambda_2 = 3185 \cdot 939 \qquad (7 \cdot 9)$$

and then from the first equation that

$${}_1x_0 = 13185 \cdot 939. \qquad (7 \cdot 10)$$

Using our equations $(7 \cdot 6)$ for the other ${}_cx_s$ we may now obtain the numerical values of as many ${}_cx_s$ as we please. Here are the first few values, with λ_1 put equal to 10,000:

TABLE III

	Young	Middle-aged	Old	Total	Income range (£)
S	$_1X_s$	$_2X_s$	$_3X_s$		
0	13,186	1,319	132	14,637	125–200
1	4,100	12,277	1,755	18,132	200–316
2	2,150	3,995	5,301	11,356	316–500
3	940	2,028	1,765	4,734	500–800
4	435	890	901	2,225	800–1,250
5	198	411	397	1,006	1,250–2,000
6	90	187	183	460	2,000–3,160
7 and over	75	157	153	385	3,160–
TOTAL	21,174	21,174	10,687	52,935	

The income scale put in on the extreme right assumes that the minimum income is £125 and that the upper limit of each income range is nearly 60 % greater than the lower limit.

It will be noted that although the equilibrium distributions of incomes for young, middle-aged and old are very different for small incomes, yet already at income levels of £1,250 and over each is rapidly approaching a Pareto distribution with

$$\alpha = -\frac{\log_{10} b_1}{\log_{10} 1\cdot58} = -5\log_{10} b_1 = 1\cdot7041. \qquad (7\cdot11)$$

This is well brought out by Chart I which shows for each age group and for all ages the following cumulative totals plotted on the double logarithmic paper.

TABLE IV

income level (£)	Number of incomes exceeding this level			
	Young	Middle-aged	Old	Total
125 . . .	21,174	21,174	10,587	52,935
200 . . .	7,988	19,855	10,455	38,298
316 . . .	3,888	7,578	8,700	20,166
500 . . .	1,738	3,674	3,399	8,810
800 . . .	798	1,645	1,634	4,076
1,250 . . .	363	755	733	1,851
2,000 . . .	165	344	336	845
3,160 . . .	75	157	153	385

We may read off from the chart that the median incomes in the three age-groups differ considerably: they are £175, £280 and £410 approximately. Yet for incomes over £500 it is clear from Chart I that the *proportionate* distributions are almost identical for the three age-groups.*

8. NUMERICAL EXAMPLE INVOLVING THE EFFECT OF OCCUPATIONAL STRUCTURE ON INCOME DISTRIBUTION

In our last model we made the assumption that every income range in every colony was accessible from every other. If we relax this assumption to state that within a certain group G of pairs (rc) every R_r in every colony c is accessible from every other, then our results will still hold, provided that the initial distribution was confined to this group.

If we maintain our other assumptions, then the effective new possibility introduced by this relaxation is the inclusion of colonies where there is an upper limit to the possible income.

This is useful when our colonies represent groups of occupations. Thus, let our society be composed of persons classified according to their main sources of income into:

1   Unskilled labour.

2   Semi-skilled work; skilled work and clerical.

3   Salaries and professional.

4   Profits, land, property.

Then we might assume that there was an effective ceiling on the incomes of classes 1 and 2, and 3. If for simplicity we ignore the complication of age considered in our last example and take broad income groups so that group R extends from 2^{r-3} thousand pounds to 2^{r-2} we might set up the following model within our relaxed assumption (see Diagram 6).

It is assumed that no one can obtain incomes higher than £500 in occupation 1, or higher than £1,000 in occupation 2. It will be seen that $_{33}p'_{rs}$, $_{34}p'_{rs}$, $_{43}p'_{rs}$ and $_{44}p'_{rs}$ assume repetitive forms when r becomes large: we might therefore expect to

* For similar charts of actual distributions see Lydall, Reports on Savings Survey published in the *Bulletin of Oxford Institute of Statistics*, Feb.–March, 1953, and other issues.

find the Pareto curves for occupations 3 and 4 to be asymptotic to straight lines.

It will be noted that $_{43}p'_{r2} > 0$ for all $r > 0$ so that (6·3) is not satisfied for finite n_3 when $c = 4$ $d = 3$ $s = 2$. Nevertheless, a solution can be found by the following method, which is similar to that of Section 7.

Pareto curves for age-groups

Illustrating Table IV

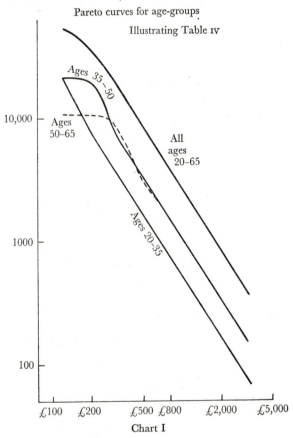

Chart I

The matrix $P_{rs}(z)$ for this example is only concerned with the values 3 and 4 of r and s. It is

$$P_{rs}(z) = \begin{vmatrix} 0\cdot020z^{-1}-0\cdot218 & 0\cdot000139z^{-1}+0\cdot01786 \\ +0\cdot180z & \\ 0 & 0\cdot030z^{-1}-0\cdot115+0\cdot075z \end{vmatrix} \qquad (8\cdot1)$$

The survival condition (6·5) is not, however, satisfied, since 1 % of those in each income group $s > 3$, in C_4, escape each year into income group R_2 of C_3. Consequently, writing

$$G(z) = \text{Det} |P_{rs}(z)|$$
$$= 0.00060z^{-2} + 0.0088z^{-1} + 0.03197 - 0.03705z \quad (8.2)$$
$$+ 0.01350z^2$$

we find that $G(1) \neq 0$ and that the non-dissipative condition (6·15) is not satisfied.

Nevertheless, two real positive roots of $G(z) = 0$ of modulus less than unity can be found and the usual method of solution proves adequate. The two roots are

$$b_1 = 0.333333 \quad b_2 = 0.100000 \quad (8.3)$$

and we calculate

$$\left. \begin{array}{l} B_{3e} = 0.30b_e^{-1} - 0.115 + 0.075b_e \\ B_{4e} = -0.000139b_e^{-1} - 0.01786 \quad e = 1, 2 \end{array} \right\} \quad (8.4)$$

to give

$$B_{31} = 0 \quad B_{32} = 0.125 \quad B_{41} = -0.18278 \quad B_{42} = -0.01925.$$

Hence we are led to try solutions of the form

$$\left. \begin{array}{l} {}_3x_s = 0.1925\lambda_2 10^{-s} \quad s = 2, 3, 4 \ldots \\ {}_4x_s = -0.18278\lambda_1 3^{-s} - 0.01925\lambda_2 10^{-s} \quad s = 3, 4, 5 \ldots \end{array} \right\} \quad (8.5)$$

It will slightly simplify the algebra to fix the scale arbitrarily at this stage by choosing λ_2 so that

$$\left. \begin{array}{l} {}_3x_s = 10^{8-s} \quad s = 2, 3, 4 \ldots \\ {}_4x_s = \lambda_1' 3^{-s} - 10^{7-s} \quad s = 3, 4 \ldots \end{array} \right\} \quad (8.6)$$

λ_1' is still undetermined and we also have still to find ${}_4x_0$, ${}_4x_1$, ${}_3x_0$, ${}_3x_1$, ${}_2x_0$, ${}_2x_1$, ${}_2x_2$, ${}_1x_0$ and ${}_1x_1$.

To find these ten constants we have the eleven equations associated with the equilibrium of ${}_1x_0$, ${}_1x_1$, ${}_2x_0$, ${}_2x_1$, ${}_2x_2$, ${}_3x_0$, ${}_3x_1$, ${}_3x_2$, ${}_4x_0$, ${}_4x_1$ and ${}_4x_2$, namely

Appendix 6

$$_1x_0 = 0\cdot856\,_1x_0 + 0\cdot250\,_1x_1 + 0\cdot050\,_2x_0 + 0\cdot050\,_0x_1$$
$$_1x_1 = 0\cdot144\,_1x_0 + 0\cdot593\,_1x_1 + 0\cdot100\,_2x_0$$
$$\qquad\qquad\qquad\qquad + 0\cdot200\,_2x_1 + 0\cdot075\,_2x_2$$

(seven equations omitted)

$$_4x_1 = 0\cdot120\,_3x_0 + 0\cdot050\,_3x_1 + 10^4 + 0\cdot200\,_4x_0$$
$$\qquad\qquad + 0\cdot370\,_4x_1 + 0\cdot010\{\lambda'_1 3^{-2} - 10^5\}$$
$$\lambda'3^{-2} - 10^5 = 0\cdot7075\,_3x_1 + 6000 + 0\cdot030\,_4x_1$$
$$\qquad\quad + 0\cdot0852\{\lambda'_1 3^{-2} - 10^5\} + 0\cdot075\{\lambda'_1 3^{-3} - 10^4\}.$$

(8·6)

Only ten of these equations provide independent information: any one is implied by the other ten. The solution of ten simultaneous equations is no mean undertaking, but in this example the solution can be found as

$$\lambda'_1 = 7\cdot29\,.\,10^6 \qquad _1x_0 = 10^7$$
$$_1x_1 = 5\,.\,10^6 \qquad _2x_0 = 2\,.\,10^6$$
$$_2x_1 = 1\cdot8\,.\,10^6 \qquad _2x_2 = 2\,.\,10^5$$
$$_3x_0 = 2\,.\,10^4 \qquad _3x_1 = 2\,.\,10^5$$
$$_4x_0 = 10^4 \qquad _4x_1 = 5\,.\,10^4$$

(8·7)

The values of $_3x_s$ and $_4x_s$ for $s > 1$ may now be found from the equations

$$_3x_s = 10^{3-s}$$
$$_4x_s = 3^{6-s}10^4 - 10^{7-s}$$

(8·8)

	$_{11}p'_{rs}$		$_{12}p'_{rs}$		
$s =$	0	1	0	1	2
$r =$					
0	0·856	0·144	0	0	0
1	0·250	0·593	0·057	0·110	0

	$_{11}p'_{rs}$		$_{22}p'_{rs}$			$_{23}p'_{rs}$				$_{24}p'_{rs}$			
$s =$	1	2	0	1	2	0	1	2	2	0	1	2	2
$r =$													
0	0·050	0·100	0·750	0·100	0	0	0	0	0	0	0	0	0
1	0·050	0·220	0·075	0·640	0·025	0	0·010	0	0	0	0	0	0
2	0	0·075	0	0·125	0·500	0	0	0·250	0	0	0	0·050	0

275

The distribution of income between persons

$s=$ $r=$	$_{32}p'_r$ 0	1	2	2	$_{33}p'_{rs}$ 0	1	2	3	4	5	6
0	0·482	0	0	0	0·132	0·1875	0	0	0	0	0
1	0·02657	0·075	0	0	0·025	0·500	0·250	0	0	0	0
2	0	0	0·05	0	0·00486	0·055	0·79956	0·020	0	0	0
3	—	—	—	—	0	0	0·180	0·782	0·020	0	0
4	—	—	—	—	0	0	0	0·180	0·782	0·020	0
5	—	—	—	—	0	0	0	0	0·180	0·782	0·020
6	—	—	—	—	0	0	0	0	0	0·180	0·782
						etc.				etc.	

$s=$ $r=$	$_{34}p'_{rs}$ 0	1	2	3	4	5	6
0	0·100	0·120	0	0·	0	0	0
1	0·0025	0·050	0·07075	0	0	0	0 etc.
2	0	0·010	0·060	0·000139	0	0	0
3	0	0	0	0·01786	0·000139	0	0
4	0	0	0	0	0·01786	0·000139	0
5	0	0	0	0	0	0·01786	0·000139
				etc.			

$s=$ $r=$	$_{43}p_{rs}$ 0	1	2	>2
0	0·500	0·050	0	0
1	0·050	0·300	0·150	0
2	0	0·0081	0·010	0
3	0	0	0·010	0
4	0	0	0·010	0
	0	0	0·010	0

$s=$ $r=$	$_{44}p'_{rs}$ 0	1	2	3	4	5	6
0	0·250	0·200	0	0	0	0	0
1	0·100	0·370	0·030	0	0	0	0 etc.
2	0	0·010	0·8519	0·030	0	0	0
3	0	0	0·075	0·885	0·030	0	0 etc.
4	0	0	0	0·075	0·885	0·030	0
5	0	0	0	0	0·075	0·885	0·030
			etc.		etc.		etc.

$_{13}p'_{rs} = {}_{14}p'_{rs} = 0$ for all r.s.
$_{31}p'_{rs} = {}_{41}p'_{rs} = {}_{42}p'_{rs} = 0$ for all r.s.

Diagram 6

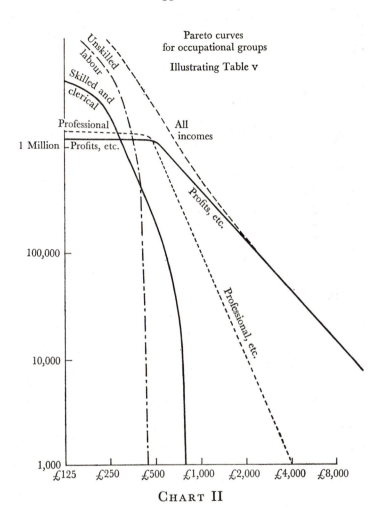

Pareto curves
for occupational groups

Illustrating Table v

CHART II

From the complete set of $_cx_s$ thus obtained, it is a quick matter to compile the following table showing for each occupation the number with incomes exceeding various levels.

The corresponding Pareto curves are shown in Chart II. An interesting feature of this solution is that the slopes of the Pareto lines for occupations 3 and 4 are not the same, that for the professional and salaried classes being much steeper than that for those whose income came from profits, land, etc. It is the latter distribution, of course, which determines the slope of the Pareto line for all incomes.*

TABLE V

Income level (£)	Number of incomes exceeding this level				
	Unskilled labourers	Skilled workers and clerical	Salaried and professional	Profits, land, etc.	Total
125 . .	15,000,000	4,000,000	1,331,111	1,163,889	21,495,000
250 . .	5,000,000	2,000,000	1,311,111	1,153,889	9,465,000
500 . .	0	200,000	1,111,111	1,103,889	2,415,000
1,000 .	0	0	111,111	393,889	505,000
2,000 .	0	0	11,111	133,889	145,000
4,000 .	0	0	1,111	44,889	46,000
8,000 .	0	0	111	14,989	15,000
16,000 .	0	0	11	4,999	5,010
32,000 .	0	0	1	1,667	1,668

9. A MODEL GENERATING A DISTRIBUTION IN WHICH PARETO'S LAW IS NOT OBEYED

The above examples are probably sufficient to illustrate the theory that the approximate observance of Pareto's law which has so often been remarked upon is not an illusion or coincidence, but has its explanation in a similarity at different high income-levels of the prospects of given proportionate changes of income.

They can do little more than illustrate the theory, since they are built on the artificial simplifying assumption that these prospects of change remain constant through time at each income level. It will be readily appreciated that any model catering for prospects which are not constant through time is much more complicated and the results obtainable are far less clear: the investigation of such models must form the subject of another article than this. The importance of such change in prospects has already been hinted at in the suggestion that changes in the income distribution affect the influence described by the matrices $p'_{rs}(t)$ just as much as the influence affect the incomes.

* For similar charts of actual distributions see Lydall, *Bulletin of Oxford Institute of Statistics*, Feb.–March, 1953.

Appendix 6

Another gap in our discussion so far has been any consideration of models which do *not* lead to a Pareto distribution. There
is a noticeable tendency recently for the Pareto curves of the
United Kingdom and other countries to curve very slightly
downwards at the tail, and it would be interesting to have a

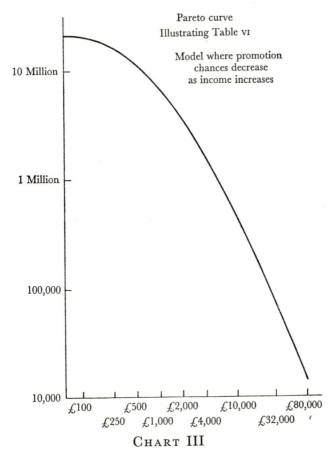

Pareto curve
Illustrating Table VI

Model where promotion
chances decrease
as income increases

10 Million

1 Million

100,000

10,000

£100   £500   £2,000   £10,000   £80,000
    £250   £1,000   £4,000   £32,000

CHART III

model illustrating how this could come about. The explanation
is probably that the prospects of increasing are proportionately less rosy nowadays for the very large incomes than for
the large incomes. This is not necessarily because the owners
of vast incomes are any less abstemious and accumulative

than their forerunners used to be, but may be because income
tax and death duties are now at a level which makes the piling
up of huge fortunes a more gradual and less rewarding undertaking.

A very simple model will suffice to illustrate the effect on the
Pareto curve that would result from a progressive worsening
of the chance of (say) doubling the income as one considered
larger and larger incomes.

We shall suppose that $R_0, R_1, R_2 \ldots$ are the income ranges
£62 10s.–£125, £125–£250, £210–£500, etc., etc. We shall
suppose that the chance of going *down* one range is the same
in all ranges (except R_0), and is 10 %. In R_0 the chance of
going *up* one range is 30 %, but in R_1 it is only 15 %, in R_2 it is

10 %, and in general in R_r it is only $\dfrac{30\,\%}{r+1}$.

The equilibrium condition for this model is

$$x_r = \frac{0\cdot3x_{r-1}}{r} + \left\{0\cdot9 - \frac{0\cdot3}{r+1}\right\}x_r + 0\cdot1x_{r+1}. \qquad (9\cdot1)$$

It can easily be checked that the solution is $r = 1, 2 \ldots$

$$x_r = \frac{3^r x_0}{r} \quad r = 1, 2, \ldots \qquad (9\cdot2)$$

TABLE VI

Income (£)	Number of incomes exceeding x
x	(Fx) (thousands)
61 10s. . . .	20,085
125 . . .	19,085
250 . . .	16,085
500 . . .	11,585
1,000 . . .	7,085
2,000 . . .	3,710
4,000 . . .	1,685
8,000 . . .	673
16,000 . . .	239
32,000 . . .	76·4
64,000 . . .	22·1
135,000 . . .	5·9

The cumulative distribution corresponding to $x_0 = 10^6$ is given in Table VI, and the corresponding Pareto curve is shown in Chart III. As one would expect, the steadily worsening prospects of income-promotion that are found as consideration passes up the income scale are reflected in a continuous downward curvature of the Pareto curve.

This example has been chosen so as to provide a very simple solution. In general, it will be difficult to obtain the equilibrium solutions in models where the promotion prospects, as reflected in the matrix $p_{ru}(t)$, vary throughout the income scale.

10. A MODEL ILLUSTRATING THE REACTION OF CHANGES IN THE INCOME DISTRIBUTION ON THE MATRIX DEPICTING THE INFLUENCES SHAPING THAT DISTRIBUTION

In conclusion, a warning must be given that although the models discussed above throw some light on the reasons why an approximate obedience to Pareto's law is so often found in actual income distributions, they do not throw much light on the mechanism determining the actual values observed for Pareto's α. It is tempting to draw conclusions from the fact that in equilibrium

$$\alpha = \frac{-\log b_1}{\log (1 + h)} \qquad (10 \cdot 1)$$

where b_1 is the positive root of the equilibrium equation

$$\sum_{u=-n}^{m} p_u z^{-u} = 1 \qquad (10 \cdot 2)$$

and h is the proportionate width of each income range. One might suppose that one had only to estimate the p_u corresponding to various economic situations in order to deduce the slopes of the Pareto lines in the consequent income distributions. But it would be just as sensible to guess at the consequent income distributions and deduce how much the p_u functions would have to be modified before that equilibrium was reached.

The point may be illustrated by a final model. Suppose that initially the income distribution is

$$x_s = 2^{23-s} \qquad (10.3)$$

where R_s is the range $2^{s/2} \, \pounds 100$ to $2^{s+1/2} \, \pounds 100$; then the total income will be approximately $2^{25} \, \pounds 100$.

Now suppose that the real income of the community is held constant and that the $p_{ru}(t)$ are given by

$$p_{ru}(t) = p_r \quad r = 1, 2, 3 \dots$$
$$p_{01}(t) = p_1 \quad p_{00}(t) = 1 - p_1 \qquad (10.4)$$

where $\quad p_{-1} = 0.3 \quad p_0 = 0.5 \quad p_1 = 0.2 \quad$ other $p_u = 0$.

The corresponding value of b_1 is $2/3$, so that the equilibrium distribution must be

$$x^s = \frac{2^{24}}{3} \left(\frac{2}{3}\right)^s \qquad (10.5)$$

which involve a total income of approximately $\dfrac{2^{24}}{1-\theta} \, \pounds 100$ where

$$\theta = \frac{\log 2}{\log 9 - \log 4} = 0.8547. \qquad (10.6)$$

The numerical value of this total income is about 3.44×2^{25} $\pounds 100$. Thus money income will have to rise in ratio 3.44, so that if total real income is to remain constant, prices must rise in ratio 3.44, so that the real income of those in R_0 will be only about 30% of what it was originally in R_0.

Now suppose that originally an income at the lower end of R_0 represented the subsistence level. Then directly prices tend to rise some policy must be adopted to subsidise those in R_0: let us suppose that prices are subsidised at the expense of prospects of increasing income. More precisely

$$p_{-1} = 0.3 + T \quad p_0 = 0.5 \quad p_1 = 0.2 - Tp_{01}(t)$$
$$= p_1 p_{00}(t) = 1 - p_1 \qquad (10.7)$$

where T is continually adjusted so as to keep prices and total money income stable.

It is intuitively plausible that this policy will lead eventually to an equilibrium distribution.

The corresponding value of b_1 is given by

$$(0 \cdot 3 + T)\, b_1^2 + 0 \cdot 5 b_1 + (0 \cdot 2 - T) = b_1 \qquad (10 \cdot 8)$$

whence since $b_1 \neq 1$

$$b_1 = \frac{0 \cdot 2 - T}{0 \cdot 3 + T}. \qquad (10 \cdot 9)$$

The total income will be $\dfrac{2^{24}}{1 - \theta}\, \pounds 100$ where

$$\theta = \frac{+\log 2}{-2 \log b_1},$$

and in order that this should be equal to the initial total income of $2^{25}\,\pounds 100$ so as to obviate the need for higher prices we need $\theta = \tfrac{1}{2}$ and hence $b_1 = \tfrac{1}{2}$ and hence $T = 0 \cdot 1$.

When we work out the equilibrium distribution, we find, of course, that it is simply the initial distribution unchanged. Hence, it is truer, under our extreme simplifying assumptions, that the initial distribution determined the $p_{ru}(t)$ than that the $p_{ru}(t)$ determined the equilibrium distribution.

Had we allowed some increase in total real income, a lower value of T would, of course, have been necessary, and had we allowed for a continuous expansion of real income an altogether more advanced model with a shifting $p_{ru}(t)$ function for low values of r would have been required.

These illustrations remind one of the impossibility of drawing any simple conclusions about the effect on Pareto's α of various redistributive policies by *merely* considering the effects of these policies on the functions $p_{ru}(t)$ representing the prospects of increase of income.

Index

Figures in bold denote pages in which the entry is a principal theme

Index

Index